DREAMS OF THE SOLO TRAPEZE

DREAMS OF THE SOLO TRAPEZE
OFFSTAGE WITH THE CIRQUE DU SOLEIL

MARK SCHREIBER

CANAL HOUSE

to Olga Sidorova
MAY ALL YOUR DREAMS COME TRUE

CONTENTS

AUTHOR'S NOTE

I couldn't, and wouldn't, have written this book without Olga's faithful assistance. But many others in the Cirque family befriended me along the way, and remain friends. I am particularly indebted to the Bazaliys for their daring hospitality, to Jesko von den Steinen and Alya Titarenko for reading the manuscript between dressing room and stage, and to Shana Carroll, *Saltimbanco*'s original trapeze soloist, for her erudite comments. How many writers can credit a trapezist as proofreader?

SERENDIPITY

imagine...

You're at Club Paradiso in Amsterdam, it's not quite midnight. A church rededicated to Bacchus and tonight, though it's only Wednesday, there's a midnight dance. After all, this is Amsterdam, and you're just around the corner from the Leidseplein, where the bars are open until four and revelers stumble over tram tracks in their sojourn to inebriation, where unicyclists and jugglers perform on the cobblestones outside the National Theater long after the official program has ended, street performers of the species which, on another continent, almost twenty years ago, inspired the Cirque du Soleil.

And a woman walks in, you don't even notice her until she tries to enter the foyer and is rebuffed by the bouncer. A wisp of a girl, crisp blond hair, a sweet face, wearing a black nylon Cirque du Soleil jacket a size too large. She looks young enough not to be admitted, though you'll later discover she's twenty-seven.

"Is it over?" she asks you with a Russian accent, pointing to the people milling inside.

"That's the jazz show letting out," you explain, standing by the ticket counter with your girlfriend, also Russian, waiting for it to open.

She joins you in line. There is no one else. She has sharp brown eyes, thin lips, a short pointed nose, pale, delicate skin. But it's the jacket that draws your attention.

"The Cirque du Soleil is my favorite show," you tell her. "I've seen it four times. Where did you see it?"

"I'm in it," she answers simply, and does not elaborate.

Of course the Cirque's in town, but you didn't know that. You didn't know it seven years earlier either, when you had first seen the troupe, when you had walked out one night from your hotel in this same city toward the Museumplein and seen the Cirque's white tent rising behind the Van Gogh Museum like an apparition from a Persian fairy tale. And now this girl has appeared before you, just as unexpectedly.

You look at her. A ticket taker perhaps. An usher. The girl who sells programs.

So you ask, just to ask. "What do you do?"

And as laconically as she answered the first question, she answers the second. "The trapeze."

The trapeze! And you look at her again, scrutinizing her this time, trying to imagine this tiny thing swinging from a bar, thirty feet in the air. And you can't imagine it. The trapeze! The quintessential circus act. Yes, there's the wire walker, the lion tamer, the master of ceremonies, the acrobats and clowns. But nothing transfixes an audience's gaze like a fellow human being dancing with calamity from the trapeze. You peer into her eyes, her sweet smile, you study her hands, but they're just hands. Yet have you ever encountered anyone so magical? There are astronauts and football players, Nobel laureates and pop stars, but a woman who flies on the trapeze!

The ticket window opens and you discreetly buy three and hand one to her. A token of admiration, of gratitude for all the trapeze artists and circus performers you've watched from afar since you were a small child, who make the world forget the world.

imagine

OFFSTAGE WITH THE CIRQUE

I want to unravel at once, like a magician's multi-colored handkerchief,, all the mysteries surrounding her. The trapeze... How? When? The star of the show, or one of the stars, yet she was here alone, at midnight! But I merely ask where she was from.

"Russia."

"Vika's from St. Petersburg," I reply.

It was the natural thing to say, but I didn't think it would impress her. After all, she must know many Russians abroad, not to speak of the other Russians in the Cirque, she must meet scores of people every day, from all over the world.

But her eyes light up and she says something to Vika in Russian and three minutes later they're still standing there, talking, as other patrons buy their tickets and file past us into the club.

Finally Vika catches her breath and turns to me. "Olga says she can try to get us tickets to tomorrow night's show. It's sold out, so she can't get us in for free, but with discount. Good seats. We should call her tomorrow at two."

We go inside and Olga writes her hotel and room number on the Paradiso stub. I thank her and ask if she has a card.

And she does! The most esoteric business card I'll ever possess.

OLGA SIDOROVA
TRAPEZE

We part, not wishing to further invade her privacy. The club soon fills and we lose sight of her in the haze of cigarette and marijuana smoke. Occasionally I look for her but, as we learn the next day, she hadn't stayed.

I decide Vika should phone her, since they had established something of a rapport. "Ask if it might be possible to go backstage after the show."

I expect a brief exchange, but they chat in Russian for several minutes. Finally Vika reports that we should go to the box office ten minutes before curtain. Olga couldn't guarantee tickets, but she would try. If we waited after the show someone would take us backstage, but Olga usually eats with the troupe, so she wouldn't be able to spend much time with us.

I couldn't believe her generosity. "She must really like you," I tell Vika. "This will be a special last night for you." Although I suspect I was the more excited.

The Cirque was no longer in the Museumplein but across from the football stadium on the edge of town. We take a taxi and wait impatiently by the ticket booth as those fortunate enough to have confirmed seats file inside. Nearly all are adults, one of the many dissimilarities to the traditional circus. Well-dressed, affluent, urbane, they resemble more a theater than a circus crowd.

But no theater has a tent like this. The Cirque's white vinyl tent, referencing the moribund big tops of the first half of the last century, but sleek and modern, almost futuristic, with one tall and several smaller peaks that shine brighter than the moon in the dark sky and stand fast against the Dutch wind.

At twenty past seven I climb the steps to the ticket window, housed appropriately in a trailer. The girl asks my name, and I tell her when she can't find our tickets that Olga might have left them in her own name.

The clerk speaks to a man with a goatee and asks me to wait while she serves those behind me. I think of the short memories, the irresponsibility I encounter daily among people with normal jobs, and that this sum could certainly be squared for people in show business and cubed for people in the circus, the most capricious of all, gypsies and bohemians who have never had to balance a checkbook or pick up a child from day care. But a minute later she calls me back and hands me two tickets and I wave them to Vika, who never doubted.

They're excellent seats, tenth row at the top of the center aisle, in front of the sound booth. But we barely have time to remove our coats before a half dozen clowns march our way, grab Vika by the arm, then me and those seated next to us and lead us around the auditorium. My clown puts her arm through mine, and I suspect it's a woman but that's all I can discern. She could be black or white, Canadian or Chinese, we've entered a new world beyond gender, race and nationality, even beyond language, for the troupe speaks a Latinate gibberish.

The clowns suddenly let go of us, rush back and claim our seats. The audience laughs and applauds. Vika is astonished.

"I hope they don't choose me again," she says, as a clown pulls off a man's t-shirt and tosses it into the crowd.

Saltimbanco is much as I remember it. When the lights come on for intermission we stay in our seats as the audience hurries out. Suddenly I notice a man in front of the stage waving at us. But he can't be waving at us. Then a small figure beside him, dressed in black, waves as well. I look behind, but the sound booth is empty.

The small figure finally runs up the steps. Olga! Her blond hair pulled back, her eyes made up with green liner, wearing a black warm up suit. She says she's glad we could come and asks if we're enjoying the show. Then she explains that she comes out at intermission to do her rigging.

She and Vika hug like sisters and we watch her run back to the stage. I can't believe she took the time to greet us, that she broke her routine. Circus performers wrap themselves in superstitions and rituals, but she seems as insouciant as a seagull, already soaring.

About ten minutes into the second act a woman dressed in a diaphanous blue costume that glows white in the spotlights emerges from a haze of smoke onto the stage, and as the band behind her plays a solemn introduction, a single trapeze is lowered from the rafters.

Neither Vika or I recognize Olga. She looks larger somehow, her hair longer, and it's impossible to see her face clearly before she grabs the hand loop and dramatically ascends.

She performs the first part of her routine without a safety line or net. A mat, much too thin, is rolled out and two male spotters stand on either side ready to catch her if she should fall. But it seems hardly adequate to the task. Couldn't they use a stunt man's mat, or a net? I've always watched the trapeze reluctantly, with trepidation, in part because of my fear of heights, in part because of the dread of witnessing an accident. And now, to watch someone I've met, not a distant performer but a new friend…

Music fills the tent, but the audience is silent, gazing with rapt concentration at the solitary trapeze. "Do you think it's her?" Vika whispers.

She's now too high to distinguish her features. But strangely she appears bigger at this distance than she had when she stood next to us at the Paradiso, as if we had just met a fraction of her last night, as if the spotlight has inflated her.

The trapeze remains stationary while she contorts herself around it. She wraps herself around one of the ropes, she hangs outward from the edge as if leaning against an invisible pillar, she hangs by her ankles from the bar.

Finally the audience breaks its attentive silence and applauds. A safety line is lowered from the rafters and Olga clasps it to her belt. One of the spotters then pulls her by a rope to start the trapeze in motion. The mat is dragged away. The music picks up and Olga kicks the trapeze still higher. Around the stage several clowns stare up, faces frozen in wonder.

Her balance seems unaffected by the motion as she swings faster and faster, standing on the bar. The audience gasps as she executes her first leap, catching the bar firmly in her hands. She folds her legs under and swings by her knees, her arms outstretched, her hair flowing down. She swings still higher, from one end of the stage to the other, the trapeze nearly glancing the rafters. She climbs back to her feet without slowing and spins and twists and lunges in rapid succession. Most of her catches are clean and effortless but once or twice she struggles. Still, the performance is so fast the audience hardly has time to gasp or applaud. Unlike a traditional two-trapeze act with discrete maneuvers, the solo trapezist swiftly flows from one action into another, much as an Olympic gymnast on the parallel bars, and an observer has little time to appraise one movement before the next, equally unexpected and thrilling, commences.

Even so, it's a long performance, and by the time she descends to enthusiastic applause I suspect I'm as emotionally drained as she. In keeping with the spirit of the show, she doesn't bow or savor the applause but hurries offstage as the next act flows on. So we were never able to glimpse her face clearly, this enigma in white, alone in the arena, without even a bull to conquer, but only her own shadows.

When the lights come on at the end of the show I wonder if we will really be allowed backstage. The audience exits quickly and we seem conspicuous in our seats.

An usher tells us we have to leave because they're cleaning up. I explain that we're guests of one of the performers and are waiting for someone to come for us. I ask if she knows the cast. She doesn't. But in any case I ask if she knows Olga Sidorova.

"She's the trapeze."

Vika and I smile with pride at the confirmation. "Imagine!" I tell her.

A few minutes later a woman approaches and introduces herself as the backstage manager. The theater is empty now except for ushers sweeping the aisles. We follow her around the curved stage into another tent furnished with two long sofas, mats, practice equipment and curtained dressing rooms. She tells us to have a seat.

We are the only visitors backstage, but no one seems to mind our presence. A woman is riding a stationary bicycle. I don't recognize her out of costume. But there's no mistaking the Argentinean boleadoros dancer. She inserts a video into the closed-circuit TV and studies her performance. She repeatedly pauses the tape to play back specific movements, which she mimics in front of the screen, her back to us. I admire the joy and discipline of these people. No audience now to impress, no coaches or trainers to goad them on. Like a golfer hitting balls after a round, except there's no leader board to ponder, no rivals to catch or keep at bay. Only their own sense of excellence to answer to.

And their sense of joy.

Vika points to a small boy, who opened the show with his parents. He tumbles on a mat beneath a chin-up bar. His older sister climbs the bar and flips off.

"They're Russian," Vika whispers, overhearing a few words.

The strongmen, twins from Poland, walk past, still in costume. But the atmosphere is strangely quiet and relaxed. Not at all the mood I would have expected after a show. Where was all the hubris of egocentric entertainers, the nervous energy and exhaustion? One might think these people had just returned from a long lunch rather than risked their necks in front of 2,500 people.

Vika and I sit down on one of the sofas. I look at the masks hanging in neat rows on the wall. There's a bulletin board near the TV covered with reminders and announcements, including a list of March birthdays.

"I know it's unlikely Olga will be able to spend time with us," I tell Vika. "But if she does invite us to do something don't say you have to get up at seven to catch a plane."

Finally Olga comes out, wearing her black warm-up again but still in make-up. She smiles at us warmly, but when I say her performance was breathtaking she shakes her head.

"I made two mistakes! It no good. If I fall I could get serious injury!"

She sits next to Vika and they speak animatedly in Russian like reunited classmates. I have no idea what they're discussing, but I don't think they're talking about the trapeze. Indeed, Olga seems to be asking Vika more questions than Vika is asking her.

I decide not to interrupt, suspecting that Olga is glad for the chance to speak Russian, despite her opportunity to speak her native language with the other Russian performers. For myself, I savor every moment. Vika leaves in a few hours. I may not see her again for months. And I may never find myself backstage again at my favorite show, the guest of one of its stars.

I anticipated Olga would merely say a few words to us before excusing herself, but five minutes later she and Vika are still talking. Then Vika turns to me and says that Olga wants to know if we want to have something to eat with the troupe.

She leaves us for a minute to remove her makeup and then leads us outside to the commissary tent. She asks us to sit down at an empty round table and brings us red wine and a large plate of fruit and bread from the buffet, which she proceeds to cut up for us like a typical Russian host. "Eat! Eat!"

The commissary, or "kitchen" as they call it, is filled with the voices of several languages. Not everyone is here. I don't see the tightrope walker or the mime. But I recognize the family that opened the show with an act entitled Adagio, the strongmen who performed Hand-to-Hand, the pretty Russian juggler. I had bought a program for Vika and now suggest she ask Olga to sign it.

Olga not only signs but takes Vika to the other tables and asks all the other performers to sign as well. I watch them go from table to table, passing the program, and I wonder who these people are. It's always difficult to extract performers from their personas, and circus people have a reputation for being the most insulated stratum of show business, perhaps because of their rootlessness and self-sufficiency, the exotic nature of their acts, including among them freaks and outcasts.

But there don't seem to be any freaks in the Cirque du Soleil, and Vika and I are the only outcasts. I wonder if the people who comprise this circus don't represent a new kind of cosmopolitanism, skimmed from the gifted, not the wretched, lacking borders and a common language, creating their own affinities.

Olga and Vika return and show me the program, now filled with unreadable comments and signatures.

"At first Olga said she hates to sign autographs," Vika informs me. "So I was very surprised when she did it!"

"People who treat me like star, I put one hundred kilometers between us!" Olga proclaims.

"But the trapeze is special," I tell her.

"It just job. Look, you have job. She has job. This my job. That's all."

"But why do you do it? Why the trapeze?"

"She left Siberia when she was fourteen to follow her dream," Vika reveals.

Olga relaxes into a wide smile and her eyes look up, as if a trapeze hung from the commissary tent. "The first time I saw trapeze I thought that's for me!" she exclaims in a girlish voice.

"How long have you been with the Cirque?"

"Since October."

"Only since October? Where did you perform before?"

"All over. In Moscow, Europe, Dubai, Mauritius, Australia. I teach now at Melbourne."

"There's a circus school in Melbourne?"

"The National Institute of Circus Arts."

"She's very well known in Australia," Vika adds, revealing in bits and pieces their conversations in Russian.

"And how did you come to the Cirque du Soleil? Did you audition?"

"No. They asked me."

"They asked you?" I exclaim. "So you must be one of the best in the world!"

"I don't like talk about it. Please eat."

Some of the performers call to her as they leave. "Are you coming Olga?"

But she waves them off. "It boring being with Cirque all time. I like get away from it. So, how long you know each other?"

I tell her ten years.

She's visibly surprised, so I explain that we met when I went to Russia to research a novel. Vika was just a girl at the time, and she and her mother had shown me the city.

"And what kind books you write?"

Vika had apparently told her I was a writer. I'm surprised by her interest in us, and her complete lack of pretense.

"I write novels mostly."

"Love stories? I like love stories. I don't like stories that not real. When I read book or see movie I lose myself in characters, but if it isn't real I just can't believe in it, you understand?"

How can I understand a woman from Siberia, now living in Australia and currently swinging through Europe on a trapeze bar, feeling uncomfortable with fantasy? "But *Saltimbanco* is filled with unreality," I point out.

"That different. I'm talking about relationships. Have you seen *Bitter Moon*? I like that movie very much."

More performers leave the tent and soon we are the only ones left. But Olga is in no hurry to leave and resumes speaking to Vika in Russian. Only when the cook begins stacking the chairs does she rise.

"Would you like to share a taxi?" I offer. "We can drop you at your hotel first."

Olga nods but seems uncertain what to do. She points to a phone and asks me to call for a taxi. I don't know the number. I've never had to call for a taxi in Amsterdam. So I call my hotel. Or try to. The number six is stuck.

"The phone doesn't always work," the cook says in English. "You can call from the security booth."

I'm surprised that Olga doesn't know what to do. "How do you usually go home?" I wonder.

"With some of the others, or by train."

"You take the train?"

"Yes, why not?"

She clears the plates herself and leads us to the gate. We seem to be the only ones left, except for the guard, who is kind enough to call a taxi. It's windy and beginning to rain, so we wait in the small security booth for the taxi to arrive.

Olga is again wearing the black nylon Cirque du Soleil jacket, as she had last night at Club Paradiso. I reflect on her transformation from a girl in a black jacket to a trapeze virtuoso and back to a girl in a black jacket. I am astonished that she's let us follow her through it all, opened up to a pair of strangers. Observing her as she and Vika laugh at something in Russian one would never know that only an hour before she had put her body through a series of perilous contortions. Only a job, she had said. But even ordinary office workers whose feet never leave the ground exhibit more evidence of stress at the end of their day. And I realize this diminutive girl I feel the need to protect from a few drops of rain is perhaps the coolest person I've ever met. As the taxi arrives and I usher them out beneath my umbrella I glance back at the shimmering white tent, buffeted like a sail by the gusting wind, lit like a mirage in anticipation of the next performance.

As we ride back into town, I in the front, the girls in the back conversing in Russian, I tell myself I couldn't have scripted a more magical night. Olga remembered the tickets, met us backstage, invited us to eat with her, and honored us with escorting her home. But in a few short minutes we'll say goodbye, and in the morning I'll take Vika to the airport, and the morning after return to the airport alone to catch my own flight.

But to my great surprise our circus adventure has an act or two to play, for when we reach the Renaissance, Olga asks if we'd like to come in for a drink. I pay the driver above her protests and we follow her into the hotel bar.

In the back a dozen Cirque members are drinking at adjoining tables. But Olga leads me to a small table by the front window. "I see them every day," she says. "What you like drink?"

She goes to order the drinks and buy a pack of cigarettes. When she returns she informs me that Vika wants to sit with the circus. "You can't say no to a woman," she muses.

Vika, whom I had feared might feel uncomfortable among this tight-knit troupe, is already perched on a stool, fielding questions. An impartial observer would have taken her for a member of the cast. Even I, who feel like an intruder in my own apartment, am made to feel I belong.

Everyone but Vika and me is smoking. "I can't believe you smoke," I tell Olga, who is stirring an ice cube into her amoretto with her free hand. She had seemed to value health at the commissary, dining on fruit and salad.

"Why not?" she says.

"It's bad for your health."

But she waves away my concern. "So is trapeze." And she raises a pants' leg to show us her bruises.

Vika's program is a big hit and gets passed around the tables. It seems these people have never seen their own program. They examine the photos and search for their names, making comments in Russian and French.

I shake hands with two men standing behind me, one English, one Scottish. They work on the crew. We talk for a couple minutes, but I can't understand a word they say. Then a woman with long black hair sitting on the far side of the next table says hello. She's Yasmine.

"Where are you from?" I ask innocently enough.

"Iran."

Okay. I spot the backstage manager at the far end of my own table and thank her for admitting us.

"She very good," Olga says. "I like her very much."

Apparently Olga likes Vika very much as well, for when I next look at Vika she's writing her name in Olga's address book. The barman brings more beer.

I find it odd to feel so comfortable among this group of elite performers. Vika at least has studied gymnastics, but I haven't done a cartwheel in years. More importantly, I've never worn masks of any kind, and what is a circus if not a mask? Literature is revelation, circus is obfuscation. One of the Cirque's shows in Las Vegas is even entitled *Mystère*. So it's a shock to me that everyone I've met so far is transparent, that a circus veteran like Olga has revealed so much of herself to us, that she yearns to de-glamorize her passion, to ignore the usual barriers between performer and spectator, star and crew. Such lack of pretense and breadth of interests would be difficult to find at any table. Recently, a molecular biologist had complained to me that his peers are so devoted to their research they can't speak to people outside their field. So I find it ironic that Cirque people, who speak an illusory language onstage and so many languages off, communicate so well.

One man at the far end of the table sees Olga's tiny glass and ask what she's drinking.

"Amoretto," she answers with a girlish grin that betrays her innocence. "Better for sex!"

The lights are turned up and last call announced.

"You're up late," I tell Olga.

But she shakes her head. "I never go sleep before two. I can't, you know. The energy after a show."

Just a job...

I assume the night is coming to an end, but a tall man with curly hair offers to continue the party upstairs and he invites Vika and me as well, although we haven't been introduced. We file out of the bar, through the quiet lobby, to the elevators. "You can sleep in Russia," I tell Vika.

The party actually divides between two rooms on the fourth floor. In one, a few people sit languidly on the floor smoking cigarettes. Olga opts for the second, which belongs to a young Spaniard from the Canary Islands who works in food and beverage. The Cirque is in Amsterdam for two months and he has planted a bit of Spain in room 423. Fluorescent blacklights illuminate glow-in-the-dark stars on the ceiling and photos of family and friends on the walls. There's a VCR player atop the TV, and beside it a mini-bar sized aluminum stereo case complete with tuner, equalizer and CD changer.

"This belongs to the Cirque?" I ask.

"No it's mine. But the Cirque transports it. I have to pay them, but only about thirty euros."

He puts on a techno CD and I feel I've fallen in with a rock band rather than the circus. Two women of indeterminate nationality are lying on the bed giggling uncontrollably at a video. An American man is slouching in one of the chairs by the window, talking to Olga. Yasmine is lighting yet another cigarette.

"So you're from Iran?"

"You know it's not like what they show on CNN," she responds, but doesn't elaborate.

"What do you do on the show?"

"I'm a rigger."

"Yasmine's fearless," someone else adds.

But aren't you all? And I reflect that if I could ask Olga one question it would be what, if anything, she fears.

Olga comes over to the king-sized bed where most of us are sprawled and sits on the edge beside Vika. When next I look at them Vika spontaneously throws her arms around the trapeze star as if they were old friends. I think of the American woman who shocked all Britain years ago when she gave the Queen a bear hug during a State visit. Doesn't Vika realize the social and economic gulf that separates her, a library clerk and art student, from an international trapeze star? Fortunately Olga doesn't seem to acknowledge the chasm either and I consider that if such Russians had taken power eighty years ago their country might have achieved its ideals of a classless society.

I take the empty chair next to the American sitting by the window. He seems lonely, and I'm curious to discover his role in the Cirque.

"I think I offended your friend Olga," he confesses. "I asked her what she did in the show!"

"So you're not part of the show yourself?

"I do IT, but I work in Las Vegas. I'm only here for a month."

"And do you like Amsterdam?"

"I love it here. Unfortunately I have to get up at seven, and work till eight."

"At the theater?"

"No. The Cirque's European headquarters is located here." He takes a sip of his drink and looks at me closely. "So you're not with them?"

"No."

"But you're a friend of Olga's?"

"Yes."

"And your girlfriend is Russian?"

"Yes."

"But you're American?" He shakes his head as if trying to solve a puzzle. "I don't understand."

But I'd much rather discover his connections than explain my own and I ask him what his job entails.

"All the computers for all the shows."

"Like the lighting?"

"The lighting's done separately."

"And the internet?"

"Sure."

"Do you like the web site?"

"The web site's not bad. But the intranet, the intranet needs work." And he laughs.

I tell him I've seen both "O" and *Mystère* in Las Vegas and admired the technical as well as the artistic wizardry in these shows.

"Which show is your favorite?" he asks me.

"Which is your favorite?"

"'O' is technically brilliant. But to me *Saltimbanco* is the real thing. It's in a tent. It travels. There's a spirit of community."

"You don't have this camaraderie in Vegas?"

"It's more corporate," he replies. "People have families and cars. They go home after the show."

I'm surprised that even a technical member of the Cirque is so attuned to its bohemian traditions.

"Of course, the problem with my job is that I have to be in the office at seven." And he reluctantly departs.

Olga is leaving too. We hug her goodbye but do not leave ourselves. We still feel welcome here, so we stay a bit longer. Our host is changing the CD player. Yasmine is smoking and drinking, drinking and smoking. The girls on the bed are still giggling, inexplicably.

When I wake, after only a couple hours' sleep, the circus will be gone. Vika will be going. And the following morning I would leave as well. My glimpse into the Cirque's esoteric world will dissolve into memory, a handful of photographs, Olga's deliberate handwriting on the Paradiso stub.

But in truth the Cirque was staying on in Amsterdam. And, as fate would have it, so was I.

AMSTERDAM

Schiphol Airport is what airports are meant to be—modern without modernism's alienating side effects, immaculate, efficient, safe, large without being labyrinthine, generously staffed with cordial civil servants, lined with useful shops, graced with a terminal casino, a five-star Sheraton and ramped escalators that allowed the weary traveler to push his cart from baggage claim to the Platform #3 train to Amsterdam's Centraal Station without having to lift a bag. It was my favorite airport in Europe, a merciful consolation considering that necessity in the form of a faithless ticket bound me to its *F* gates for something like eternity.

I was flying stand-by, that wretched designation for travelers without confirmed seating. I'd flown stand-by before, I was a stand-by veteran. My sister-in-law's cousin worked for Delta and sometimes gave me passes. I'd gotten on flights after being told the flight was closed. I'd been bumped and re-routed. I'd missed a 6:30 AM flight with plenty of seats due to the wrath of the Equipment Failure gods. I'd even been asked to leave an aircraft just as I was perusing the in-flight magazine.

So when the check-in clerk informs me Flight 39 to Atlanta is over-booked by 28, I merely return her smile. To emphasize her pessimism she asks me to put my check-in bag on a solitary cart in front of the desk. It seems a sort of punishment, and I glance back at it on my way to Passport Control, worried it will be left behind. How wrong I was.

I really did think I would get on. After all, Schiphol is a transit hub and most of today's passengers would be coming from different cities. If you consider that the aircraft seats 252 passengers, and add the inevitable missed connections to the usual compliment of last minute cancellations and no-shows, we would need less than twelve percent to miss for all the stand-bys to travel. But when I reach the gate it seems enough anxious passengers are crammed inside to fill a football stadium and my ride home appears no larger than a commuter plane. March 19, 2002, a banner day in the annals of air traffic control.

I don't mind. Not at all. While the other stand-by passengers clamor at the desk and watch the loading ramp disengage from the plane with a sense of impossibility, as if witnessing an earthquake, I calmly recline in my chair, thinking only that a sort of emotional equilibrium is being restored to offset my ecstatic night at the Cirque. Besides, there was a flight to New York in three hours.

I make good progress on Brian Greene's *Elegant Universe*. I walk the long terminals. I return to the New York gate and take my place at the back of a very long line waiting to go through security. I take a seat by the desk as boarding commences and the gate attendant announced that the flight is full.

"Think we'll get on?" an American with a scraggly beard asks me nervously as the Business Class passengers file by.

"A couple weeks ago I was going to New York with my sister," I tell him calmly. "She had a ticket and I didn't. The gate attendant told me I wouldn't get on, so I told my sister I would take the next flight and meet her at the Yale Club. But I got on."

"I don't know," he muses, as general boarding begins. "There aren't any more flights after this. What happens if we don't make it? Do you have a plan?"

But how could I have a plan, looking backward as I was?

The morning before, at Passport Control, Vika laid her head on my shoulder and then she was gone. I'd hardly slept after our magical night at the Cirque, so I checked in to the Schiphol Sheraton and pulled the shades. When I woke the airport shops were still open, so I went to find Olga a present. I didn't want to send her flowers. As a performer her room was probably filled with flowers. So I thought of a stuffed animal. All women like Teddy Bears. You can't go wrong with a bear. Unless, perhaps, the recipient hails from Siberia, where people are doubtless devoured by bears every day. No, a Teddy Bear could be quite traumatic, like giving an Australian a plush white shark. With that in mind I had asked Olga between amorettos what her favorite animal was. She answered dogs, and Vika later added that she had a poodle in Siberia.

So now, in Hamley's Toys at Schiphol, I look for a stuffed dog. I am surprised to find a selection, including poodles. I have one wrapped, take a train into the city, and leave it with the concierge. Soon it will be showtime at the Cirque. I imagine Olga putting her makeup on, doing warm-up exercises in the backstage tent. How quickly would she forget us?

I consider waiting at the bar for her return, but I don't want to over-stay my welcome. And I have an early flight...

Some of the stand-bys get called. They leap to the desk like acrobats and grab their tickets with rude jubilation. The gate closes. About eight or ten of us remain, in groups of two or three. My bearded acquaintance and I are the only ones traveling alone and he's eager to form an alliance. It's comforting to find allies at such times, but I would prefer to be left alone. Still, I feel bad for him. He's taken the train from Switzerland because the flights in Zurich were overbooked, and now he's stranded another night in another city. Furthermore, he has the burden of his snowboard. But he appears less stressed than the others, as one would expect a snowboarder to be. We walk to baggage claim, which is completely empty of passengers. He collects his snowboard and suitcase from the far carousel and asks if I'm going into the city. I tell him I think I'll stay at the Sheraton another night, and we say goodbye.

The carousel continues to turn, revolving the same two pieces of luggage, neither of which is mine. I talk to the KLM baggage clerk, but she can't help me. And the Delta baggage desk is upstairs, which means I have to go through customs. If I leave I can't return.

So I wait. I've been here seven hours, what are a few minutes more? Fortunately one of the men who had worked the Delta flights comes over. He takes the two suitcases off the carousel and wishes me luck for tomorrow. I tell him my bag hasn't arrived and he seems surprised. He makes a call on his mobile.

"They've sent it to Atlanta."

"Atlanta! I thought the airlines aren't supposed to send unaccompanied bags?"

"It happens," he says with a shrug and wheels his cart away.

I am alone in baggage claim in one of the busiest airports in Europe. Even the carousel has stopped moving.

The official at customs watches me approach with only my carry-on. "Where do you come from?" he asks.

A rather philosophical question for a Saturday afternoon. Ask instead, quo vadis?

I check back into the Sheraton and phone home. Then I call my friend Mariska, a writer herself who'd translated two of my novels into Dutch. She had been gracious enough to help with Vika's visa and we had gone out to dinner one night with her and her husband. But she doesn't answer. So I walk over to one of the airport restaurants for a sandwich and fresh-squeezed orange juice. Fortunately I don't need clothes. I always keep underwear and a t-shirt in my carry-on, as well as a swimsuit—you never know when you'll run across a swimming pool. And indeed the Sheraton has a spa. But I haven't the energy to properly relax and I ride the atrium elevator back upstairs. I've been unnecessarily upgraded to a club room, which only exacerbates my solitude. I think of Vika miserably restored to her communal flat in St. Petersburg and wish I could send her some square footage. I'd be content in a capsule hotel. All I need is a mattress, vitamin C, and an offering to the Stand-by gods.

I think of Olga limbering up. Did she get the poodle? Will I ever see her again? Probably not. I think of my orange and black Head bag endlessly revolving on a carousel in Atlanta and try to recall its contents. Will I ever see it again?

I close the curtain on this wasted day, but leave the curtain to my window open. I stand before it for a few minutes, gazing at a spectacle every bit as wondrous as a flip on the double tightrope or a twist on the solo trapeze. Airplanes departing.

Deja vu. The security people look familiar, the clerk at the counter remembers me— "It looks bad again I'm afraid, but you never know," she says with a smile. Even some of the passengers look familiar.

The snowboarder sits beside me and tells me about the hotel he found in Amsterdam for fifty dollars. He's pleasantly fatalistic, a welcome contrast to the other stand-by passengers, hovering around the counter like buzzards. But when he informs me he works for Federal Express I think he might do better to assume a sense of urgency. I envision piles of undelivered packages engulfing his cubicle.

As for myself, if I was bumped another day it would hurt my bank account, I would have to buy some socks, another book to read, but that was all.

This becomes my mantra as the last call for boarding is announced and a few lucky stand-by passengers are given seats, but not me and my new friend from Fed-Ex.

We have to wait for the flight to close before we can talk to the desk agent about our options. But we are at the end of a long line. There are more stranded stand-bys than there had been yesterday.

The New York flight is overbooked by thirty and Monday looks worse. I ask about alternate airports, but the gate agent shakes her head. "Paris is oversold by fifty. Brussels is bad, London is bad. They're sending passengers here from other cities! It's Spring Break."

Who goes to Europe on Spring Break? What about all those reports about people not flying? I ask if Tuesday looks better and am told all the flights for the week are overbooked.

"But you'll get out," she assures me with a smile, like an attorney boasting about the appeal to his jailed client. "Connections are missed all the time because of fog or rain. Just last week a flight was oversold by twenty and it left half empty. You may even get on the New York flight."

I ask where I stood on the stand-by list. I was last. "But I've been bumped three times! Don't I move up?"

I knew there were different classes of stand-by. Pilots, obviously, received preference over baggage handlers. And my class I knew was the lowest. But I believed within each class priority was given to those who listed first, or had been bumped. But I learn instead priority was given to employees with seniority, and my sister-in-law's cousin had only worked for the airline one year! I would always be last.

If I hadn't spent all my euros at the Sheraton I would have bought stock in Delta, because everyone shows for the New York flight and a couple dozen distressed stand-bys file back through passport control, eyeing one another like the schoolboys in *Lord of the Flies*.

"You may want to buy a ticket," I tell the snowboarder, who is listed one place before me. But my motives aren't entirely self-serving, for when I return to the terminal I go to the counters of several other airlines myself, hoping for a discount fare. But Northwest, American and United are all booked solid. Spring Break I'm told. I picture the beaches of Daytona and Cancun lying deserted, every freshman in America having come to rain swept Europe.

For the first time I have to admit to myself that I might be facing an extended stay. Much as I like the Sheraton, I can't afford to reside there indefinitely. So I return to the city in search of my friend's fifty-dollar hotel.

But by some mysterious deviation in the laws of demographics, there are no budget rooms to be had in Amsterdam. I try ten before becoming wearied, despite the fact that I am unencumbered with luggage. How could it be that everyone was leaving Amsterdam and staying in Amsterdam at the same time? I finally book a room at the three-star Botel, a floating hotel that never leaves the Oosterdok, a perfect metaphor for the stranded traveler.

The alarm sounds at 6:00 AM. Monday morning, time for work. I have to get up earlier, now that I'm not staying at the Sheraton. At home I rarely go into the office before eleven, but that was at home. That was before I became Supervisor of Overbooked Flights at Schiphol Airport, the important duties of which included ensuring no seats were left unoccupied on Flight 39 to Atlanta and Flight 81 to New York, listening to boarding announcements to make sure Economy wasn't called before Business, observing that gate agents closed all the doors that needed to be closed, that the ramp completely disengaged from the fuselage, and that the aircraft successfully maneuvered onto the runway. Furthermore, I had to make sure Passport Control stamped my passport every single day so future Passport agents would suspect me of being a drug courier.

I had to make sure the security agent asked me when I had packed my bag and if it had been with me at all times even though I had packed it days before and had been unable to monitor it properly due to the fact that it was in another country, but that I was reasonably certain no one had added anything to its contents, although it may well be that some of its articles had been removed.

My work day began at eight when I attempted to check in for Flight 39 to Atlanta. After a leisurely lunch I attempted to check in for Flight 81 to New York. After which I had only to go through the formalities of documenting that the flights for the next day were overbooked as well and return through passport control and customs, with a quick stop at the desks of other airlines to spy on the competition. I was usually done around three, not even an eight-hour day excluding commuting time. True, I didn't receive wages and had to pay my own expenses, but everyone smiled, and how many employees can claim such sympathetic co-workers?

As the final passengers hurry onto the New York flight I find myself effused with a Zen-like calm. An Asian woman is screaming at the gate agent. Screaming. I tune her out. I will not go home today. Perhaps not tomorrow. I must ride back into the city, check back into my hotel, if there's a room. But what is the stress of these last days compared with somersaulting from the Russian swing or diving nose first on the Chinese poles or flipping on the double tightrope or letting go of the trapeze? If Olga can ascend to her lonely bar night after night, surely I can plumb the depths of this fateful airport day after day.

"Man, this is serious!" the snowboarder complains. "I've got to get back to work. If I can't get home tomorrow I'm going to have to buy a ticket!"

But the gate agent informs us there aren't any available seats until after Easter. Easter! That's ten days!

Back in the terminal Northwest has a ticket for $1,499. Martin Air has no availability to the U.S. But they have a $218 fare to Cancun. Cancun! I'll never get home from there. I have a vision of a modern Odysseus, taking twenty years to return to Ithaca on a stand-by ticket.

I go back into the city, check back into my hotel and call the number

Olga had scrawled on the Paradiso stub.

Monday is the Cirque's day off. Olga is just waking up. "I thought you went home," she says.

"My luggage got on the plane, but not me," I explain.

"Do you need anything?"

"Thanks, I'm fine. I was wondering if you had plans today?"

"I have to get massage. And tonight a group of us has reservations for a comedy club. How long you staying?"

"I don't know."

"I can get you ticket for show tomorrow. A free ticket this time. I don't know if you want see it again, but we can go out after."

"That's very nice of you. Thanks."

"And thank you for dog. Whose idea was it, yours or Vika's?"

"Mine. I hope you like it."

"It made me cry."

It will be some consolation to see Olga again. I can afford to stay another day. But I've been bumped six times. I can't afford to lose the whole week, and I certainly can't stay here through Easter. So I visit a travel agency not far from Club Paradiso and buy a discount ticket to New York on Singapore Airlines for Wednesday morning. From New York I'll use my Delta ticket to get to Columbus, or rent a car. I'll still have to go to the airport tomorrow to change my stand-by pass and see about getting my baggage re-routed. But I won't be taking the 6:30 train. Someone else will have to receive the commiserative smiles of the gate agents, someone else will have to watch the ramp disengage from the fuselage. The snow-boarder perhaps. The Asian girl.

I've been bumped six times. I wonder what the record is. Certainly more than six. But consecutively, for a trans-Atlantic flight. And what about consecutive days spent going to the airport? I took Vika on Friday, the next three days I was bumped, Tuesday I have to change my ticket, and Wednesday I finally depart. Six days at the airport. Six times bumped. I regard the Schiphol stamps in my passport like so many bruises. Olga isn't the only one who needs a massage.

Around midnight I walk to the Renaissance. There's a driving rain, a gale wind that pulverizes umbrellas. Maybe the Spring Break crowd will go to the beach next year.

I enter the bar thinking Olga might have returned from the comedy club, but it's nearly empty. I say hello to Yasmine, who's talking to the barman, and sit alone at a large table. Soon an elegant young woman with short auburn hair and pale skin walks in, has a few words to say to Yasmine about the Iranian woman's mini-skirt, and asks in an Australian accent if she can share my table.

Her name's Sue and she works in costumes. But she doesn't make them, she's quick to inform me. That's all done in Montreal.

"The costumes are an integral part of the show," I point out.

"It's all right," she says with a modesty I'm beginning to think is endemic to the Cirque.

"It must be an exciting life, to be immersed in such a creative environment, among such people."

"The people are wonderful, but it's a bit tiring after a while. I've been with the Cirque three years now. The Asian tour, the North American tour, now the European tour. You reach a point you want to put down roots."

"In Australia?"

"In Montreal."

"And work for the Cirque there?"

"Actually I want to open a wine bar specializing in Australian wines."

I'm eager to hear her elaborate but instead she asks about me. When I tell her I'm a novelist she pushes her stool closer to mine and asks my name. I give her my card, but insist she reciprocate. "I'd love to read one of your books," she says, and tells me about the Nick Hornby novel she's reading. "I'm always reading a book. I've gone through the Cirque library, but half their books are in Russian and Chinese. Have you read..." And she proceeds to mention several young British authors, and I mention a few others and we talk about literature until a good looking young man with long flowing hair, her Canadian boyfriend, joins us with his parents, just in for a week from Montreal. They don't speak much English. But

Daniel speaks excellent English with a soft French accent.

"Mark's a writer. He's had a book published in Canada and a film made there," Sue tells them.

I think it ironic, being the subject of their attention when they're the ones in show business. "Daniel would like to make documentary films some day," Sue reveals.

"What do you do for the Cirque?"

"I'm the stage manager."

I'd met the backstage manager the first night, and ask the difference between the two.

"The stage manager gives cues and makes sure the show runs according to schedule. Also, I'm responsible for any problems that come up. I don't actually work backstage."

Daniel's parents are tired from their journey and the party heads upstairs. Yasmine too has left. I slowly finish my beer, looking out the window, waiting for the rain to subside, hoping Olga will emerge from one of the approaching taxis. But the rain doesn't subside. One of the characters in *Quidam*, another Cirque show, is a headless man holding an open umbrella. That's the part for me, I think, as I battle my way back to the Botel, invariably against the wind.

MAY ALL YOUR DREAMS COME TRUE

I have to wait until five minutes before showtime to be handed a ticket, or rather a slip of paper with the seat number scrawled in by hand above the words "last minute" and someone's signature. I am surprised for the second time that Olga has remembered this detail and hurry to my seat as the lights go down. The clowns are already performing their preliminary tricks in the audience. Indeed, it isn't just the performers who confront primal fears in *Saltimbanco*. Stage fright is among the most prevalent of phobias, and coupled with the element of surprise, it can be truly terrifying. Imagine sitting in the spotlit tent enjoying the show and suddenly the spotlight turns on you. An anticipatory hush descends. You notice the band has stopped playing, the spectators in the rows ahead have turned around, even the clowns on stage are watching you. You take a deep breath, a nervous laugh, you glance around. But you can feel the heat on your neck even when you're looking away.

And the mime is throwing an imaginary ball to you. He wants you to catch it and throw it back. Well how hard can that be? So you toss your arm. But he shakes his head and motions you to stand. You have to stand. He's waiting. Twenty-five hundred people are waiting. You're delaying the show. Or you've become the show.

All right. Somehow you rise. Catch the ball, throw the ball, sit back down in blessed darkness. You can do it. But your imaginary throw is off the mark. The mime watches it go over his head like a center fielder watching a Barry Bonds' home run. He doesn't even attempt to catch it.

He glowers at you. Even from the distance of the stage you can see his burning eyes, scalding you like the spotlight. And the tent is no longer silent but shaking with laughter. They're laughing at you. You can't even throw an imaginary ball.

So they've had their fun. On with the show. Except the mime goes looking for your ball. It's a circular stage, with the seats going about 270 degrees around, and your ball has apparently shot from one side to the other. Another spotlight follows the mime as he scrounges through the rows, but there's still a spotlight on you. No point sitting down, you'll only have to stand again.

After an eternity the mime finds the ball and returns to the stage. This time he signals you to settle down before throwing you the ball. But how can you settle down? When you reach out to catch it the audience cheers. What now? How long can this go on? You throw the imaginary ball, which strangely weighs more in your hand than any real ball ever has, and this time the mime makes the catch. The audience applauds. The band plays. The spotlight releases its grip. Enjoy the rest of the night.

Audience participation is a staple of Cirque du Soleil shows, but *Saltimbanco* is the worst offender. You think the pre-show clowning is all there is and settle comfortably into your seat when the first act comes on. But after intermission the mime appears and the spotlight makes its perilous circuit through the audience. The ball toss is a deceptive preliminary to the main event, when an unlucky spectator is led by hand onto the stage. It's unclear whether the victim is willing or not. I suspect not. Often performers will surreptitiously ask audience members if they wish to participate, but I've never spied any whispering. Besides, what language would the Cirque use? Maybe the mime reads body language. In any case, the participant must assume he'll only be onstage a few seconds, a minute maybe. After all, there are well-trained acts waiting in the wings. But the mime's act is the longest of the show, and this routine, with a solo audience member plucked seemingly at random, and definitely not a plant, is the greater part of the mime's act. Imagine!

And imagine having attended the show twice before, knowing all that will come. Maybe I should have just waited for Olga in the Renaissance bar. The other night the clowns had taken Vika and me from our seats and stranded us in the aisle, but that was good fun. Not cause for stage fright. But I recall Vika's fingers digging into my arm a little while later as the spotlight froze on a man seated two rows in front of her and her breathlessly whispering into my ear, "I thought it was coming for me!"

My seat tonight is in the fifth row on the far side of the circular stage. It's interesting to see the show from different vantage points. I can see the band better from here, and glimpse the performers entering and exiting from the wings. One of the four rigging columns is a few feet to my left. I follow it up and across and spot the crane bar that will hold the trapeze limply hanging high in the dark rafters, waiting to swing down.

I stay in my seat during intermission and watch the riggers prepare for the second act. Yasmine, dressed in black, her long dark hair flowing freely, hurries over to the column by me and starts winding cables like a sailor during an America's Cup race. The crane bar lowers to the stage. She combines sex appeal with brute force and I shudder to think what would have become of her had she remained in Iran. She doesn't see me and I don't disturb her—I wouldn't want the morning's headlines to read: TENT COLLAPSES AT CIRQUE DU SOLEIL.

A minute later Olga comes out, wearing her black warm-up as she had the other night. She attaches the trapeze to the crane bar and then diligently inspects the cables. When she looks over I catch her eye.

"You came!" she exclaims.

I take this as an invitation to approach.

"Do you like show?" she asks in a relaxed voice, as if she were just another spectator.

"Of course. Thanks again for the ticket."

"When you going back?"

I can't believe that just a few minutes before her act she is asking me when I am going home. What about athletes' superstitions, performers' backstage jitters? She has just done her rigging, a serious task. And now she's smiling at me and chatting.

"I leave tomorrow morning."

"Well, you come backstage after show."

I give her a hug. I want to wish her luck, but maybe she once fell after someone wished her luck. Maybe she does have superstitions, and my well-meaning words will be the last she ever wants to hear from me. Maybe I shouldn't be here at all.

When Vika and I had seen Olga perform the other night we hadn't been sure it was she. And we had only made her acquaintance the night before. But now I was prepared for her appearance and we were better acquainted. We had spent an evening together, talked on the phone. She was becoming a friend.

I've always found it difficult to watch trapeze artists. As a child I feared witnessing a death or injury. When I pass an accident on the highway, while everyone else slows down with morbid curiosity, I look away. Even when football players are injured I can't bear to watch the replay. We desensitize ourselves with images of other people's pain and then wonder at man's brutality.

I've seen the Cirque du Soleil six times now, and this is my third time watching *Saltimbanco*. I've managed to appease my fear of other people falling, reminding myself that these aren't fly-by-night circuses rigged by fugitives but a highly professional organization. In the first part of Olga's act she has a mat beneath her and two men to break her fall. Well that must be good enough. And in the second part, when she begins to swing, she's attached to a safety cord. As my new sprightly friend emerges from the smoke in her diaphanous suit like a wingless fairy, I convince myself the trapeze is a very safe profession. The most dangerous part of Olga's day is probably her commute to the show. Indeed, I had read about a flyer at the Cirque's Las Vegas Show *Mystère* who was killed—when his SUV overturned.

Nonetheless, it is quite a thrill when you personally know the woman ascending to the trapeze. Afterward, backstage, alarmed by her performance, she would accuse the audience of indifference. "They don't know me!" she would exclaim. "I am no one to them. What they care if I fall?"

And it's true. Circus performers are alienated from those who watch them. They never address the audience, they're far away, and those who do have contact with the crowd, the clowns, never speak. Only the ringmaster talks, and in the Cirque du Soleil there are no ringmasters in the usual sense. There is no billing at the Cirque du Soleil, no hyperbolic introductions. There are no large screens showing replays in slow motion as there are at sporting events. Even televised circuses don't feature many close-ups. And circus performers, whether from a traditional wariness of the outside world, or a calculated desire on the part of promoters to preserve their mystique, rarely give interviews. If you are old enough to remember the great performers of the traditional American circus, Emmett Kelly and the Wallendas, you probably can't recall many details about their lives. Have you ever heard their voices?

The Cirque du Soleil comprises Olympic athletes and world-class acts but they don't advertise this fact. "O" features a gold-medal winning synchronized swimmer, but I only learned of her participation long after seeing the show.

But now I've peered within the tent that protects the circus from the stormy world outside. I know the woman languidly sitting on the trapeze. She is not a nameless figure shrouded in makeup. I have heard her voice and held her hand and looked into her eyes. I have seen her not as she is now, tensed with concentration, flowing through her maneuvers with a graceful rapidity difficult for the layman to follow, like an alien creature dancing for an unseen mate. I have seen her in repose, a woman like any other, making jokes and laughing, her eyes gentle and wandering.

She attaches the safety, which hangs down from the crane bar. As her spotters push the mat away an assistant onstage pulls a rope, which is also attached to the crane bar, starting her swing. Then the rope falls away and Olga kicks the trapeze higher, swinging in a long arc, almost touching the rafters. I watch with pleasure, relaxed, having reassured myself she can't be hurt. But then, hanging from her knees, she leaps up, spins, and almost plunges! It's a standing pirouette and, as I'll later learn, Olga is the only trapezist in the world who performs it. She catches the trapeze's right rope with her right hand and pulls herself on. The audience hardly has time to gasp before she continues, with only a moment's pause to regain her balance.

I gaze at her with admiration and sudden agony. During Wimbledon one always sees parents in the friends' box suffering like victim's of an Inquisition through their child's match, with peril spelling no more than a missed overhead or double fault. Imagine how much more wrenching it must be to watch someone you care for leap from the trapeze! If I came to know Olga better would I still wish to watch her?

Olga performs the rest of her routine flawlessly. As she descends on the safety and runs offstage I wonder what went through her mind after the near-miss. Was she fearful? Embarrassed? Did she consider terminating the performance? I don't intend to ask her these questions, however. Perhaps she will be in no mood to see me, will talk to no one, will go straight back to the hotel and gulp a couple amorettos before turning in early.

Doubtless the coping mechanisms of circus stars are as individual as the performers themselves, but whatever they are, we need to give these people a wide berth. They're taking these risks for us, after all, to make us forget the dangers inherent in our own lives. And unlike the prize fighter, who has months to recover from a knockout punch, or a motorcycle daredevil, whose broken bones have ample time to set before the next stunt, Olga has to walk out onstage in less than twenty-four hours and once again thrust her hand into the looped rope that will lift her to the indifferent trapeze.

After the show I wait for the backstage manager, but she doesn't come. I talk to the ushers, who are busy sweeping. They are temporary employees, working only the Amsterdam engagement, and so they are not familiar with the cast and crew. One of them offers to get a supervisor.

A minute later a man wearing a headset comes over and says hello in a heavy English accent. We had met at the bar the other night. We chat for a moment until he's called away, but he promises someone will come for me.

I stand by the stage. One of the performers, whom I don't recognize, wearing a t-shirt and sweats, practices circling on the German wheel. He isn't doing very well. Maybe he's trying something new, or it isn't his discipline. Maybe he's not in the cast at all, but his physique makes me suspect he is. Another man, equally muscular, follows his wobbly circuits, making suggestions. Then a small young woman with short black hair walks onstage. She sees me and says hello.

"We met the other night," she says. "How are you?"

"Very well. What's your name?"

We exchange names and I ask her what she does.

"Bungee, Russian Swing and Chinese Poles. Are you waiting for Olga? You can go back. It's okay, really. Follow that way."

I follow the curve of the stage and leap over a low protruding ramp, my only acrobatics of the night. I see a tent flap just beyond a lone rack of costumes and venture inside.

Again, I am the only guest backstage and again it's very quiet. No music, no shouting, no carts of props being wheeled to their boxes. The masks hang neatly in rows from their hooks, the television is off, the curtains of the dressing rooms don't even rustle.

The only person I see is Sue, who doesn't seem at all surprised to find me here. "Olga should be out shortly," she assures me.

When Olga does come out I can tell she is preoccupied. Her face is clean and she's wearing her black Cirque jacket. She doesn't even greet me or sit down but leaves the tent and crosses to the commissary.

"Did you see? I almost fall!"

"I don't think the audience noticed."

"It means nothing!" she shouts. "You understand? Their applause won't save me! They don't know me! I no one to them. What they care if I fall?"

"But it's safe, isn't it? I mean, for the first part you have spotters and the mat, and for the second you have the safety."

"If I fall to mat I probably won't die, but I be hurt. And with safety it depends on how I fall and how my assistant reacts. If he pulls too fast or doesn't pull quickly enough I could be seriously injured, even killed!"

So much for my earlier reassurances. "Have you ever been injured, then?"

"Of course. In Belgium my first year with Moscow Circus I hit stage because assistant slow to pull safety. Not everything hit, just legs. I need surgery later. Out one year."

Just a job, I want to remind her, but keep my silence.

She climbs into the commissary tent and stands in front of the salad bar, eating croutons one at a time. I wonder if I should leave.

"Come on," she says, and hurries out.

A taxi is waiting, but there are already four cast members inside, including one of the boleadoros dancers.

"She sprained her ankle tonight," Olga whispers to me.

She asks the driver if he can take six, but he can't. "I said I go with them," she tells me by the open door. "Sorry."

"Do you want me to meet you at the hotel?" I ask. "I have to call a taxi anyway."

She hesitates for a moment, then tells the others she won't be coming. "I want get away from Cirque," she says.

So tonight we go to my hotel, my old hotel, predating my stand-by fiasco, the Park Hotel near the Leidseplein. They have a cozy bar with plush furniture, soft music and large windows overlooking the Singel Canal.

It's quiet tonight and we sit on a green sofa beside an antique stove. Olga appears more relaxed now and starts to smile, lighting the first of what will be half a dozen cigarettes. She doesn't wait for the hostess but goes to the bar and buys the drinks herself.

"No amoretto?" I ask as she hands me my beer.

"White wine."

But she doesn't seem to be much of a drinker, and after taking a sip she lets her glass rest on the long coffee table, and asks me about America.

"You'd like America, or at least America would like you. We love blonds, especially natural blonds, and youth, and twenty-seven may be old for the Russian gymnastics team, but it's still young in America. Besides, you look sixteen. And we like size zeros. You know, it's odd, Americans worship thinness and fried chicken at the same altar. But we're a very ambitious nation. In Australia you have the tall poppy syndrome. The tall poppies are cut down to size. But in America it's the short poppies that are uprooted. Which is the primary reason America would love you. You're special. You say you're not a star, but if you ever want to be a star, America's the place."

"I don't want be star. I can't understand why people don't treat me like normal person."

"Speaking of Australia, why don't you have an Australian accent?"

"I knew a little English before I moved Australia."

"Did you study in Russia?"

"No, I never opened book. I just learned."

"That's amazing!"

"I was in England for year with the Billy Circus. I very popular with everyone. I know nothing in English, so I learn one sentence—may all your dreams come true. And every time I meet someone I say, 'May all your dreams come true!'"

We laugh. She lights another cigarette.

I'm surprised by our casual intimacy, the degree to which she has relaxed, so soon after her shaken performance, and her apparent trust in me. I am also surprised she has not asked about Vika.

I had come to consider Olga more Vika's friend than mine. After all, the other night they had mostly spoken to each other, in Russian. And Olga had not asked for my contribution to her address book. I assumed her chief interest in me was as an accessory to her new friend, and I wouldn't have been surprised had she not wished to see me at all.

Indeed, when she invited me to the performance I expected her to act with more reserve. Perhaps we would find nothing to talk about, perhaps she would be suspicious of my attention. I've been careful not to talk about the trapeze, to let her guide the conversation. So I'm particularly surprised when she turns the subject to love, sex and men.

"Do you write love stories?" she asks with a faint smile.

"Sometimes."

"And do you believe you can love more than once?"

"You mean at the same time?" I tease.

"You have many girlfriends?"

"Have you had many boyfriends?"

She looks away, at nothing in particular. "I can't count."

I can't tell whether she's joking or serious. "How many, really?"

She clings to her cigarette for a moment as if debating whether to tell me. "Two. An Australian in Gold Coast, and a Russian when I lived Moscow. I don't know if I love again," she says sadly. "It difficult for me with men. I'm very strong woman. I like be in control."

"But you're a wonderful person," I reply. "You're lovely and sweet and talented. Any man would be happy with you."

She rolls her cigarette between her fingers. "I don't take compliments well. I just ordinary person."

"You're far from ordinary," I argue. "You're gifted. And you're more than gifted. Many performers and athletes leave the best of themselves on the stage and the field. When you meet them they're disappointing. But you're more beautiful without your stage makeup, and you're even more fascinating on the ground than you are in the air!"

She blushes. "You good talker." And she laughs. "So will you send me one your books?"

"Do you read much?"

"No. But I read your book. I won't read it to understand the characters but to understand you. You very interesting person."

I, contrary to her, take compliments without complaint, but I can hardly credit her words.

"How old you?" she asks.

"Forty-one."

"That not old for a writer. But twenty-seven very old for trapeze."

"How long will you stay with the Cirque du Soleil?"

"I don't know. I decide at end of year. But I can't perform too many more years. It very hard on body. You use same muscles in trapeze. Do you know the trapezium muscle in your back? I use that muscle. I use certain muscles in my arms, but not others, so some get very strong. And when they get strained you have no time rest them. You can't substitute, you understand? And each year it take longer recover. Beside, no one wants watch ugly old woman on trapeze!"

"You'll never be an ugly old woman," I tell her. "But what will you do after you retire?"

"I want have children. That my dream. It's something I have to do. But I don't know if I'll love again."

I've always read about circus people bound to the tent and the road, so I'm surprised that Olga dreams of settling down, of doing what everyone else does.

"Won't you miss the trapeze?"

"Of course. But I can still teach."

"But why do you feel such an urgency to be a mother? You're one of the best trapeze artists in the world. Isn't that enough?"

"No. You're a man. You can't have baby. But I can. So I need do it."

Her words reflect the triumph of biology over sociology. Despite the pill and women's ascent in the workplace, despite the rhetoric of the Feminist Movement that marriage and motherhood are not their raison d'être, it's rare to find a woman of Olga's age or older who finds her career sufficiently fulfilling. The world is filled with men who devote their lives to their work and view their wives and children peripherally, like the blur of cottages to a Grand Prix driver as he races through an obscure country village. But women want to excel both in the world of speed and the world of stability.

A song comes on by Madonna and Olga reveals her admiration for the way she's managed her career and become a mother.

"And yet you despise stardom. If Madonna sat down in this chair," I challenge, "you wouldn't treat her like a star?"

"I would treat her like one woman to another."

"You think she's an ordinary person?"

"Why not?"

"Do you think Madonna would take the train to work?"

"Yes, I think she would!"

She lights another cigarette. She seems quite content. She hasn't looked at her watch or talked about the Cirque. Neither have I, but of course I have many questions and I decide the time is propitious to ask one or two.

I start with her hobbies and she tells me she likes gymnastics and surfing. "Are you an adrenaline junkie? Do you sky dive or parasail or bungee jump?"

"I sky dived once but it was boring."

"I've never heard anyone describe skydiving as boring! What about bungee jumping, or motorcycle racing or mountain climbing? Are you attracted to danger?"

"I been rock climbing. But I don't want do anything might hurt me for trapeze. I can't take risks like that, you understand? One injury and my career be finished."

"What do you do when you're sick? How can you gather the strength to grab the bar and swing upside down when you're ill?"

She thinks a minute. "I've never been sick when performing."

"That's extraordinary! Not in your entire career?"

"No."

I feel a heightened sense of responsibility now. What if I keep her out too late, fail to shelter her from the North Sea wind? The trapeze will hang limp for the first time in her life.

Nevertheless, I move closer to her rather than farther away and ask the question that's been mystifying me all night.

"Tell me what went through your mind when you almost missed the rope?"

"I, angry. There no place on trapeze for mistake."

"Were you afraid?"

"No."

"You weren't afraid at all?"

"I angry."

"Did you want to stop? Were you afraid to continue?"

"Of course not."

"But didn't your near-miss weigh on you? Didn't you think about it during the rest of the performance?"

"There was no time think of it."

"So when you perform you don't think at all?"

"Of course I think. But only about what I am doing next."

"You don't find yourself in a zone, like many athletes do, when their body takes over and they execute without conscious effort?"

"In trapeze you has to think. You cannot do anything unless you have time to think about it first. Where your hands are going, when your body is going to turn, when it time bend your knees."

"Even after all this time, as well as you know the trapeze, you still think your way through your routines?"

"For me it is only way. My thoughts have to concentrate completely on next move."

"But you don't seem that intense. When I saw you during intermission you seemed very relaxed and even asked when I was going home. Most performers wouldn't do that. There are actors who lock themselves in their dressing room until they're called."

"People say I too focused," Olga admits. "It was good for me talk to you."

The barman announces last call, but she still hasn't finished her first glass of wine. "You think it torture for me be up there, but it just my job," she insists. "I love to do it, it what I know. If I was afraid I wouldn't be on trapeze. But it natural for me. Just as it natural for him to work in bar," she says, pointing her cigarette toward the barman. "People different. I don't know how make drinks. I would be nervous to stand behind the bar. You understand?"

"Yes, but the only thing he might shatter is a glass."

I look away for a moment and pitch my next question slowly, hoping she will not duck from the weight of it. "If you're not afraid of falling, what are you afraid of?"

She looks at me squarely, as if I've asked the lightest of questions. And she considers it carefully, as if no one's ever asked her before. Then she laughs. "Men!"

"You're afraid of men?"

"I don't trust them. I don't trust them at all!" she repeats slowly and emphatically. "I stay away from them," she confesses intently.

I respectfully neglect to remind her that she's revealing this vulnerability to a representative of the accursed gender, a veritable stranger at that, in a strange bar, in a strange city, at one o'clock in the morning.

"I told you it difficult for me with men. I like be in control. I am in charge of my own life. I don't even have manager. But I don't want weak man either. I had weak men. Stupid men before. I need someone who strong but respect my strength."

"When you are on the trapeze you are in control," I realize. "But love is a state of uncertainty. When you're in love you relinquish control."

"Do you think I love again?" she whispers.

"Of course. And the man you love will be very lucky. You must only choose more wisely."

"But when you love you close your eyes."

We might have talked all night had the lights not come on to break the spell. I lead her out to a taxi and when we arrive at her hotel I escort her to the lobby.

"Thank you for your company," she says in a sweet voice.

She presents her pale cheek for me to kiss and then hugs me with strong arms. And like a fairy in a fading dream she says, "May all your dreams come true!"

SIBERIA

Her first aerial act occurred in the town of Ishim in Central Siberia when she was still a child, in the hours between midnight and dawn, outdoors in the crisp April air, with only the stars in attendance, and ended in her arrest.

Her father, the son of a general, had wanted a boy. An independent farmer married to a school teacher, Uri Sidorov already had two daughters from a former marriage and one daughter from Olga's mother when Olga was born. What was he going to do with another girl, and such a tiny creature at that? What crimes had he committed that fate dealt him four daughters?

And what of Olga's fate? Life in the Soviet Union was hard enough. In Siberia it was unimaginable. To survive you had to acknowledge that the Twentieth Century was not your century. And for a woman that meant little schooling, an early marriage, subservience to men, a premature old age.

But Olga ignored fate, as she ignored everything that did not fit beneath the canopy of her dreams. Perhaps she heard her parents' wishes while still kicking in the womb. If her father wanted a boy, then she would be a boy.

She played like a boy, worked like a boy, dressed like a boy, fought like a boy. She vowed to cut off her breasts when she became a teenager. A photograph she would later show me in her hotel room in Barcelona reminded me of a street urchin in New York during the Depression. Short hair, baggy trousers, a drawn face with thin lips drawn defiantly together.

The Sidorov's lived in a village of less than a thousand souls, ten miles from the city of Ishim. They lacked electricity, running water, paved roads. Moscow wasn't merely at the far end of the country—it was another country. As Brezhnev let the Soviet Union wither from his Politburo office, the people in Olga's town might have still been living under the czars.

Not that they were impoverished. True, Olga couldn't remember ever having clothes of her own, but she had her own bed and never went to sleep hungry. She received a good education and credits her mother for her intellectual curiosity. She had friends, she had leisure, and her ignorance was a kind of bliss. For you could not compare Olga's town to a town in Alaska or South Dakota. American children in small towns know what they have and what they are missing. But Olga wasn't exposed to television, magazines, billboards. She wasn't bombarded with advertisements and didn't encounter people who had traveled anywhere farther than she. Moscow wasn't even a concrete image in her mind. It was only a word. And the circus wasn't even a word. Other than being a boy, Olga didn't know what she wanted. Siberia provided too little raw material to construct a dream. She stumbled through her childhood feeling only a vague dissatisfaction, a sense that she had been dropped into this desolate place from the skies and that she must somehow climb her way back.

For her thirteenth birthday her father bought her a bicycle. It was her first bicycle, none of her friends had one. Blue, with chrome handlebars, not a hand-me-down but hers alone, one of the few new things she had ever owned. With it she could ride to Ishim and back in an afternoon. And who knew how much farther she could travel?

She couldn't contain her joy. She mastered the bike the first day and rode until her legs ached. She lovingly cleaned it at night and carried it into her bedroom. But the third day it was stolen. She had ridden into Ishim and left it on the street while she went to visit friends. When she came out it was gone.

Tears in her eyes, she hitch-hiked home. But she gathered her emotions together before walking through the door. When her father asked about the bike she said a tire had blown and she had left it with a friend. She couldn't bear to tell her father it was gone. Even though it wasn't her fault she felt responsible. And as much as she missed the bicycle itself, her father's disappointment saddened her more.

The following day she returned to Ishim and resumed her search. After hours spent scouring the center of town, stopping people on the street and inquiring in shops, she spotted a blue bicycle with chrome handlebars on a third-floor apartment balcony. She stood watching it for a long time until a crazy plan formed in her young mind.

She went home and enlisted the aid of a boy she knew. A boy who liked her, a boy almost as wild as she. They borrowed a long coil of rope from his parents' house and snuck out of their bedrooms after dark, meeting on the road to Ishim.

It was a ten mile walk. It was after midnight and they were two young teenagers dressed in black carrying a length of rope. In the silence of the countryside they had hours to reflect on the foolishness of their enterprise. But Olga could only think of her bicycle, her father's sad eyes. And her friend could only think of her.

The center of Ishim was lined with concrete tenements five stories high built in the oppressive, unadorned Soviet style. There were no locks on the main door, or the door to the roof, and at this time of night all the city was asleep.

Olga and her friend hurried to the roof, where she tied the rope securely around her tiny waist. Her friend tied the other end to the railing and lowered her down. She had never belayed before, she didn't know the meaning of the word. Had she fallen she would have surely been killed. But she didn't hesitate for a moment or contemplate the risk she was taking. As she eased down the tenement wall her only worry was that she wouldn't be able to maneuver onto the balcony.

But she landed on the balcony like a cat and motioned for her friend to untie the rope. Her plan was to tie the rope to the balcony railing and lower herself down to the street with the bicycle. But when she turned to get the bicycle she realized with a shock that it wasn't hers after all. She had only seen it from afar, and in her excitement had never considered that it might belong to someone else. This was a characteristic of Olga that age would not remedy. Her intelligence hovered somewhere between street smarts and book smarts. In relaxed conversation, when talking about any number of subjects, she could be surprisingly lucid and exhibit a critical reasoning more characteristic of intellectuals than circus stars. And yet there were grave lapses, impulses she took without the slightest thought of consequence, inexplicable and often trivial, not for risk or reward, such as talking for many hours on a hotel phone when she knew it would be much cheaper to use a phone card, or renting a car in a strange city and declining the free map.

So she stood alone on a stranger's balcony in the middle of the night, a rope tied around her waist, staring at a bicycle that was not hers. It didn't occur to her to take it. She wasn't a thief. She had come here in the manner of a collections agent to reclaim her property. Now the only thing to do was to lower herself to the ground and begin the long walk home.

But when she turned around she knocked something over and the sound echoed throughout the building. Her friend had already hurried down from the roof, but Olga was still trying to secure the rope to the railing when she felt a powerful hand encircle her arm.

Olga turned with a start to see a huge man in his pajamas glaring down at her. But he must have been the more surprised to discover that his prowler was a tiny girl he could have lifted with one hand.

When the police came they naturally asked this most diminutive of criminals what she was doing on a third-floor balcony in the middle of the night with a rope tied to her waist.

"Climbing!" she replied.

"Couldn't you climb in an empty building?" the policeman wondered.

Fortunately the man on whose balcony she trespassed turned out to be a friend of her parents, so no charges were filed.

Olga saw the circus for the first time one year later during a visit to her grandmother's in the city of Omsk. She didn't even know what a circus was when she took her seat in the theater. But she understood everything immediately, as if flashing upon a past life or, more aptly, stumbling upon a future one, as if the circus ring were a crystal ball that reflected her adult life with mystical clarity. Awestruck, she watched the animal trainers, the acrobats, the jugglers and clowns. And then the lights dimmed and a spotlight shot upward and a lone woman climbed a rope to a metal bar suspended far above the floor. Later Olga would learn that this wondrous sport was called "trapeze." But before she knew the word she knew her destiny. "That for me!" she promised herself.

But the distance from the sawdust to the bar was nothing compared to the distance from Olga's town to circus school, or the emotional distance from rural Siberia to the cosmopolitan world of show business.

Most circus performers come from circus families or have trained as gymnasts. Olga had neither circus connections nor gymnastics' training. She didn't even know where the nearest circus school was located. She had no allies. Her parents were conservative and practical. Her sisters, her grandmother, her friends were all walls she had to scale on her way to the trapeze. Even the friend who had recklessly lowered her onto a stranger's balcony in the middle of the night wouldn't help her run away to the circus.

Olga began to feel she had been born in exile, imprisoned and ignored. Her parents didn't take her pleadings seriously. No one understood her.

She knew where she wanted to go, but no one could tell her the way. She knew there were many circuses in Russia, and many circus schools. She knew the best was in Moscow, but Moscow was too remote to even consider. In her entire life, she had never been farther than the hundred miles' distance to Omsk.

As a child and as an adult Olga contained contradictions as vast as the land of her parents. She was dangerously impetuous, yet could also be studiously patient. She was sweet and temperamental, harsh and forgiving, capricious and loyal, stubborn and flexible, foolish and wise. What else but these vast contradictions that marked the contours of her character could account for the strange fact that while she ran away from home without knowing her destination, she did so with great deliberation? Unlike most runaways, who are impelled by impulse, Olga postponed her departure for months. She would need at least a little money and, not being a thief, would have to earn it. And she needed an act.

The trapeze hung at the end of her road, not the beginning. For now she needed a simpler skill to gain her admittance to a circus school. For a few days she tried juggling with stones and fruit, but having no one to teach her, quit in frustration. She thought of animal acts. That was something she could do. Not with tigers or bears, but a horse perhaps, a dog.

Her father refused to buy her a dog, so Olga went to Ishim and befriended a tiny shaggy mongrel she spotted at a refuse dump. It followed her home, where she washed it and named it "Lassie," after a dog she had seen in a movie.

Her father said, "You can't take care of yourself! How are you going to care for a dog?"

But Olga proved to be a good master and proceeded to train Lassie with a determined patience she rarely accorded humans. In no time at all Lassie was standing and playing dead. Olga would make her climb the stairs one at a time. If Lassie failed to stop on a step until given permission to continue, Olga would make her start all over. By the end of the month she had an act.

Now all she needed was a train ticket to Tyumen, her first stop on the road to Moscow. She had no money of her own and certainly couldn't approach her parents. There weren't many jobs available for a young girl, and she was still attending school. She and her friends had bought lollipops from gypsies in Ishim, but none of the townspeople sold them. So one day Olga asked a gypsy woman how they were made and went in to business for herself, stealing sugar from her parents' kitchen. The first batch was awful, but the second was good enough to sell to her friends. Her father kept asking where all the sugar was going. To this day he doesn't know it financed her escape, the first yellow brick in her long road.

On a sunny day in August she informed her parents she was leaving home. She told them at the breakfast table, over porridge. Her sisters were already grown and living elsewhere, so their influence could not be brought to bear against her. Not that it would have mattered. Her father could have locked her in her room, but for how long? Until she was married? He had wanted a boy and had gotten a man.

"Let her go," he told his wife, whose tearful pleading was no more effective than his own threats. "She'll be back tomorrow."

In the history of runaway children, has there ever been a case more singular than Olga's? No stormy battles, no hurriedly packed suitcases, no open windows in the middle of the night, no pillows thrust under the blankets to gain a few more hours. Olga rode to the train station in the light of day with her dog and her parents, and observers on the platform could be forgiven for thinking this model family was sending their daughter off to a relative's for a weekend. But had they looked closer they would have noticed the desperation in her mother's eyes and realized her tears were not tears of leave-taking but tears of loss. And the Siberians on the platform, had they perceived the unique domestic drama unfolding before them, would have surely protested the parents' acquiescence. How could they let their daughter, a girl who had to leap to reach the steps of the carriage, leave home accompanied only by a mongrel dog, for destinations unknown? How could they conspire in her delinquency, blowing kisses and waving goodbye to the diminutive figure behind the window as if they were sending her to summer camp? But then these observers didn't know Olga Sidorova, and her parents knew her too well.

When she looked at them through the window tears filled her own eyes and she too felt a sense of loss. She loved her parents. She loved her sisters, her friends. Unlike other runaways, she had fond memories of her village. She even liked school.

As the train pulled away from the station and her parents receded into the past, Olga realized the enormity of what she had done. Rather than being overcome by a youthful exuberance or eager anticipation of the adventures that lay ahead, she felt a grave sense of responsibility. She realized with a sudden clarity that from now on she and no one else would be responsible for her life. That it didn't matter what happened in the outside world, neither war nor revolution could alter the course she had embarked upon.

She was fourteen years old.

BARCELONA

I began to feel a new rhythm in my life, measured out like a metronome in the long graceful arc of Olga's trapeze. Just as a yogi uses breathing to restore equilibrium, so I used Olga's flight. When I found myself becoming anxious I imagined her dropping to her knees and swinging upside down. When I felt myself hesitate before a new uncertainty, I pictured her letting go of the ropes, knowing she would catch them again. I glanced at the clock and wondered if she was at that moment in the midst of her performance, a human pendulum swinging between aspiration and attainment.

I phone her from Columbus and we talk for almost an hour. I lie awake thinking about the road I have chanced upon. I set aside my notes for a new novel and begin to write about her. Soon the Cirque will be in Barcelona. I decide to join them. They don't know I'm going to join them. But I have to go back, and soon, before I lose my chance. I have to see Olga again, and wander through all-night parties in hotel rooms. Only then will I discover if I've unearthed not merely a few pages of impressions but a book.

I could have fabricated an excuse for coming to Spain. The troupe would have welcomed me as they had before and willingly revealed themselves. But I lacked the journalistic instincts that allow some reporters to exploit friendships. Particularly with Olga. She already distrusted men. Yet she had opened her heart to me. If I bared her thoughts in a book, her relations with the opposite sex might suffer an irreparable tear. Faithless boyfriends, then a faithless writer...

I had to tell her. I had to tell them all in due course and let them choose whether to be included. They could say yes or no. Except for Olga. I decided that if she said no I would not write the book at all.

The rain in Spain falls mainly in Barcelona. I had thrown a windbreaker and umbrella into my bag only at the last moment. After all, I wasn't going back to Amsterdam and all the guidebooks asserted May was the best month to visit Catalonia. But it rained the day I arrived and the day I departed—or I should say the day we arrived and departed, for I came to Barcelona with my father, who was lured by his own circus dreams and my exaggerated account of the impression I had made upon its trapeze star.

"Who? Who are you? Mark? I don't know Mark."

This was two days before our flight. I had not been able to reach Olga since deciding to come to Barcelona, and she had not responded to several e-mails. I had talked only to Sue, who told me where the troupe was staying and wished me luck. I decided to make one last effort to contact Olga and woke her at 1:30 on a Tuesday morning. It was a feature early on in our relationship that she never returned phone calls or correspondence and was never in her room except for a few unpredictable hours when she was sound asleep. So I would either get the hotel's voice mail or a whispering murmur more remote than the voice of a dead aunt at a séance.

"I'm sorry I woke you. Go back to sleep."

But Olga was always kind enough to talk to me when I had woken her, even when she had forgotten who I was.

"How I know you? How you know call me here?"

"Mark, from America. The writer. We met in Amsterdam, at Club Paradiso. Your friend."

"Friend?" she wondered in a stronger voice. "I only talked to you once or twice. I don't know you."

"But you do remember me?"

"Yes, I remember. How are you?"

"Did you receive my e-mails?"

"Yes, but I never answer e-mail."

"So everything's okay?"

In my last e-mail I had declared my intentions to write a book, but this isn't the time to discuss it in detail. "I'm coming to Barcelona in a couple days. With my father."

"You're very brave," she says with a laugh.

Brave or foolish, I begin to think.

I was wrong to assume the weather would be warm. I was also wrong to assume the reason the Cirque's hotel was located in a southwestern suburb of the city, far from everything but the football stadium, was because that was the area where they were performing. In fact they were performing in a northwestern suburb and required a chartered shuttle bus or a fourteen stop metro ride to make the commute. No one I met could explain the booking, but if the hotel was geographically undesirable, the hotel bar was very suitable, located at one side of the bright, expansive lobby. From the bar or one of the comfortable booths, I could look out onto the lobby and front desk and observe everyone coming and going. Over the course of my visit I would witness three different acrobats trip on the marble steps leading to the entrance, and one on the perfectly flat revolving door. Being sensitive, I never brought this to the attention of the troupe but privately concluded that if accountants don't balance anything in their free time, why should acrobats?

After checking into our own hotel, the newly opened Grand Marina in the harbor, and investigating the drainage properties of cobblestones on la Ramblas, we go in search of Olga. She doesn't answer her phone, of course, so we take a taxi to the Hotel Senator.

Olga has already left for the show. Sue greets me in the bar and introduces me to a pleasant woman with long gray hair, visiting from Quebec. She's the assistant costume designer for all the shows, a demanding but highly creative job. I ask her about the new show, *Verakai*, which just opened in Montreal.

Sue complains about the late show times—nine on weekdays and ten on Friday and Saturday. Fortunately the troupe persuaded the hotel to keep the bar open until three. She then asks if we're staying at the Senator and suggests Olga might be able to get us the Cirque rate.

Yasmine stops by and we say hello. Unlike Olga, she does remember me. I ask about the Food and Beverage manager in whose room we had partied. I'm told that after Amsterdam he went to Italy for a frisbee tournament and broke his legs in a fall. All these bungee jumpers, acrobats and aerial performers and the worst injury of the year is sustained in a park by Food and Beverage.

I tell Sue about my plans to talk to members of the troupe. She's supportive but skeptical.

"A number of people over the years have approached the Cirque about writing a book," she informs me. "The Cirque always says no."

But I'm not going to ask.

Barcelona is an insomniac's town. Dinner from eight till twelve, bars that stand empty before midnight, choruses of automobile horns at 2:00 AM. North of the center, the Olympic Harbor is flanked by the high-rise Arts hotel on one side and rows of late-night restaurants on the other, and fronted by cookie-cutter clubs set next to each other like canal houses in Amsterdam. I've never seen anything like it. The clubs have picture windows and open doors so you can hear the music as you approach— disco, house, reggae—and peek inside before moving on. There are muscle-bound bouncers but no cover charges. Club hopping has never been easier. These are dance clubs for couples, but many feature young women in bikinis dancing on small platforms. I'm reminded that the reason I'm here at all is because I entered a dance club in Amsterdam. Who knows what stories await should I cross these thresholds?

I wake Olga up the following afternoon. It's three o'clock but I'm greeted with the familiar whispery hello.

"It's me. Mark. Do you know who I am?"

"Of course I know who you are. How your flight?"

"Fine. How was Siberia?"

"It was nice see my family. But I cried for two days!"

"Do you like Barcelona?"

"I don't know. I haven't seen Barcelona. What can I do for you?"

"I'd like to see the show."

"Yes, of course. And maybe you can watch the set-up. I think you find it interesting. I don't know about tonight, but maybe Saturday. You can come for matinee and stay for night show."

My father and I spend Friday exploring the Gothic Quarter and the art nouveau architecture in the neighborhood known as the Eixample. *Saltimbanco* signs hang from street lamps, and on the Plaza Cataluna there's a *Saltimbanco* billboard several stories high on the side of a building. I had given Olga my number but, naturally, she doesn't call. And Saturday afternoon I prefer to risk not getting tickets for the show to waking Olga yet again. It was a small risk, in my view, since we could always go on Sunday. But it turned out to be a much bigger gamble than I had imagined, and would jeopardize both my book and my friendship with Olga.

The tickets aren't a problem. I step up to the trailer that serves as their box office a few minutes before the show and give both my name and Olga's. They don't have my tickets, but this had happened in Amsterdam as well. I am asked to write Olga's last name and, after a supervisor is consulted, I'm handed two passes.

My father had seen "O" and *La Nouba*, but both those shows were in permanent theaters. There's something special about seeing a circus in a tent. Ringling Brothers and Barnum and Bailey had made the circus tent an American icon in the first half of the twentieth century. The tent symbolized the nomadic and independent nature of the circus. There was also something magical about it, which Ray Bradbury captured in *Something Wicked This Way Comes* and Cecil B. DeMille in *The Greatest Show on Earth*. In a nation that was still mostly rural, the idea of this esoteric, rootless tribe building its city in a day and then tearing it down and moving on was dangerous and enchanting. Dangerous because it tempted the sons and daughters of farmers and merchants to abandon generations of pragmatism for a life that produced only gasps and smiles. Today the entertainment industry is just that, an industry, as respectable as manufacturing or agriculture. But in the first half of the twentieth century entertainment was a kind of scandal, and respectable people kept it at arms' length. Children who run away today are seeking a well-defined dream and have thousands of models, however unrealistic, from television and movies, to graft onto their future. But the children who ran away to the circus in pre-World War II America, or in Siberia in the 1970's, might as well have been traveling to Mars for all they knew about life under the big top.

The tent disappeared in the sixties, as the American circus flirted with extinction. Barnum and Bailey merged with its great rival, Ringling Brothers, and although they still traveled by train, they discarded the big top for basketball arenas.

When the Cirque du Soleil was formed in 1984 it brought the circus into the age of computers, rock-and-roll, extreme sports and Twyla Tharp. It discarded the animals, the carnival, the bombast, the juvenilia. But it resurrected the tent.

At intermission, after Olga has done her rigging, I introduce my father and she gives us hugs and asks where we're sitting. I had brought binoculars to observe her facial expressions while performing, but unfortunately they had fallen through the gap beneath my seat before the first act. So when Olga ascends to her trapeze she's as inscrutable as the first time I had seen her.

This is the first matinee I've attended and there are many children in the audience. They're predictably rambunctious, but when Olga starts to swing they don't make a sound. *Saltimbanco* has an original score, played by a costumed band on a platform behind the circular stage, with a female vocalist who sings words which belong to their own language. The score relies heavily on synthesizer, drums and electric guitar and each act has its own song. Most songs are upbeat and energetic, but Olga's is plaintive and slow, like an Italian love song. The vocalist walks out beneath the swinging trapeze and sings while looking up, as if relinquishing a lover. The creators probably had something completely different in mind but, for me, one of the charms of the Cirque du Soleil is the play it offers to one's own imagination, eliciting deep and often contrary emotions. To watch the trapeze in a normal circus setting is astonishing enough, but it's a discrete event. You are sitting here, she is flying there, with nothing in between. But the music, the costumes, the choreography, and the use of cast members as witnesses creates a narrative framework that pulls everything together and brings tears to one's eyes.

Olga's performance this evening is the best I've seen, but she won't listen to my compliments.

"Don't talk to me about it," she says. "What does it mean?"

Later she will tell me she invites criticism even from people unfamiliar with the trapeze and that her coaches in Moscow never said an approving word. And I would recall her telling me in Amsterdam that she was not comfortable with compliments. The reason, I realize, is largely cultural. In America we're very supportive. We tell our children they can achieve anything and scorn demanding parents. But then ours is a nation of individuals, of entrepreneurs. Russian culture, on the other hand, has been one shorn of opportunity, where the masses are beaten into line and suffer without hope. What other major city in the world would dare to turn off the hot water for two months every year? It doesn't happen in Jakarta or Cairo, but the municipal leaders do it in St. Petersburg during July and August and the citizens stoically bear it.

Olga would tell me she approved of Olga Korbut being beaten by her coach, that their training so hardened them that the actual performance was a relief. But I would counter that America has the best athletes in the world and we spoil our athletes.

I find it ironic that so many of the performers in the Cirque, which is a celebration of individuality and harmony, human potential and liberation, are products of a culture that tries to beat them into the ground. And that while they've confidently hurdled the low expectations ranged against them, they defend this ethos as though it made them.

I don't see Olga backstage, so we go into the commissary tent. I say hello to several performers who remember me from Amsterdam before spotting Olga sitting at one of the large round tables with the juggler, who is also Russian.

She's one of the people I hope to eventually talk to, since I admire her act and am interested in her views on being a woman in a field traditionally dominated by men. The fact that she's also young and pretty doesn't influence me at all. Which leads me to respond pre-emptively to discerning readers who might ask, "Is the Cirque du Soleil composed then only of women? Where are the men in your story? Perhaps this entire enterprise is just a scheme to meet Russian girls. Speaking of which, where is

Vika?"

To which I answer, "I'll talk to the men in due course, but there just happen to be a lot of women here, in the crew as well as the cast. As for Vika, I haven't forgotten her. She just couldn't get a visa in time."

But I have another reason for wanting to talk to the juggler. I'd like to ask her some technical questions. After deciding to embark upon this path I thought it would be a good idea to learn a circus art and, being wary of heights and allergic to dogs, I took up juggling. If nothing else it would improve the toss on my tennis serve. In fact I found juggling to be mesmerizing and relaxing, a kind of moving meditation. And, unlike, golf, you don't have to walk so far to retrieve your balls.

But I'll have to wait for my talk with the juggler because she leaves. Olga, too, excuses herself, saying she has to get her ankle wrapped.

"Help yourself to food," she says. "It's cheap."

There's no beer in the commissary tent. No cigarette smoke. All poisons ingested and inhaled the night before are purged with Cirque green tea, cantaloupe and couscous. "How health-conscious these people are," the backstage observer might be forgiven for remarking.

We sit down at a table across from two young women, whom I haven't seen before. One is from Australia and works in Costumes. The other has an Ace bandage wrapped around her right hand. Did she sprain it while diving head first from the Chinese poles? Maybe she jammed it against the trapeze bar after mis-timing a bungee catch. Or maybe she skidded off the mat after leaping from the Russian swing.

But she doesn't look like an acrobat. She's too tall. She has red-streaked hair, a sharp nose, crystal blue eyes and speaks English with Western European proficiency.

"I was pushing a wardrobe cart and cut my hand on a door," she confesses.

That was my fourth guess. What kind of alternate universe have I stumbled into? The only injuries of the past two months have been Food and Beverage and Costumes. I'm beginning to think the safest place in this strange company is the high wire!

After expressing sympathy with the straightest face I can manage, I ask about her background. She tells me she used to be a fashion model. I ask if she ever fell off the runway.

I find it interesting that someone who was used to being the center of attention, pampered and dressed, was now dressing others. And not because of circumstance but by choice. She had been modeling since she was fourteen and now, at twenty-three, had burnt out. She had gotten her present job through a friend and had been with the Cirque for less than a year. She found it refreshing and glamorous and loved the camaraderie. I asked her how it differed from the world of high fashion. After all, she had worked for some of the top designers in Paris, New York and London and had been photographed for magazine and television ads as well as doing shows.

She enjoyed modeling and admitted the lifestyle was also glamorous, but she thought the Cirque was more fun. "Many of the models were lonely," she said. "Crying all the time."

"What about your ego? Not being in the spotlight anymore?"

"I prefer being behind the scenes."

"And the money? You can't be making much in your present position."

"I'm not doing this for the money!" she answers with pride and scorn.

It's easy to understand what compels the performers from Russia and China, for even a demanding life on the road is preferable to the life they left behind. But here was a woman who had already made a good living by her twenty-first birthday, who had traveled the world and made important connections. She could be lounging on the Seychelles, trying her hand at acting, starting her own business.

And I wonder what it is about the circus and the Cirque du Soleil that inspires even a fashion model to run away from the runway. For what promises and rewards?

But I know.

There's only ninety minutes between the six o'clock and ten o'clock shows. I pass Daniel, the stage manager, in the corridor leading from the backstage tent, where the unisex rest rooms are. He doesn't seem at all surprised to find me here and we chat for a few moments. I look forward to seeing him in action, but he informs me he works in the light box and I won't see him again until after the show.

Normally the stage manager gives the cues to the actors and makes sure the show runs according to schedule, as well as taking care of emergencies. He's the person responsible for the show once the curtain rises. But Daniel doesn't appear at all stressed. Where is the walkie-talkie to relay instructions? Where are the cast members bombarding him with requests and complaints? Why has he stopped to talk to me?

"So you don't give cues to the cast?" I ask.

"No, more the lighting and music and rigging. I really don't do that much," he says modestly. "The show runs itself."

He excuses himself and I lead my father to one of the two long sofas set at right angles in the backstage tent. The tent is about sixty feet in diameter and thirty feet at the peak. There are six small corridors of dressing tables radiating from the perimeter, closed off by translucent curtains. But the main area is unpartitioned, so that from our sofa we can view all the activity at once.

But the activity is not at all what I had imagined. Only a few yards separate the rear of the stage, where the band plays, from the entrance to the backstage tent. In fact there is no door to the entrance, perhaps a flap, but it is never closed. Unlike traditional theaters, there are no wings, so performers enter directly from the backstage tent.

I had expected more tension, more silence. I anticipated that I would have to remain glued to my seat and not say a word. But the atmosphere is...like a circus, and a deeper discipline expresses itself in the self-discipline of the cast and crew.

There are no relatives of the performers backstage. No VIPs. My father and I are the only guests.

The backstage manager, whom I had briefly met in Amsterdam, comes over and asks whom we are with. I tell her Olga, and expect to hear a list of backstage rules: no eating and drinking, no fraternizing with the cast, no standing or walking, no photography, no trying on the costumes, etc., etc. But she walks away without another word.

The show is so finely timed I expected performers lined up like runners at a starting line. But there isn't even a clock in the tent, and after the backstage manager calls out, "Ten minutes till animation!" and, "Three minutes till animation!" we hardly hear her voice again. Performers are constantly coming and going, scrambling like shoppers the day before

Christmas.

Daniel wouldn't be the only one to tell me the show runs itself, that *Saltimbanco* has been on the road so long its performances are practically automatic. But what I see are 2,500 paying spectators with high expectations. I see performers with joint pain, costumes that tear, wires that cross, nerves that fray. So what if it runs automatically? Computers run automatically but they still crash. We have to back them up regularly. But you can't back up a live performance. A live show is always perilous, and I'm impressed with the understated professionalism of the troupe.

Indeed, not five minutes before curtain a visitor enters from the rear, a petite young woman bearing a backpack nearly as heavy as she. I would later learn she had been an acrobat in *Saltimbanco* for three years and had just returned from Mexico. Many performers, surprised by the arrival of their old friend, greet her with shouts, hugs and kisses. "What are you doing here?" "How are you?" "Where have you been?" Half the cast congregates by the rear entrance. Not five minutes before the show!

But the greatest surprise for me was how much I enjoyed this experience. One always has to raise the bar and, after getting backstage in Amsterdam, I had to ask myself what I wanted in Barcelona. Of course, I wanted to see Olga again, and to become better acquainted with the troupe. But I needed a dream, and the dream I settled on was to watch a performance from backstage. I didn't think I would be allowed, and would have understood perfectly if Olga or Daniel or the backstage manager had said no. But I had to try.

Still, despite being a dream, and sharing this moment with my father, I assumed it would be extremely boring. Illuminating, certainly, but not the sort of experience I would wish to repeat. Two-and-a-half hours of sitting in petrified silence watching cast members walk out and walk in. The sort of experience that doesn't encourage or reward repetition.

And yet how wrong I was. The hours passed too quickly and what I witnessed was as wondrous as what the 2,500 watched a few yards away. A show unto itself.

THE SHOW BACKSTAGE

The backstage manager inserts a new tape into the VCR. Each show is recorded for safety reasons. If something goes wrong they can determine the cause. Of course, cast members sometimes wish to review their performance for technical reasons, as I witnessed one of the boleadoro dancers doing in Amsterdam.

The two long sofas are perpendicular to each other and face the TV. Our sofa also faces the entrance to the stage, so it is easy to watch performers come and go. Across the tent to our left is a practice wire, about twenty feet long and three feet high. Beside it are some mats and horizontal bars for stretching. Directly to my right is a table with a backgammon board, currently being used by two acrobats in swirling blue and yellow spandex costumes. Directly behind me are table-high mats on which the strongman twins from Poland are meditating on their backs, side by side, beneath identical blue afghans.

The middle of the tent is covered with thin mats and holds a chin-up bar and a practice trapeze five feet high, the only apparatus—aside from the plastic chess set on the other couch—that will go unused during the show.

Behind the resting strongmen are racks of costumes. On the other side, if I crane my neck to the left, is a massage table, where Olga is currently being taped up, a stepping machine and stationary bicycle, and a small wooden table with two computers, which cast members use to check e-mail.

In the minutes before the show some of the cast are in the curtained dressing rooms, but most are within view. In all there are fifty-two performers. Thirty-seven acrobatics and characters, four musicians, two singers—who alternate shows—a family of three gymnasts, a pair of strongmen, a mime, a juggler, a wire walker and a trapezist.

But to the audience the number of cast members seems even larger because many of the performers play multiple roles. Members of the acrobatic troupe may appear in Chinese Poles, Russian Swing and Bungee, but are difficult to recognize individually and sometimes even by gender because of the costume changes. Indeed, I would later be surprised to see the juggler return to the stage after her act in the passive role of a masked character in a blue costume. And I would be shocked to see Olga take shape as a green cavalier who sits on the stage admiring the bungee jumpers at the end of the show. Wasn't the trapeze enough? But, as she would later tell me, her participation as a character wasn't required. After all, the wire walker didn't play a character. But Olga volunteered because she liked to watch Bungee.

We can hear the audience taking their seats, but the commotion backstage seems just as great, especially with the surprise arrival of the backpacker.

The clowns who perform the pre-show antics have already gone out. We can hear the audience's laughter.

The backstage manager says, "Thirty seconds!" The music begins, but the chatter backstage continues. Onstage, Dreamer, a blue-costumed character with a paunch and a tail, pulls a rope that rings an imaginary bell.

Saltimbanco is Italian for "street performer," a reference to the Cirque du Soleil's roots. Analogous to a musical as well as to a traditional circus, *Saltimbanco* is a series of discrete acts connected by an underlying narrative. The acts can be changed without affecting the show as a whole. Thus, the Asian tour included a rhythmic gymnastics act and Olga's solo trapeze was preceded by a duo trapeze. But the music, characters, costumes and symbols lend the show cohesion, however vague.

You can be forgiven for not comprehending the story; there's no effort at explication, and if you haven't purchased the program you wouldn't know the man in the lion yellow costume with the green cape who screams once but doesn't speak is the ringmaster, or that the blue fellow with the tail is called "Dreamer," or that the character wearing leggings and striped bat wings is the "Baron." You wouldn't know the white fabric covering the stage in the beginning of the show represents the primordial earth, or that the characters evolve from Worms to Baroques, who sleep under bridges. I've seen the show four times and I've yet to spot a bridge. And the psychedelic arm chair that complements the flower-power circular stage and serves as *Saltimbanco*'s centerpiece, what does that mean? Since when do street performers have arm chairs?

But then mystery has always been a part of the circus, and in this respect at least the Cirque du Soleil is loyal to tradition. The Baron walks out with a silver tray. He lifts the lid to reveal a scale model of the chair.

Then, without being prompted, the Russian family walks out for the first act—Adagio.

The wife is dressed in a body-tight hooded blue outfit, with holes cut for her ears. The husband is wearing yellow, their six-year-old son, Maxsim, white. They perform slow, fluid acrobatics without props. The father and mother form a pyramid, supporting the son, like a flower blooming, the approach of new life. Then the son stands on one leg on his parents' outstretched palms, then the father holds the son by his outstretched calves and the mother hangs upside down from the father's waist. Then he holds her horizontally and the son does a handstand on his father's palms. Finally they form a column on each other's shoulders, then descend like a bird landing. They melt into one another, forming a small circle, the father holding the mother in one arm, the son in the other in a touching gesture of family unity.

Except that the fourth member of their family is still backstage. Initially their daughter had performed in their act, a complex part because the child character returns throughout the show, lending it continuity. But Dasha had outgrown the role and it went to her younger brother. Now twelve, she still participates, but as a cavalier, and in between seems happy quietly cavorting backstage on the mats and horizontal bars.

Backstage, the acrobatics' troupe, who had been casually idling until the last moment, playing backgammon or sitting on the sofas, line up and run onstage.

A full-scale plastic psychedelic arm chair is wheeled out. The parents leave the stage, but Maxsim doffs a red baseball cap and sits in the chair. Two characters spin him around and push him toward the band, but when the chair is spun back to the audience Eddie, the mime, is sitting in Maxsim's place, similarly dressed.

Backstage, the husband seems upset about his wife's performance, but I can't make out their words. In any case, they must be speaking Russian. He disappears behind one of the curtains. When Maxsim comes backstage his mother takes him to one of the mats and begins slowly stretching his limbs. He lies very patiently and doesn't say a word.

The wire walker is also receiving a massage, from her male Chinese assistant a few feet away. I don't see Olga and, with much of the troupe onstage, our tent is suddenly quiet.

Chinese Poles consists of four aluminum poles planted vertically on the corners of a trapezoid. The music picks up, featuring a wailing electric guitar, as sixteen members of the troupe, in their reptilian costumes of yellow, red, green and blue wavering vertical stripes slither up the poles or crawl along the stage.

First a single climber ascends, then leaps to another pole, which he or she catches between his or her legs and slides down head first. Then all twelve climb, three on each pole. After they descend a single climber ascends using his hands only, spinning around the pole. Then six climb and dive head first, stopping just inches from the stage. Then two climb halfway and lean out so that their bodies rest perpendicular to the poles. Then one climbs upside down and dives back. Then two attach one foot to the pole by a cord so that they can stand along it and, using another cord connecting their wrist to a partner's, spin them rapidly in the air.

Finally all twelve ascend in step to the music and strike poses, concluding with a synchronized salute, their bodies held at a forty-five degree angle with their arm outstretched, like a squadron of Blue Angels ascending.

The mime is so quiet I don't even notice him go on for his baseball routine. But the troupe make a lot of noise coming back and the tent is once again lively and the dice rolling on the backgammon board.

The wire walker finishes her massage. She doesn't speak to anyone. For a moment I catch her eye but she seems inscrutable.

Beside the mat where the wire walker had been lying, the juggler, still wearing sweats, carefully lays out her electric blue uniform before opening a wooden box which contains eight bright white silicon balls. Her mother, a thin, dark-haired woman who doesn't interact much with the rest of the cast, pulls up a chair by the side of the tent, and watches her daughter practice.

The juggler starts with one ball and slowly progresses to six. Then she goes down on one knee and juggles off the floor. She's been doing this since she was eleven, in Moscow. Four years ago, at fourteen, she joined the Cirque. Her mother serves as coach and chaperone. I wonder where the father is.

The juggler completes her practice and methodically folds and unfolds her costume before taking it back to the dressing room to change. I have been told her routine backstage is just as structured as her onstage act and requires her to touch certain objects in a certain order.

Without being cued, without hugs and kisses and good will wishes, the Chinese wire walker departs. I watch her on the television, as do some of the others. Indeed, I'm surprised to find so many of the cast turning to the screen for a few minutes here and there.

Wearing rose stockings with a matching mini-skirt and a top featuring a textured bustier, and lightly holding a small pink umbrella, the tightrope artist slowly walks up a diagonal wire from the stage to her platform.

She acknowledges the audience's applause before stepping off from the platform. There are two high wires, the second parallel to the first and three feet lower. There is no net, but she has a safety attached to the back of her waist.

After walking back and forth along the higher wire and doing some traditional movements, including a straddle and a flip, she gathers her inner energy, tests her balance and then, miraculously, flips from the higher wire to the lower. The audience gasps and applauds. Then, even more miraculously, she flips back to the higher wire.

I haven't seen her miss yet, and tonight's performance, to my untrained eye, seems her cleanest. But it's not over. A unicycle descends by wire from the rafters. She rides it for a moment, then steadies herself and does a backward flip onto the wire. The unicycle flails back up to the rafters.

Then, as the audience is still applauding, she returns to the platform, extends her umbrella, and slides down the ascent wire to the stage.

The audience is still applauding when she re-emerges into the backstage tent. But no one congratulates her and she appears perturbed. Her assistant confronts her, or she confronts him, and they speak quietly but firmly to each other in Mandarin, in the middle of the tent.

No one seems to notice but my father and me. Olga is playing cards on the mat with Maxsim, who has finished his stretching. I find it odd that she hasn't come over to say hello, but I ascribe her behavior to her discomfort with friends attending the performance.

I have no idea what the wire walker and her assistant are upset about. It's the second show of a long day, but her day should be over. Change into jeans, have a hot fudge sundae, a couple amorettos, dash off some e-mails to the good folks in Shanghai. But no, it's back to the practice wire, where she'll stand and turn and walk back and forth for the rest of the show, like a rose-colored sparrow on a telephone wire, in Kansas, on a hot summer day.

The juggler stands ready to go, three shimmering white balls in her right hand. Onstage Dreamer is sleeping, and his dream takes the form of a procession—a skeletal horse, a wooden cart, clowns and cavaliers.

Olga does four chin-ups on the horizontal bar. Then she does something I've never seen before. Two one-handed chin-ups with her left hand braced on her right wrist!

The music changes and the juggler dashes out. After throwing a baton, she juggles the three balls to her platform, the same wooden cart featured in the procession. She climbs the four stairs to the top. The clowns gather around to watch and to toss her additional balls. Her movements, even without the balls, are elegant and precise, like a ballerina's, her gesture for an additional ball or her reluctance to accept a seventh or eighth ball theatrically exaggerated.

After throwing seven balls up she bounces eight down against the platform and departs by bouncing five balls against the stairs as she descends. I've never seen her miss, but she misses tonight while throwing seven in the air.

She storms into the backstage tent like a commissar at Stalingrad. No one speaks to her, except her mother, who doesn't seem to be offering words of reassurance. A moment later she's back at her station, practicing before her mother's critical gaze.

The Polish strongmen have long since roused themselves and are practicing their balancing movements on the mat. By turning my head slightly to the left I can see the entire scene—the wire walker, the juggler, the strongmen, all a few feet apart and oblivious of one another. The only three-ring circus in the Cirque du Soleil!

The boleadoro is a Spanish dance performed with bolas, cords with a ball at the end originally used by caballeros to entangle the legs of cattle. The two female dancers, dressed in identical red leggings and short skirts with a flame theme, come from Argentina and Canada. They perform beside each other on flat circular platforms, a bolo in each hand. After performing together, they do solos, the band no longer playing, the only sound the sharp rapping of the bolos against the wooden platform.

But we can't hear it backstage. Despite the shattered morale of a few, the mood of the many remains lively. Maxsim is standing behind the costume racks with the mime, trying to master paddle ball. The ringmaster is chatting with a pair of acrobats at the backgammon table. Olga is doing a handstand on the mats.

No announcement is made for intermission. The band come back and the tent becomes even noisier. Everyone stays in costume, except for the clowns, who remove their masks, and the juggler, who has changed into a Cyrillic t-shirt and is listening to a Walkman while climbing the stepping machine. And Olga, who has put on the familiar black sweats to check her rigging.

The second half begins with an up-tempo rhythm for the Russian Swing. Six members of the troupe give momentum to a long plank, which swings from a metal frame, and take turns flying off, landing on a crash pad several yards away, while eight other members of the troupe catch or spot them or look on with fixed fascination.

The theme of the show, the evolution of beings from faceless worms to willful Baroques, can be glimpsed in the costumes for the Russian Swing. In Chinese Poles the troupe wore identical, androgynous reptilian body suits, but now each member has his or her own style, and the sexes are clearly defined. Like a band of pirates wearing their latest spoils, they sport a mishmash of frilly dresses, striped trousers, cuffed shirts, bustiers, pencil-thin ties, hippie vests, flaming wigs and derby hats.

In keeping with their individualistic attire, this act is more improvisational than Chinese Poles. It begins with one jumper leaping twenty-five feet into the air and landing on his feet on the crash pad. Then three members form a tower in front of the pad and the six jumpers take turns leaping over them freestyle. Some shake their arms and legs, some twist, some flip. Then a jumper leaps to the human tower and is caught at the waist by the top man.

For the finale one of the men raises a ten-foot pole and another climbs atop it. A jumper, now wearing a safety, leaps to his shoulders and stands upright. It's as difficult as it looks and I've seen them take three attempts to make it, but tonight it works on the first try and the audience applauds wildly.

Olga appears in her costume, which I'm surprised to see is diaphanous blue with patches of white. Onstage it had appeared completely white. She isn't talking to anyone and I avoid making eye contact, not wishing to disturb her concentration.

The music softens and deepens as the troupe run back in and Olga, without speaking to anyone, walks out.

We watch her performance, my father and I and several of the troupe, who relax on the sofas. She catches everything clean, but she too seems upset upon her return and disappears into the dressing rooms.

Onstage Death razes the clowns with his stare, the only ominous note in the show. But then he removes his mask to reveal Eddie, the mime, who then ventures into the audience to find his final victim.

A woman with glasses and short red hair, whom I haven't seen before, is talking to one of the acrobats about the shuttle to the hotel. They are standing behind me and, when the acrobat leaves, I ask the woman if it would be possible for us to take the shuttle. I hope to see Olga after the show, but I recall how difficult it was to get a taxi in Amsterdam.

After asking who we are, she tells me the shuttle is only for the Cirque and that the first one is always full. But we may be able to get on the second.

A moment later she sits down on the sofa across and watches the show. When I ask what she does, she answers, "Artistic coordinator," but does not elaborate.

I ask if she was the original artistic coordinator. She tells me she has only been with the Cirque for three years. Her duties are both administrative and creative and include monitoring the quality of the show and hiring replacement cast members or new acts.

"So you hired Olga?"

"Yes. Olga's quite rare." But again she does not elaborate.

"And the show doesn't bore you after all this time?"

She had been laconic and inexpressive, but now her face breaks into a smile and she takes her eyes away from the screen to meet mine. "*Saltimbanco* is like therapy!" she confesses. "When I'm feeling down all I have to do is watch the show and it lifts my spirits!"

The twins go out next, bare-chested, wearing matching pants and boots. Their act is called Hand-to Hand. They carry what look like swords with a padded grip and place them in the center of a raised circular platform. They do one-handed handstands from the posts, then one of the twins does a horizontal handstand while the other does a headstand with outstretched arms on the back of his neck. Then they take out the posts and #2 does a handstand on #1's raised hands. Then #1 lies down, raises his legs and #2 grabs his feet and lifts himself to a handstand. Number 1 slowly lowers his legs and twists himself onto his stomach. He now lies flat, while #2 maintains the handstand. After a moment #1 lifts him back up.

Their act is followed by a brief parody from Ringmaster and Dreamer.

Backstage I notice Olga in a green cavalier costume, her tiny face dwarfed by a Pinocchio nose. No one gives her a cue to go on.

Onstage two members of the troupe climb ladders to the rafters. Four trapeze are lowered, and four pairs of thick nylon bungee cords. The north/south trapezes are nearer to each other than those east and west, so each pair of fliers performs a slightly different routine. Cavaliers in costumes of white and yellow, pink, green or turquoise with crescent hats march onstage as other members of the troupe tie the cords to either side of the waists of the prone jumpers, who are dressed in white, hooded body suits. Then they're slowly lifted, lying on their backs as the singer begins the final song.

They slowly bounce up and down in unison before catching the trapeze, drawing on the cords to control their lift. The cavaliers, the clowns and rest of the troupe watch below.

The leapers stand on the trapeze, facing each other, then jump off at the same time, executing flips before returning to the bar. Then they leap singly or in pairs before swinging toward one another. They jump, flipping with outstretched bodies in an elliptical path caused by the arc of the trapeze.

For the finale they fall together and grab hands, like skydivers.

Still joined, they are lowered and disconnected from their cords. The music becomes more whimsical and, a few moments later, the two forgotten troupe members in the rafters unexpectedly jump down from bungees of their own. Spotlights shine up from the back of the stage, a clown does flips to the center and the music abruptly stops.

Consistent with the ensemble nature of the show, the performers take their bows as a group. They emerge from both sides of the stage and run along the main aisle, then converge in the center aisle and spread out along the perimeter of the circular stage. There doesn't seem to be any priority to placement. Both Olga and the wire walker are off to the side, Olga still in her cavalier costume but with the nose removed. This is why I couldn't spot her in Amsterdam. I had been looking for her trapeze costume.

Backstage my father and I are almost alone. We can hear the applause and whistles in the theater. But backstage, for the first time all night, it is quiet.

THE GRAND MARINA

The backstage manager removes the tape and turns off the TV. Daniel appears and asks how I liked the show. The performers make their way back and go to the dressing rooms or commissary tent. I stop Olga and thank her for the experience.

"Don't thank me. I didn't know."

"I'm sorry if there was a misunderstanding."

"No, no, it's all right."

"Are you going back to the hotel? Would you like to do something?"

"Sure. Whatever you want. Maybe we can get Chinese."

It's 12:30 AM and I suspect there are no Chinese restaurants open, even in nocturnal Barcelona. But if she wants to search for one I'll be glad to accompany her.

"I can call a taxi if you like," I offer, knowing I'll need a taxi in any case.

"No, I have a car."

"You have a car?"

"I just rented it today. Meet me outside in ten minutes."

I can't believe my luck. I got to go backstage, and share this experience with my father. We ate in the commissary, watched the show from the sofa of our choice, and now we're going to be chauffeured by the trapeze artist!

I chat with Yasmine and Daniel outside, who are waiting for the shuttle. I tell Daniel I hope my presence wasn't an inconvenience, but he says I'm welcome any time. He just doesn't think I'll get the Cirque's permission to write a book.

But who is this Cirque, I wonder? It's a private company, headquartered in Montreal, staffed, Daniel tells me, with attorneys who fiercely protect their brand. Well, why shouldn't they? The owner is Guy Laliberté, one of the two founders. He was in Barcelona just last week.

"For the show?" I ask.

"For the Grand Prix."

It would have been interesting, of course, to have met him. But now, even if given the opportunity, I don't know if I would want to. I imagine someone as innovative and creative as he would welcome my efforts, but you never know. And the last thing I need at this exciting but delicate stage of my endeavor is discouragement. Besides, the people I'm really writing about are the people in *Saltimbanco*—Daniel and Yasmine and Olga. If they're talking to me, what more do I need?

It's been a long night. I don't know it yet, but it's going to get much longer. I reflect on what was involved for the cast and crew to put on two shows in one day. In Amsterdam Olga had nonchalantly told me the trapeze was a job like any other, but even better, a dream job, only ten minutes a day.

"It's great! They pay me for what? Only ten minutes a day!"

Now I've seen how long those ten minutes last.

She appears as promised and leads us through the gate to a white Toyota Corolla. She doesn't know where the lights are, so I show her. I don't ask if she wants me to drive, knowing her penchant for control. Besides, she has to learn the route.

She spots some crew members getting into a van and asks for directions. They tell us we can follow them if we wait a couple minutes. Olga agrees, but a minute later, without explanation, she drives off. I'm not sure what this reveals about her character—surely someone who trained for years to learn the trapeze can't be labelled impatient—but I view her rashness in this case as a significant insight into her nature.

Soon, of course, we are hopelessly lost. We are looking for the Ronda de Dalt. We enter the first highway we come to, but it is not the Ronda de Dalt and we don't see the cut-off. Olga is undoubtedly the slowest driver in trapeze history and I have to keep telling her to get out of the left lane. She's such a goulash of contrasts, this girl, that even without the circus she would be an endless source of fascination.

The highway is taking us toward the sea, past the Grand Marina. I should suggest stopping there, but we stick to the original idea of going to her hotel first and then deciding what to do. I've taken a taxi to her hotel once, but am uncertain about the exit. When I finally advise her to turn she drives on, despite her modest speed. I know the airport's coming up and we definitely don't want to go there.

"What should I do?" she asks, leaning over the wheel.

I tell her to take the next exit. I'm not familiar with the road, but at least this leads west, in the general direction of the Hotel Senator. Unfortunately, I didn't bring my map. I open the glove compartment, but it's empty.

"I didn't want a map," Olga explains.

"You're supposed to decline the collision damage waiver, not the map!" I point out. Why would someone driving alone in a strange city decline the free map?

I don't ask.

Just yesterday my father had remarked how easy it was to get around Barcelona. We hadn't gotten lost once. Even the Bari Gotic with its maze of alleys and squares was navigable without a map. There seemed to be landmarks everywhere in the city. The sea, the Columbus monument, the two cathedrals, Montjuic, the TV tower on Mount Tibidabo. But Olga leads us into a Landmark-Free Zone, which we will tour for over an hour without seeing a single hill, street, building or sign that has constituted our knowledge of Catalonia.

Actually, I should take the blame, for Olga, usually so controlling, has deferred to my judgment.

"Which way?" she says at every exit or intersection. "Right? Straight?"

Until one time my guess leads us in a circle and she mumbles, "Ah, you don't know any more than me!"

But at the next intersection she asks again. "Right? Straight?"

Despite being lost, she doesn't seem particularly frustrated. Her earlier impatience, when she left the lot instead of waiting to follow the van, is matched by her coolness now.

"Maybe you want to stop somewhere?" she says. "A bar, a Chinese restaurant? It's up to you."

But all I see are warehouses. We've managed to find the only place in Barcelona without nightlife. Finally we approach a gas station and I suggest asking directions.

Not even the taxi drivers know the Hotel Senator, so I ask the clerk which way to the football stadium.

"Which football stadium?"

Somehow I know the difference. It turns out we're very close. To reach the Ronda de Dalt we only have to go through two intersections. The problem is that those intersections are roundabouts, and there's no sign for the Ronda de Dalt.

At a traffic light I roll down the window and ask a motorcyclist directions. He motions to follow him and soon enough we are on the Ronda de Dalt. Olga remarks how fast motorcyclists drive, how dangerous motorcycles are. Imagine!

So now all we need is exit sixteen. We pass nineteen, then twenty. I sit back as Olga changes lanes for the next exit. All we have to do is turn around and we'll be at the Hotel Senator before you can sing, "Spanish Eyes."

Unfortunately, the exit takes us onto another road, leading away from the Ronda de Dalt with no chance of escape for another mile. And this unnamed road too has no direct means of re-entry. So now we are hopelessly lost again.

Europe may criticize the export of American culture with some justification, but they can't build roads. For every golden arch there should be a green highway sign. For every Michael Jackson album there should be an interstate. Tell me what you miss about home. Baseball, Sunday shopping, attentive waiters. I miss overpasses. Those non-descript bridges we never even notice unless we're riding a Harley in the rain.

Finally, somehow, we see a sign to Barcelona. Where have we been? We follow it into the center and I suggest we go to the Grand Marina, which we had passed in a former life. At least I can show off the suite.

Olga wants to go to the bar, which is preparing to close. We sit on a plush red sofa—a night of sofas—for one drink, and then go upstairs. Something's wrong with this picture. She should be the one with the suite, like Greta Garbo in *Grand Hotel*. (Garbo's character also had a driver.)

From the balcony I show Olga the port and the city, which she has not seen before.

"It's lovely," she says.

"Maybe I can give you a tour Monday."

"Yes, that would be nice."

She asks how much the suite costs. Later, when I ask about her own salary she will take offense.

"It's not so much as you think! I'm not rich but I have what I need. I know you asked this question to Sue... You shouldn't do that."

But apparently hotel suites are fair game.

We order room service, minestrone all round, and sit at the dining table. Olga asks my father three times if he minds her smoking. "You look so young!" she tells him. "I can't believe you're his father!"

We chat for a while, until the minestrone comes. Olga tries to pay, as she always tries to pay, but I sign it to the room.

Lighting another cigarette, she looks at me and says, "So, what you want to know?"

I bring her a small bottle of wine from the minibar and soda for my father and me. "Tell us about Siberia."

She talks for three hours, pausing only to scream, "Why you ask such stupid questions?" after I've interrupted her narrative to seek clarification on an important point, such as the lack of her older sisters' influence on her decision to run away.

"They were living in another house, they had their own lives. If my parents couldn't make me stay, how could they? Why you ask such stupid questions?"

But despite these occasional outbursts, and her chain-smoking, Olga is remarkably relaxed. Especially for a woman being entertained by two men in a strange hotel room in a strange city at five o'clock in the morning.

At 5:30 she says good night to my father, and I walk her down to the lobby. My plan is to accompany her back to her hotel and then return by taxi. But she refuses. So I suggest hiring a taxi to lead her home. But this offer too she rejects. I remind myself that she's just told me how she ran away from home at fourteen.

"Whatever other judgments you form about her character," my father would later tell me, "remember that."

But I can't understand her present recalcitrance. She's not insensible to danger, but rather cautious in matters not related to the trapeze. She drives slow, she drinks in moderation, she's wary of men. I can only conclude that she doesn't perceive the risk in driving alone through unfamiliar streets in the dark. The good news is that soon it will be dawn and she can navigate by daylight.

I ask for a map at the front desk, and this time she gladly accepts it. I walk her to her car and kiss her good night.

She doesn't say, "May all your dreams come true."

But they have.

SACRED FAMILY

Monday morning my father and I check in to the Hotel Senator. We had spent Sunday exploring Barcelona. I had decided not to bother Olga, but now I phone her excitedly, hoping she will still wish to spend her day off with us. I haven't made any definite plans. With someone as capricious as Olga, reservations are a waste of time. But I had stayed away Sunday from the Segrada Familia, hoping to take her there, as well as on an architectural tour through the Eixample and down to the Bari Gotic. And of course a Chinese restaurant would figure in the day's itinerary. As for the night, if she wanted, I would take her to the street of dance clubs on the Olympic Port for an appropriate closure to a circuit that began at the Paradiso in Amsterdam.

I phone from our room, my father unfortunately sitting nearby. It's 1:30 PM. I hear the familiar somnolent hello.

"Hi, it's Mark. Sorry to wake you."

But she wakes up in an instant and I would later imagine her sitting up with a jerk. "Mark, I do not think you are natural person!" she screams in a voice I have not heard from her before. "Do you know what I mean? You lied me twice! Why didn't you tell me about book? You lied me about book and you lied about artistic tent! Darling, I don't want see you anymore!"

Her voice is so loud I have to hold the receiver away from my ear. I'm sure my father can hear, and I'm embarrassed, as well as shocked. If only I could explain. If only she could explain. But she hangs up.

I phone her again but she doesn't answer. For a moment I consider going to her room, but if she won't answer the phone she won't answer the door. Or she'll open it only long enough to throw something sharp at me.

I stare at my father. There is nothing to say.

If I were alone I would probably go to the airport, but my father still hasn't seen the Segrada Familia and for once it isn't raining.

On our way out we spot Sue and Daniel eating breakfast at the bar. "What a night!" she says. "We didn't get to sleep till six-thirty!"

"Is there something wrong with Olga?" I ask. "Did she say anything?"

"No. Why?"

"I was supposed to show her the city today. But I just called her and she said she doesn't want to see me. She said I lied about the book and going backstage. But she knew about the book. And the artistic tent was just a misunderstanding. She wasn't upset at the time. Do you think something happened yesterday? Maybe someone said something to her about it?"

"Who would say anything?" Daniel asks casually, eating his omelette.

"Give her a day," Sue suggests. "Talk to her tomorrow."

But there are people who, once they've made up their minds, never change them, and I suspect Olga will not give me the opportunity to resolve whatever conflict has arisen between us. If her parents' pleadings couldn't stop her from running away, how could I?

"If there's something I need to apologize for, I will. I just can't imagine what happened."

"Olga's unpredictable," Sue remarks.

"Very unpredictable!" Daniel adds.

"Please tell her I'm her friend. I didn't come here just for the book."

A cruel sun reflects off the fairy tale spires of the Segrada Familia, but it's a Grimm tale, filled with dark forests, witches, cauldrons. What is now the most visited site in Barcelona, to which Antoni Gaudi devoted the last forty years of life, was begun by the architect F. de Viller after the Association of Followers of St. Joseph purchased land in the Eixample with the object of building a church dedicated to the sacred family. But two years later Gaudi was brought in and, inspired by Catalon nationalism, religious faith, mysticism and boundless imagination, he drew plans for a church that was to cathedrals what Mad Ludwig's Castle was to palaces.

The floor plan, shaped like a Latin cross, is largely traditional and features five naves, three transepts, sacristies, chapels and an exterior cloister. But the phantasmagoric sculptures and futuristic bell towers are visionary.

Unfortunately, little more than the crypt, one facade and one bell tower had been completed when Gaudi was killed by a tram in 1926. The cathedral has been slowly rising since then, with the addition of more bell towers and the construction of the exterior vaults.

A few cranes stand on the site, but this isn't a Hong Kong skyscraper and Gaudi's masterpiece may never be completed. But sometimes unfinished works are the most poignant and respectful. And I think of my own plight and wonder about projects never begun.

When I had first come here, just after the Olympics in '92, I had climbed one of the interior circular stairways, which ended in a platform that overlooked the vacant interior and a pair of columns supporting nothing. But it's the exterior that's most interesting. The eight soaring bell towers shaped like rockets, capped with brightly colored ceramic fruit. The Nativity Facade, one of the three entrances, gaping like the jaws of a surrealistic shark, cluttered with statues of angels and birds that take shape from the vault like figures in an Escher drawing. It's an engaging marriage of the wondrous and grotesque, and had we come here yesterday I might have considered it a metaphor for the circus.

Sacred Family.

But I have no patience for it today.

We circumnavigate it in silence and move on.

We walk across the Eixample, the suburban landscape of gridded streets and chamfered buildings designed in the 1880's by I. Cerda. Unlike American city blocks, these buildings are rarely taller than six stories, with stone facades, bright ceramic mosaics, turrets, iron balconies, tiled roofs. And the diagonal corners open the street up, revealing a faceted view of entrance ways and windows.

Gaudi's most expressive houses are here—tenements and office buildings. But there are fascinating structures on every block, equally deserving our attention. I look at my map as we stare up at a brick building with elongated windows and massive towers rising on the corners topped with brimmed spires that look like hats. It's Josep Puig Cadafalch's Terrades House. And then we approach the Museum of Music, an undulating structure with dragon-lair doorways, green woodwork and mosaic insets like pieces of candy beneath the windows.

"Wow!" my father says.

Any other day I would smile at such a playful creation. "Yeah. Wow."

Not far away Gaudi's six-story apartment building, Casa Mila, wraps around the corner, as bound to the earth as the Segrada Familia is inclined toward heaven, an even more undulating structure than the Museum of Music, but strikingly uncolorful, its sand-colored stone and curved compartments reminiscent of Hopi cliff dwellings.

"Do you want to take the tour of the roof?" I ask. There are fanciful chimneys."

"No, I'll wait here."

But I don't want to tempt fate today by walking on a roof. I tap my umbrella against the pavement. Why doesn't it rain?

I try not to think of her but I can think of nothing else. People are flawed equations, yet we never cease trying to solve them. Fused to my anger is a dread that I am to blame. Her accusations are irrational, and yet it will be unfortunate for her as well as me if her suspicions are not corrected. Always wary of men, how will she trust anyone again if she believes I have betrayed her?

She had been so solicitous, so sweet. Charming, dependable enough, generous with her time. I was in her debt. What can I do?

We come upon Gaudi's Casa Battlo and Cadafalch's Casa Amatller standing side by side in mute rivalry on the Passage de Gracia. We had seen them the first day, my favorite Gaudi with it's masquerade railings and dragon-back roof of red, green and purple tile, breathing against Cadafalch's symmetrical step gables and virgin pink plaster facade. Move on.

We eat a late lunch or early dinner at a Chinese restaurant. We are the only customers. The empty chairs filled with ghosts of Olga.

I miss her terribly. I fear I will never see her again. Indeed, she was hard enough to find when we were friends. Staying at the Senator will be unbearable. I imagine the Cirque will shun me, now that I am out of favor with its trapezist.

My father observes that Sue and Daniel were supportive.

"I'm not going to write the book," I say.

"Of course you'll write the book."

"I don't want to write it without her approval."

"You're taking this friendship thing too far. You're a writer," my father reminds me. "Do you think Norman Mailer ever worried about hurting someone's feeling?"

"That's why I'm a novelist. I'm too thin-skinned for real life."

"You are."

That evening we go downstairs for a drink. Orange juice and hot tea. We sit at a table away from the handful of Cirque people standing at the bar. It's not late, but this being the Cirque's day off, cast and crew members are continually coming and going.

My father looks up and says, "There's Olga!"

I didn't expect she would be here. I'm both eager and anxious. This is my chance to speak to her. But there are glasses within reach. Cutlery.

I follow my father's gaze to the lithe figure approaching the bar. How can such a tiny thing destroy so many hopes? An atom bomb.

Then she turns her head. She sees us. And waves. She waves!

She waves with a bright smile, like the old friends we are. And turns to order a drink.

"We're in the Twilight Zone," I tell my father. "How do you explain it?"

"I don't explain it."

Women! Russians! Siberians! Trapeze artists!

But there's a lightness in my step as I go to greet her, as if I'm being reunited with a lost love. I want to throw my arms around her.

"Can I buy you a drink?"

"I can buy my own drink."

She's drinking sangria and smiles at me while waiting. "How was your day?"

How was my day? How was World War II? We visited some South Pacific islands, swam in the lagoon, played a little volleyball on the beach.

She follows me back to our table and greets my father. Maybe she was talking in her sleep this morning. Maybe I dialed the wrong room.

We chat about Gaudi for a few minutes. Then my father excuses himself.

"I thought of calling you to apologize," she confesses. "I'm sorry for this morning. But I don't understand why you come Barcelona. I think to see me, or for holiday."

"But I told you—"

"Everyone knows you are writing book but me."

"Everyone? I only told two people."

"This is the circus! You tell two people you tell everyone!"

"Anyway, I did tell you. In an e-mail. I sent you three. The second explained my idea for a book. Then when I phoned you I asked if you received my e-mails, and when you said yes I assumed everything was okay."

"It doesn't matter."

"And I'm sorry about the artistic tent—"

"Yes, but you should ask me! You can't just come, I have to make arrangements!"

"So that's why you didn't talk to me backstage."

"The manager says to me, 'Are these your guests? You have to let me know in advance.' But I didn't know myself. Then she says what if twenty people ask for tickets in your name? I told her good, let them all see show! It's Cirque's fault if they can't sell out!"

"You didn't say that?"

"Mmmm."

We laugh for a long time.

Then she leans conspiratorially close to me and says, "I think it's good idea, this book. But you shouldn't have told people. Now no one will talk to you. You should have come as friend and talked to people naturally, then they would open to you."

"Yes, but I didn't want to misrepresent myself. Besides, you're the main person, and I wanted your consent."

"I will be glad help you. But you've made a mistake. You don't understand psychology. Why are people going to tell you about their lives?"

"In America everyone wants to tell his story. Don't you watch Jerry Springer?"

"Darling, this isn't America!"

I take her point. The close-knit circus troupe suspicious of outsiders. Many from countries where a microphone means an interrogation room, and a biography is a file in an apparatchik's office. I remember Russian-immigrant neighbors on a street where I once lived. They would chat on the corner, even in the depth of winter, because in Russia they never felt alone in their rooms.

"I think I'll lie low for a while," I say.

"Yes, that is a good idea. Let me think about it. Maybe I will talk to people. They need know you first."

Yasmine comes over and invites Olga upstairs to a party. Olga asks if I want to come along. "Maybe it is interesting for you," she says.

The party is in one of the rooms, I don't know whose. Except for Yasmine and Olga, all the people are unfamiliar to me. Because of the masks and makeup, it is difficult to recognize many of the performers offstage, and I can only guess if a particular person is cast or crew. Olga drifts in and out, as she did at the parties in Amsterdam. Then she leaves without saying goodbye.

One of the guests standing by the stereo smiles at me and signals me to come over. He puts his arm around me and says he understands I'm a writer. He then goes on to explain that I'm welcome to stay as a friend but everything that happens tonight is off the record.

But nothing is happening. Nothing at all. And it isn't even his room. He isn't even in the cast. He isn't even listed in my program. I ask him who he is and he tells me. He still has his arm around me. He's seen too many mafia movies. So I agree. What else can I do?

I sit on the couch. Or maybe it's a futon, a chair, a chaise longue. Maybe we're listening to Snoop Doggy Dog. Or maybe it's Beethoven. Maybe that's a Trek mountain bike by the window, or maybe a racing bike. Could be black or luminous green. My lips are sealed.

Actually, nothing I see or hear would even make it into my notes, let alone a book. I'm not using a tape recorder or jotting down quotes during discussions. I thought that would be distracting and intrusive. Of course, in Olga's view my simply being a writer is intrusive, and she's right. But I believe that approaching people without the usual tools of journalism is an advantage, as long as memory holds out until I can get back to my room.

After an indeterminate time I ask who the host is and thank him for having me. I then say goodbye.

He says, "So you're the writer!"

I've always wanted to be famous. Just not in this room.

He puts his arm around me. Maybe it's the left. Maybe it's the right. "Sit down. Have a beer."

I figure this guy trumps the other guy because it's his room and he's in the cast.

"What do you write?" he asks, handing me what I can categorically state is a beer. Bottled, not canned. Michelob.

"I'm doing an exposé of the Hotel Senator after receiving a tip that there aren't actually any senators staying here."

"I hear you're writing a book about the Cirque. I might be interested in telling you my story. But I don't know anything about you. I'd want to read something you've written. What you write has to be real."

"Okay. Good night."

"If I'm going to talk to you I have to know who you are, and if your writing is any good. I don't read much, but I know good writing. And there's going to have to be a lawyer involved. And it's going to be my lawyer."

"Swell. Good night."

"I've been through some strange shit, man. I lived on the street for years. I could tell you stories. I was a drug dealer. I sold marijuana. I got into the Cirque because when I got out of juvenile the judge said I had to perform community service and find an activity. I'd taken gymnastics as a kid, so that's what I picked."

I suspect this is how he got arrested. Talking before his lawyer arrived.

The traditional American circus was peopled, at least in the popular imagination, with runaways, vagrants and criminals. That was one of the reasons it made me uncomfortable as a child. The Cirque du Soleil, on the other hand, was a class act. Sophisticated artists, aesthetes, Olympians. But what do I uncover beneath the tent?

Runaways. Vagrants. Criminals.

THE MANAGING DIRECTOR

The following afternoon I give the thumbs up to my father and open the curtains to reveal a marvelously gloomy sky—the Barcelona I've come to love. I don't try to call Olga—no, I'm not going to do that again. We only have two days left, but in a sense I feel it's two days too many. Get out of Dodge before the hangwoman changes her mind. Yet I do feel more secure, knowing that Olga is amenable to reason. Indeed, the strangest part of the whole episode was her friendly wave last night—the fact that her anger passed of its own accord, before I could offer an explanation. Thank God my father was here. Otherwise I might be back in Columbus by now, hurling my juggling balls into the Oleantangy River.

While waiting for a taxi in the lobby's plush arm chairs, Cirque life unfolds around us. The juggler, dressed in sweats, nods at us without expression as she walks to the front desk. The model waves with her unbandaged hand. Sue informs me she's given up smoking. I congratulate her and make a mental note to keep my distance. Yasmine scoots out on her skateboard. Another crew member rolls his mountain bike across the marble floor. Outside it's begun to rain. Wonderful.

In the taxi I recount the night's events. My friendship is saved, my book is saved, but I'm also relieved for my father. Although he wouldn't have complained, I wanted this trip to be special for him and I would have felt bad had it ended ignominiously.

I ask him if he wants to see the show again, but he replies that we can't top the other night and in any case it would be better for my sake not to further impose myself. "Your relationship with Olga is the main thing, and you don't have to see the show for that."

We go to the Picasso Museum but I find the line too long and don't want to stand in the rain. We buy some souvenirs, check e-mail, walk along la Ramblas and the harbor. By the time we return to the hotel it's pouring. We change clothes and take a taxi to the Inter-Continental. Frommer's says it has a superb dinner buffet and we have it all to ourselves.

"It's not the commissary tent, but sometimes you just have to slum it," I remark.

Indeed, the ambiance is lovely, but no one's doing handstands by the salad bar or juggling the fruit. "I'm going to miss the Cirque," I confess.

"It's become your social group," my father, a former social group worker, observes.

I haven't belonged to anything since Little League. My relationships with friends are one-on-one, my sports are tennis, cycling, squash, golf—individual sports. I usually travel alone. My girlfriend lives in St. Petersburg, the one before in Costa Rica. At home I never hang out. I never go to parties in people's rooms. The pages in my address book are separated by oceans.

"I find this lifestyle exhilarating," I remark. "I mean the social aspect. But I can see how over time it can be tiring, even boring. Apart from the performing, just being on the road, in unfamiliar countries. And it's not as though they have assistants and guides. These are young people, mostly in their twenties. And, except for the juggler's mother, no one seems to be watching over them. They're stuck with one another, day and night. I can understand why Olga wants to get away from the Cirque after the show."

"But she wears the jacket."

"You know, if she hadn't been wearing her Cirque jacket that night in Amsterdam we wouldn't be sitting here now. She would have asked me if the dance was over and I would have said no and she would have quietly waited in line behind us and that would have been the end of it. In fact the only reason I was at the Paradiso at midnight was because I had promised Vika I would take her dancing. I'd never been there before. And to go back still further, I shouldn't have been in Europe at all then. I came to Amsterdam in January to meet Vika, but she didn't get her visa in time. So I cut the trip short, flew home and re-scheduled."

"And you wouldn't have met Vika if it weren't for me!" my father points out.

Which is true. In 1991 I had been staying at my parents' house and had just finalized an itinerary for a month-long trip to South America. There weren't any Grand Marinas or Inter-Continentals in the picture, just a hammock on a cargo boat that plied the Amazon from Iquitos to Manaus.

I went downstairs to tell my parents my plans. They were listening to the strange denouement of the failed Soviet coup. Gorbachev's rescue, Yeltsin's heroics, the cartoon schemes of the reactionary plotters, including a meeting in McDonald's to discuss the perils of capitalism.

I said this would make a fascinating backdrop for a novel, and proceeded to explain how I would write it.

"Forget Brazil," my father said. "Go to Russia."

So I went to Russia.

"I'm impressed how well everyone gets along," I say, getting back to the subject at hand. "On a rock tour you have four musicians and they're at each other's throats. Here you have fifty artists and no prima donnas."

"Rock bands don't do flips on the high wire," my father replies. "These people depend on one another for their life. They have to get along."

Later that night I go down to the bar to await Olga's return. My father stays upstairs, saying it will be better if I see her alone.

I sit at one of the tables and drink orange juice and write postcards, as well as a note to the backstage manager explaining that the other night's misunderstanding was not Olga's fault.

Because they travel by shuttle, the troupe comes in like a wave. But Olga, who has a car, isn't with them. Some of the cast greet me on their way to the bar, but I stay where I am. Although I only have two days left, I'm not impatient to talk to them. That can wait until Vienna.

When Olga enters I cross the lobby to meet her. She smiles at me and asks about my day. Then she says she has to go to her room with one of the costume assistants to alter a dress and asks me to come up in half an hour.

I walk her to the elevator and go back to my postcards. A few minutes later a distinguished-looking man wearing a beige sweater, whom I have not seen before, steps over to my table and sets down his beer.

"Are you with the Cirque?" he asks.

I realize I'm wearing an "O" t-shirt. "I'm a friend of Olga Sidorova's," I reply.

"Olga!" he says in an approving voice. "Do you mind?"

He sits down next to me in the booth. He has a full face, light eyes and curly hair. He's too old to be in the show himself, and appears too affluent to be in the crew. I wonder what his connection is, as he must be wondering about mine.

"Have you seen the show then?" he asks.

"Oh yes. Many times. And "O" of course, and the others." I decide it's better not to say anything about being a writer. But I tell him the story of how I met Olga.

"That's very interesting," he says. And he asks me a few more questions about my views of the show.

Finally I ask what he does.

"I'm the managing director," he answers casually.

"The managing director! So you're in charge of everything?"

"Well, the European shows," he answers with typical Cirque modesty. "We used to have two shows touring Europe, *Quidam* and *Saltimbanco*. But now it's just the one."

"And you're headquartered in Amsterdam?"

"That's right. But every couple weeks I come out for a few days."

"You do a great job!" I tell him.

"Yes, well *Saltimbanco* is an old show. It was first staged in 1992, then was retired in 1997 and revived a year later. So it runs by itself. I don't have much to do."

Where have I heard that before? Daniel only gives a few cues, Olga only works ten minutes a night. A colony of goldbrickers.

The managing director! I had decided to concentrate my book on the cast and crew of *Saltimbanco*, but if I had wanted to interview the corporate side of the Cirque, the managing director would have been at the top of my list. He would have been the one who never returned my calls.

And he had come to my office! He had asked permission to sit at my desk! He had introduced himself to me and seemed in no hurry to leave!

I couldn't believe my good fortune. But what should I ask him? And then it occurred to me that he might have ulterior motives. Perhaps he had been told I was a writer and had approached me to warn me off. He was sitting dangerously close. Perhaps in another moment he would put his arm around me and say, "So I hear you're the writer."

Maybe he's feeling me out and it would be best to come clean. Hold on—you've been around Russians too long. He's a decent guy just trying to get an outsider's perspective of the show.

But what should I ask him? This is a great opportunity, but what can he tell me that I can't learn elsewhere?

The Cirque du Soleil was founded in 1984 by Guy Laliberté and Daniel Gauthier, former street performers. After touring Quebec and then the rest of Canada in an eight-hundred seat tent with a show called *La Magic Continue*, they dreamed of a more ambitious production in a larger tent. After being turned down by bankers, they received a grant from the Canadian government, and gambled it all on a single performance at an arts festival in Los Angeles. The crowds loved them and Laliberté's creative team staged *We Reinvent the Circus* and then *Nouvelle Expérience*, both since retired. The subsequent shows, all running, include *Saltimbanco* in Europe, *Mystère* in Las Vegas, *Alegría*, currently touring Japan, *Quidam*, touring the U.S., "O" in Las Vegas, *La Nouba* at Disney World, *Dralion*, touring the Pacific Northwest, and *Varekai*, premiering in Canada.

"Do you see Laliberté much?" I ask. A stupid question, perhaps, but it will give me some sense of the management style.

"A few times a year," he answers. "Not much."

"So you don't have to go to Montreal on a regular basis?"

"I go every now and then."

"One thing I admire about the troupe is their camaraderie. I was speaking to someone who worked in Vegas and he told me the atmosphere was different there."

"Yes, it's true. And *Saltimbanco* is a very European show. It plays very well here."

"Everyone is so proud to be a part of it. They wear their Cirque jackets everywhere."

"That's because it saves them the expense of buying a coat."

He smiles at me, but I'm not sure he's joking. He has a very pleasant manner, but intense eyes. I appreciate that he doesn't look away, despite the fact that we are surrounded by his employees. I have his undivided attention. What will I do with it?

"What's it like working with the Cirque? What are the people like?"

"Oh, like anywhere else I suppose."

But I don't believe that. "Isn't the corporate culture different from other businesses?" I pursue. "Isn't the Cirque unique?"

"Well, it's a business like any other."

"Yes, but I mean if you're a manager for a drug company and you move to a computer company or a chemical company it's pretty much the same thing. How would you characterize the corporate personnel at the Cirque?"

He smiles candidly and puts an index finger to his temple. "You have to be a little twisted to work here."

I laugh. "You too?"

"Of course!"

He spends about fifteen minutes with me before taking his glass and saying good night. I too have to go, late for my date in room 316.

Olga's bicycle is in the hallway and I notice the poodle I had given her in the basket. I knock on the door and she tells me to come in.

She's in the bathtub and the bathroom door is cracked open. I sit at the table to wait for her, but she starts talking and I can't hear. So I walk back to the bathroom door. It's one-thirty in the morning and I'm a cartwheel away from a naked trapeze artist!

She asks about my father and tells me to help myself to the refrigerator. "Are you hungry? There's fruit. Take what you like."

One of my wishes has been to see her room, but I haven't had the temerity to ask. Even in Amsterdam, before I decided to write a book, I wanted to see her room. You can tell a lot about a person by observing where she lives, and I believe a hotel room can sometimes be even more revealing than a home because the traveler is reduced to essentials.

I'm stunned. But nothing about Olga should surprise me anymore, and I should have the sense to stop making assumptions. I was certain the theme of her room would be chaos. After all, wasn't her life chaotic? She was an athlete, not a homemaker. She could be impulsive and forgetful, and such people are rarely organized. I expected clothes strewn on the furniture, open purses and drawers, the bureau covered with makeup and coins, a pack of cigarettes and a brush on the night stand.

Her room was spotless! The cleaning woman had made the bed, of course, and cleaned the ashtrays. I couldn't credit Olga for the lack of empty bottles or crumpled papers. But I didn't even see a suitcase! Or one article of clothing! Even the fruit had been carefully placed in the refrigerator. And the table, the night table and dresser were completely bare, except for a box of biscuits beside the TV. One could be excused for thinking she had just checked in for an overnight stay rather than a visit of one month. There weren't even any pictures on the walls.

I think of the Food and Beverage manager who had brought his whole world with him to the Amsterdam Renaissance. Whatever Olga brought with her was carefully concealed. The neatest runaway in history.

She comes out toweling her hair, dressed in a jade robe, her face pink, her feet bare.

"Have something to eat," she says, putting the fruit on the table. "Do you want wine or beer?"

"Juice is fine."

"Do you like biscuits?" she asks, handing me the unopened box. "You can take these with you."

I smile, recalling her hospitality when Vika and I ate with her in the commissary tent. It was a Russian custom for hosts to feed their guests into submission.

"Your room is so clean," I remark.

"Yes, I hate if anything is out of place. Do you mind if I smoke? I open window. So, tell me about your family."

We sit across from each other at the table, I with my juice, she with white wine and Marlboros. She rests her elbows on the table and looks at me with a sweet smile while I answer her questions about my family.

After about an hour she opens a drawer and takes out a pile of scrapbooks. "Do you want see my pictures?" she offers, moving to the bed.

I sit next to her as she shows me press clippings from Australia. She had performed in a resort casino on the Gold Coast before moving to Melbourne to teach at the National Institute of Circus Arts. I'm surprised to read in one article that she didn't speak much English at the time.

When I ask about salaries Olga scolds me for my curiosity. She won't tell me what she makes but states she makes far less than I imagine and is not rich. But then she immediately defends the Cirque.

"I am not complaining, you understand? They treat us well, they pay us well. Where else can we do what we dream and be paid for it?"

Refreshing thought. There was a time when baseball players said the same thing. But that was about a hundred years ago.

Interesting though. She doesn't want to be a star, she doesn't want to be treated differently. And she could certainly get a lot more press than she does. Yet she's kept all these articles.

The other albums are filled with photos and are extremely revealing in both contexts. There's one of her parents, not small at all, like her, but solid, prosperous. Their home more elegant than you would imagine a Siberian farmhouse to be, with striped wallpaper and lacquered tables. There are photos of her sisters, her grandmothers. And then a small boy—but no, it's she! Standing squarely in the yard, her hair darker and cut short, wearing suspenders and baggy trousers.

I discover Olga is a chameleon, no easier to qualify on celluloid than in any other aspect of her life. In each photo she appears different. The only common denominator is her bare feet.

"I hate shoes!" she says.

I'm most surprised by her femininity. She wears makeup for the show, of course, but not afterwards, not even lipstick. Her nails aren't polished, she doesn't wear jewelry, or seductive clothing, preferring slacks, long skirts and pullovers. She doesn't style her fine blond hair but pulls it back indifferently.

But she's very photogenic and her albums reveal a side of her I never would have imagined. Many of the photos were taken professionally, in studios with white backdrops or in scenic settings. A sophisticated gaze through a pair of glasses, a seductive pose in a long dress, smiling in a bikini on the beach. The most striking is a shot of her straddling a boulder in a short white dress, her legs showing to her thighs. Hmmm.

"But you don't want to be a star?" I tease her.

"I like take pictures," she replies. "And try different looks."

Yes, but it's too bad we in the audience can't see her face. She has so many faces. Her smile is her brightest feature. Even in the two quick photos I took of her in Amsterdam I was dazzled by her uninhibited smile.

I also perceive that nearly all the photos are of her alone.

"I didn't know I had this!" she admits almost at the same moment, discovering a snapshot hidden behind a newspaper clipping.

And she shows me a photo in which she is not standing alone. A tall, handsome Australian man towers beside her.

"You destroyed his photos?"

"I can have a very bad temper. We were not good for each other. We always fighting. One time I threw the TV."

"When he left you for another woman?"

"I destroyed the whole room."

"But you didn't leave him?"

"I loved him. What could I do?"

"But he was your assistant. How could you trust him to hold your safety when he cheated on you?"

"It not easy find good assistant."

She puts his photo back in the album.

"Do you ever talk to him?"

"Oh, I called him yesterday."

"You called him? I don't understand you!"

"He's stupid and not good for me, but I love him. What can I do?"

I continue looking at her photos as she talks to me, occasionally glancing up to meet her eyes.

"At least you had the sense to leave him."

"After he began seeing this other woman he asked me to meet her."

"You're kidding! You didn't do it?"

"Of course."

"What was he thinking?"

"I don't know."

"But he knew your temper. Is that when you threw the TV?"

"No, that was before."

"So what did you do? Did you hit him? Her?"

"I was curious. So I went to her apartment and she said, 'Hello, how are you?' just like that, in a sweet voice."

"And you spit in her face? You kicked her in the groin?"

"I smiled back and said, 'May all your dreams come true!'"

"You didn't!"

"Mmmm. And I said 'Goodbye,' and closed the door."

"You poor thing. You must have been very depressed."

"I drove to Sydney. We were on the Gold Coast and I took the car at night to Sydney. And I checked into a hotel to kill myself."

I wonder how a trapeze artist kills herself. But this night is too special to spoil with dark memories. I'll save it for another time. "You're lovely," I tell her, handing back the last album. "You photograph like a model. The Australian guy was a fool. And listen, I know you've confided a lot of intimate details. Such as when we were in the Park Hotel in Amsterdam and you were talking about your mistrust of men. You said you never open for men, even in bed."

"I only open for one man."

"Yes, well I want you to know I won't put that in the book."

She looks at me and shrugs. "Put it in. Why not?"

Had someone observed a man departing Olga's room at 4:30 in the morning they might have been forgiven for suspecting an intimate tryst. Indeed, they would not have been completely wrong. But what my friend revealed to me on her bed was far more personal than what lay beneath her robe.

HARLEQUIN

Our last full day. Fortunately Olga appears in the lobby as we're waiting for a taxi. I don't know if my father will see her tonight and this gives them a chance to hug goodbye. I invite her to lunch but she has to get a massage. Then she points to a back room and tells us there's a computer set up for the Cirque and we can use it to check e-mail. I thank her, but I've had enough behind-the-scenes experiences for one trip.

It's only drizzling outside. We go back to the Picasso Museum, and either the line is shorter or my patience is longer this afternoon. Housed in a series of restored mansions in the Gothic Quarter, the collection features Picasso's early works and traces his influences and development as an artist in Catalonia.

The catalog explains that in his twenties Picasso began to frequent the Medrano Circus in Paris, and the acrobats and clowns deeply influenced him, transforming his work.

The Cirque has certainly transformed my work, and even my life. Imagine, you have always held a profound curiosity about life, history, culture, science, art. And, of course, the performing arts have always attracted you. Theater, film, music, dance. All but the circus, which you felt undeserving of your attention. And then one day you see *Saltimbanco* and weep. And five years later meet a trapezist and laugh. You find yourself juggling, walking on balance beams in the park, trying to do a one-handed chin-up. You begin to re-evaluate long held assumptions about high culture and low, sport and entertainment, exploitation and transcendence. And all the unmeetable extremes in life—competition and cooperation, recklessness and caution, holding on and letting go—converge in the tiny person of Olga Sidorova.

I ponder a portrait of a harlequin more deeply than I would have before my experience with the Cirque. The man is very pale, with patchy, close-cropped brown hair, and his eyes are almost mournful. But then this is not a clown at all but a Russian ballet dancer posing in a muted pastel diamond-patterned suit. Yet another example of the convergence of high culture and low.

The circus certainly influenced Picasso, but Picasso also influenced the circus. Only it would take decades, it would take the Cirque du Soleil to finally comprehend how Picasso's re-shuffling of the world could transform something grotesque into a thing of beauty.

That night my father goes to sleep before the Cirque returns. We have an early flight tomorrow. I go downstairs and wait for Olga. She's happy to see me and sits on the couch in the lobby beside my arm chair.

"What are you drinking?" I ask.

"Sangria."

For once she lets me buy her a drink. When I return she's talking to Sue about nicotine gum.

"I'll give you some if you want to try it," Sue says, taking her stash out of her purse.

But Olga shakes her head. "I want stop, but not now. I don't know how my body will react. How it will affect the trapeze."

"How's it going for you?" I ask Sue.

"Oh, it's all right."

"You're not frustrated being surrounded by hardened smokers?"

"Actually everyone's very supportive."

She leaves and Olga lights up. A moment later the juggler passes and Olga motions her over. She's wearing a white sweater, blue jeans and six-inch black platform heels. I've never seen her down here this late and wonder where her mother is.

She smiles at me and sits on the arm of the sofa between me and Olga, her clunky shoes nearly touching my knee.

They speak in Russian for several minutes without interruption. Then the juggler rises, nods to me, and goes upstairs.

Olga takes a drag on her cigarette and leans closer. "She won't talk to you," she states. "She doesn't like talk to reporters. She's tired of the same questions."

"But I'm not a reporter. I'm not asking the same questions."

"I know. But she doesn't know why she should talk to you. We need a plan. The problem is they don't know you."

"But they know you."

Olga's eyes light up. "Maybe I could do interviews for you. I could use tape recorder!"

"You would do that for me?"

I'm genuinely touched, although that's not what I want. "How about this?" I then offer. "It's my last night, I can't do anything more in Barcelona. But I can come to Vienna. If that's all right with you?"

"Of course."

"I can write a letter when I get home and e-mail it to you. I'll explain who I am and what I'm writing and that I'll be in Vienna if they should want to talk to me."

"That's an excellent idea!" Olga exclaims. "I can put it on board in artistic tent."

I smile at the idea of being on the board in the artistic tent.

"I'm grateful for all your help," I tell her.

"I'm glad to help. I think the book is very good idea. You just didn't think the right way to go—boom, boom, boom. But now I think it better. I think it will work."

"In any case I don't need to speak to everyone. You're the center of the book. You deserve a book of your own."

"That your decision," she replies. "I'm just ordinary person."

"Listen. If you ever want to come to the U.S. you can be my guest. I'll take you wherever you want to go."

"I was in the U.S. one time only, in December. I went to Florida to see friends."

"You have friends in Florida?"

"I have a Russian friend who does trapeze for Ringling Brothers. But she not in the show now because she pregnant. And I know a coach in Jacksonville. And I have friends in *La Nouba*, the show at Disney World. But you know, I don't care so much go U.S. but I'd like see "O". I've never seen it."

"I'll take you if you like."

"Yes, I can get us free tickets. But I can't go after Barcelona. Maybe after Vienna, or Brussels."

"Whenever you want," I tell her, surprised by her seriousness. I don't expect she will ever come, but I'm flattered by her intention.

It's three o'clock and the bar's closing. I walk her up to her room and hug her goodbye. A few minutes later I return and leave a gift outside her door. I didn't want to buy something ostentatious, which might make her uncomfortable. And knowing her minimalist decor I didn't want to give her something she wouldn't want to keep. But then at the Picasso Museum I spotted an ash tray. A smoker can never have too many ash trays.

"Guess what?" Olga says when I call her a week later from Columbus. "I stopped smoking!"

"That's great! Congratulations! When?"

"Yesterday!"

Neither of us mentions my ash tray. I hope she threw it out the window.

"How are you doing? Are you taking the gum?"

"I got patches. Mark, it so hard! It changes so much your body! You know I been smoking fourteen years!"

"Why did you decide to quit now? Did Sue get to you?" Or my ash tray? I want to add.

"I've wanted stop for some time. But I'm afraid about performance. What it will do. Last night was the first time without smoking. I don't know what will happen. Will I shake? Will I be dizzy? Will I fall?"

I'm always surprised when Olga mentions falling. I'd always read that people who trade in danger are stubborn optimists with a superstitious antipathy for considering bad outcomes. Yes, they take precautions and know the risks. But a fighter pilot won't tell his friends, "Well, I hope I don't crash tonight." Or after nearly crashing, he'll say, "No, it was a just a patch of turbulence." You never hear the running back fresh from rehab tell reporters before the game, "I sure hope I don't re-injure my knee." Or the fire fighter or the cop or the solo sailer or the balloonist or the stunt man or the wire walker. But especially the trapezist.

And yet here was Olga, able to envision disaster and still go up. This made her appear even cooler in my eyes and more enigmatic.

"But you did it?" I managed to ask.

"Yes, of course. But today, oh, it terrible. I wake up, I want cigarette. I eat, I want smoke. Imagine, every hour for fourteen years I had a cigarette!"

"But you can't smoke at the Cirque."

"Not in the tent. But outside."

And then the chain smoking after, I think. "But didn't smoking restrict your breathing? I don't know of any athletes who smoke. Yet you've told me you can run ten kilometers. How could you be a smoker and run?"

"Well, I would run five kilometers, stop, smoke a cigarette, run five kilometers..."

"You're strange! Did anyone ever tell you you're strange?"

"So how are you? How your father?"

"Both well, thanks. I wanted to tell you I'm going to Ringling Brothers tomorrow. They're in Columbus for the weekend."

"Oh, you must tell me about it! I've never seen it. You know my friend is in the show. But not now, she pregnant."

"Yes, I know. And they have a trapeze troupe called Angels of Fire. Ten men and two women."

"Yes. They from Russia. A lot of us trained together. Sometime I'd like go and see different circuses. In England, in America. And I want we should go see "O" and *Mystère*. Maybe after Vienna."

It's another of Olga's countless contrasts that she yearns to get away from Cirque people and often protests when I ask about the trapeze, yet wishes to spend her vacation watching circuses and visiting old friends from the Moscow school. But, unlike some of her other contrasts, this one I understand. After all, when you spend twenty-four hours a day with the same small group of people it's natural to want a change. And yet her dedication to the circus is so great she can't spend more than a few days away from it without suffering a withdrawal perhaps equal to or even more profound than her withdrawal from nicotine. And nearly all her friends are from the circus. I would have thought that someone as well-traveled, gregarious and charming as Olga would have scores of friends, would meet new people every day. But this is a fallacy we on the outside often harbor about people in show business. In fact Olga finds life often lonely and appears genuinely grateful for my attention. She once confided to me that she only has a few close friends, most from the past, other trapeze artists and coaches. I told her I was honored to be included in such rarefied company.

I don't think I went to the circus more than two or three times as child. I was more interested in Pete Rose and Oscar Robertson than the colony of acrobats and clowns that rolled through Cincinnati every spring or summer. Of course, I knew about Ringling Brothers and Barnum and Bailey, and there were books and movies and cartoons. But the sixties was a difficult decade for the circus. In fact, I can't recall if I ever actually saw Ringling Brothers.

The only clear memory I have is being taken by my Aunt Dee to see the Shriners' Circus at the Cincinnati Gardens when I was five or six. I remember the carnival outside and my distaste for the unwinnable games. I recall a five-dollar bill wrapped around a wooden block slightly larger than the ring which was supposed to encircle it. I got the impression that none of these barkers had children of their own, or if they did they had met with some unspeakable fate.

And then there was the madness inside. I was accustomed to watching basketball games with scoreboards and time outs and a single ball, the movements of which were followed religiously by the spectators. But here was complete chaos, rigging in the rafters, simultaneous stunts, crying babies, endless movement in the aisles. The clowns doubtlessly made me laugh and who doesn't like elephants and horses, but I nevertheless felt uncomfortable. I don't remember any details of the trapeze act. Only that I couldn't take my eyes away, but wanted to. There are few things more instinctively unsettling than watching a fellow human being fall from a great height. And yet everyone seemed to be having a good time.

I managed to keep my feelings to myself, not that I would have been able to express them at that age. I suffered a vague melancholy, a sense of alienation. My final memory of that night was of my Aunt offering to buy me a balloon. They were quite special, oblong translucent balloons containing another balloon shaped like the head of Mickey Mouse. I'd been looking at them all night, but I couldn't let her buy me one, not simply because they cost a dollar but because they were filled with helium and the rafters were painted with them—so many metaphors for loss, for running away, for unwinnable games.

But I was not one of those children who was frightened by clowns. Indeed, I didn't even appreciate the exoticness of the circus in my youth. My passions were dinosaurs, monsters, aliens. Only as an adult did I acknowledge the uniqueness of clowns, animal trainers, contortionists and aerial acts. So much so that I resigned myself to the fact that our paths would never cross.

So I attend Ringling Brothers and Barnum and Bailey with the sense of curiosity and anticipation I should have felt in my childhood. The first thing I observe is that I've forgotten to bring a toddler. I'm surprised they let me in. The only other unaccompanied adult I spot is a bald man wearing a clown nose. Good for him!

Indeed, why aren't there more like us? Why aren't there teenagers? Why do we cling to the notion of the circus as the province of small children? Sure, it's not the ballet, but neither is *Star Wars*. Of course, I can understand the lack of teens. Like Disney, the American circus suffers from wholesomeness. It isn't cool. And yet the opening act is a troupe of indoor freestyle skiers, who fly down a watered polypropylene ramp, and the star clown, Bo, rides a wire on a motorcycle and climbs a swaying pole, from which he hangs interminably.

And what about adults without children? Adults who don't have to worry about being cool but can simply admire the artistry of Bo the Clown. There are a pair of female solo trapezists from Bulgaria. Of course they aren't as good as Olga. But they're good. And the Floating Balance Beam group are good, and the Angels of Fire are very good, exercising triple somersaults and the longest throw I've ever seen. Indeed one can see the influence of Disney on the parade and musical numbers and the influence of the Cirque du Soleil on the polish and presentation of the aerial acts.

True, it's not the Cirque. The sawdust may be gone but there's still enough kitsch to keep P.T. grinning cynically in his grave. But it's unfair to make such comparisons. It is what it is, and by the end of the show all

I can think is how hard these people trained to learn their skills and how hard they work to make the world forget the world. No exploding cars, no shoot-outs, no alien genocide. Just a few exploited animals whose fate seems no worse than that of the children of activists not allowed to visit circuses and zoos.

In short, I was wrong. I was wrong!

FALLING

Olga has fallen in love. With a Dutch bartender she met in Amsterdam. He's come to visit her for a few days in Barcelona and she's very happy. "He loves me very much!" she says. "He loves me too much! I don't like someone love me too much, you understand? I want love him. Next week we get married. Will you come?"

"You're joking!"

And she laughs an uninhibited laugh, like a child who can't stop laughing and gets the hiccoughs. This transatlantic laugh roars through the phone louder than her screams.

"Does he want to marry you?"

"Yes."

"Where would you live, Amsterdam?"

"No, Australia. If he come to Russia, for example, it will be no good. He doesn't speak language and will always be following me. The same in Holland. I will be following him. In Australia we are the same."

"And will you have children?"

"I want twins. Twin girls. I will teach them gymnastics!"

"Not trapeze?"

"Oh no! No way trapeze! My children be two trapeze, la, la, la! It would be awful! You know how boxers get hit in the head so many times and get Parkinson's? Well it's the same with trapeze, but the shoulder."

"You have a bad shoulder?"

"Of course, always. All trapeze have."

I ask about her boyfriend. She says he is not interested in the Cirque.

Only in her. She didn't even notice him at first. But he noticed her. And when she came down to the bar one night in her bathrobe and bare feet for a bottle of wine he fell in love with her.

He doesn't like to see the show. It makes him nervous. But it is hard for their relationship if she stays with *Saltimbanco*. She will have to try to get him a job on tour, which is difficult even for someone in her position, or they will have to content themselves with a few days in his city or hers.

I sympathize, but only so much. After all, they are both in Europe. My girlfriend is in Russia and needs a visa to go to the bathroom. I am more concerned that Olga will be hurt again, although I should be worrying about the Dutchman. The Dutch are famous for their mildness, their moderation, their maturity. The drug addicts and vagrants in Holland are mostly foreigners. Where else can you attend a soccer rally and among the throng of fans on the Leidseplein only spot two cops, leaning against their car, smiling?

And, of course, my own interests press upon my unspoken thoughts. What will this do to our friendship, to the book? What if he's jealous? What if he tells her he doesn't want me to write about her? My father will later reply, "Good luck telling Olga anything!"

But she's been tied down before, by men. She breaks away eventually, but it takes time. At least this guy's Dutch. If he knows how to pour a Heineken he can't be all bad. She could have chosen much worse. A hot-tempered Catalan. A bullfighter! A Russian gangster! Or, worst of all...another writer!

I'm surprised she's found a boyfriend so quickly, fallen in love so precipitously. But I shouldn't be. I recall our talk in the bar of the Park Hotel. "I don't think I can ever love again," she had confessed.

Had my assurances served as a kind of permission? Had my encouragement given her strength to finally forget her last boyfriend and start anew? I'd like to think so.

But she doesn't say. And I don't ask.

When it comes to love, Olga forgets the wisdom of the trapeze: patience, preparation, concentration, understanding. She becomes a bungee jumper who neglects to inspect her cord.

"I fell!" she says.

The first words out of her mouth, as soon as I say hello. Before I can say, "It's me!" she says, "I fell."

And she proceeds to explain, clearly and calmly, what happened to her in the air. She has fallen before, of course, most recently in Australia. And I have observed a couple near misses. But she has not fallen in *Saltimbanco*. She confesses that since she quit smoking she has experiences several lapses in concentration. She has lost her credit card, she has forgotten her keys. Once, while driving, she had to pull off the side of the road and rest. And one night after finishing her fixed routine, she was waiting for one of the characters on the stage to pull the rope that starts the trapeze swinging. But he didn't pull. Then she felt something hit the back of her head. For a moment she ignored it before she realized it was her safety line.

"Can you imagine! Can you imagine!" she exclaims. "I forgot put my safety on! And then, last night, I didn't feel right, I mean my body was fine but my mind was spinning. Usually I am concentrating perfectly, everything in a line—bam, bam, bam! But last night... I still went up, I thought, oh well... And during the fixed I just felt lost, my eyes were everywhere, my head was spinning, I wanted let go...

"I began to swing, at least this time I remembered the safety! But now my knees felt weak, all strength left me... And I fell!"

I imagined her badly hurt, being carried off by the clowns as the audience sat breathless. But with characteristic resolve she went back up and finished the routine.

"Were you injured?"

"I hurt my knee. But I'll probably be okay next week."

"What will they do for the show? Will they fly out someone else from Montreal? What about the twins?"

"One of them is still recovering from surgery. Since it's only a few days, we won't have trapeze. We'll have Diabolo instead. Mark, you don't know how hard it is to quit smoking! I don't know what to expect from my body. I'm so angry with myself. I just let go."

But she recovers on schedule and returns to the stage without trepidation. Her performances for the rest of their run in Barcelona are without incident. Offstage, however, her behavior remains erratic, as evidenced in an e-mail I receive one morning during her holiday before Vienna.

Hello Mark

Thank for the e-mail. Right now I am in Holland and it is good practice write you letter even if you don't understand everything. My girlfriend she is professional writer like you. She been read your book about boy and cancer. She very disappoint. 1. It is no feelings, don't touch. 2. She think it is translated for different language. I definitely like you send me things what you write about circus. OLGA.

If a meteor had crashed through my roof at that moment I wouldn't have been more surprised than I was by this e-mail. How nice, I had thought, an e-mail from Olga! Who was this girlfriend of hers? How could she say such things? No one else had ever found such faults in my writing. Maybe English wasn't her native language.

I couldn't ignore Olga's complaint. If she didn't have faith in my writing she wouldn't cooperate with my book and I would have to let go, as she had let go of the trapeze. I felt she had a right to read what I had written so far, and I had looked forward to showing it to her. But now she was prejudiced against me. Maybe she would show the Cirque chapters to this same friend. I was doomed.

And I'd already bought my ticket to Vienna.

So I wrote back that I would be glad to show her the Cirque book but that I hoped she would read my work herself.

I expected the worst. But the heading of Olga's next e-mail made me smile.

MY FIRST BOOK ENGLISH!

Hello Mark! I am so happy that you write this e-mail to me. Am nearly finishing reading this book and I really like. Olga

So I too had fallen and survived!

In Vienna Olga would confess with a guilty grin that she had fabricated the first e-mail to test me, and was very pleased with my answer. Although her second e-mail was equally specious—she still hadn't read the novel.

Of course, such tests can spell the end of a friendship, if not a book. But to my surprise I felt no anger, only relief. Olga may have a temper that drives bears back into their caves, but when she laughs she looks like an angel and how can anyone reproach her? Besides, one must give a wide berth to people who swing through the air upside down.

VIENNA

I arrive in Vienna with low expectations. I've brought the first three chapters of the book. If Olga doesn't like them I'll feel like Joseph Cotton in *The Third Man*, fending off Orson Welles atop Vienna's famous Ferris wheel. And the vicissitudes of Barcelona are still fresh in my thoughts. Olga's mercurial temper. The troupe's general suspicion once they learned I was a writer. The juggler telling Olga she didn't wish to talk to me.

I had received one piece of good news. Olga informed me word got back to Montreal that I was writing a book—she didn't say who told them. And the good people in Montreal replied that I wasn't to conduct interviews backstage. What else? That was all. They could have threatened me, asked to see my work, told the cast not to talk to me. I felt relieved, completely unencumbered. Why did I need to go backstage when I had the bar, the terrace, the pool, the eighth floor Jacuzzi, the river promenade at the salubrious Danube Hilton?

I arrive in the evening, while everyone is at the show. The Danube Hilton is on the outskirts of town, within walking distance of the Prater, Vienna's historic amusement park where the aforementioned red Ferris wheel presides over more modern rides. The Grand Chapiteau—the Cirque's tent—is also a short walk away, which makes for much better logistics than Barcelona and Amsterdam.

Indeed, when I go to the lobby bar to wait for Olga just after eleven I see a crowd of Cirque jackets. And a blond pixie with her back to me wearing a purple bathrobe. I had assumed that my entire relationship with Olga—however long it lasted—would be characterized by my waiting for her, by my phoning her. But in Vienna she would often be the one waiting, and more mornings than not would call me to invite me up to her room for breakfast.

She gives me a big hug and I smile back in relief.

"I came down to look for you!" she admits, which explains the bathrobe. "I'm so happy you come!"

"Thanks. It's good to see you again."

"Where is your room?"

"Just around the corner. Number 123."

"On this floor?" she asks, impressed. "I'm on fourth floor! How you get this room?"

"I have good connections!"

She says good night to the woman she was talking with and invites me upstairs for wine. "You know my sister's here. She came yesterday. I haven't seen her in five years!"

Of course I didn't know. Had I known I would have re-scheduled, not wishing to get in the way. But as it turns out the three of us would spend a lot of time together, and my presence may have served to ease the inevitable tensions between two Russian sisters who haven't seen each other in five years. I would also serve as a tour guide for Tanya while Olga was working, and she in return would provide additional insight into Olga's past.

Tanya is sleeping, so Olga brings a bottle of Australian white wine down to my room and we sit across the table from each other and talk about her sister and her boyfriend and Vienna, and her favorite restaurant, which serves schnitzel so big it hangs off the plate.

"We have to go one day and eat schnitzel!" she says. "I can't believe you're on first floor! How you get this room?"

"I told them I was a friend of the beautiful trapeze artist."

She opens the window and looks at my view of the front entrance.

"What this?" she asks a moment later, looking at my books on the desk.

I had brought the celebrated Pevear and Volokhonsky translation of *Crime and Punishment*. Dostoevsky, it turns out, had been exiled to Omsk, the same city where Olga had first seen the circus. Four years of hard labor and four years in the army. But Olga is unaware of this fact. I had always imagined Siberia as a frozen wasteland dotted with wooden barracks. I wonder if the circus was there in Dostoevsky's day. One person's prison is another's paradise.

"You want play tennis?" Olga says, taking one of my racquets and hitting a ball against the wall. I had brought racquets because I thought I would have a lot of free time, since no one wanted to talk to me, and the hotel had courts. As it turned out I would hardly be alone for a moment, but everywhere we went Olga would try to get me a game, asking performers, crew, even waiters if they played tennis.

I deliberately don't ask about her injury. Obviously she was back in the show, she appeared happy. Recalling the petulance with which she often greeted my questions about the trapeze, I decide not to raise the subject tonight.

But I do show her the first three chapters. She reads the title and the first paragraph and smiles. "The Paradiso! Can I copy it? Can I show it people?"

"It's yours. Do what you want."

"I'll make a copy at the Cirque. Thank you."

I breathe a bit easier. She's read the first page and she's still talking to me.

She pours the wine and sits across from me at the table, examining me with a curious gaze. "So, how are you?"

"Fine."

"Oh? I think something bothering you. How your girlfriend?"

"She was supposed to come to the U.S. Instead she went to Switzerland to see someone else."

"How old she?"

"Twenty-one."

Olga shrugs and replies with characteristic candor, "I think if I her age I do same thing." She drinks her wine. "So, who you want talk?"

The Cirque is an embarrassment of riches. Scores of artists, as well as crew and staff from all over the world. The problem is that I don't know what I may be overlooking. The program lists only name, date of birth and country—and even this can be misleading. Jean-Paul Boun, for instance, is listed as Canadian. If it hadn't been for Olga I never would have learned he was Cambodian, his family having escaped the Khmer

Rouge when he was a child. Nor would I have known Elena Grosheva, whose entry simply says, "Russian Swing, Chinese Poles, Bungee; April 12, 1979; Russia," had won an Olympic medal had someone not happened to mention it in my presence. Nor would I have know Yasmine, the rigger, was from Iran had she not told me herself in Amsterdam.

I'd like to talk to the wire walker, of course, but this is problematic. She doesn't speak much English and she's still a Chinese citizen. I'd have to be careful what I ask her and the interpreter who, for all I know, could be a Party member, might respond with quotations from Mao's *Little Red Book*.

I'd like to talk to the juggler and her mother, to the family that opens the show with Adagio, and to the Olympian. Olga nods patiently. Of course, if I had to list the people I thought least likely to consent it would be these same performers. The juggler because she has already said no and her mother seems stern and aloof, the family because they also don't seem to interact much with the others and are doubtless protective of their children, and the Olympian because she told my father not to walk on the mats when we were backstage in Barcelona.

But I would discover these assumptions to be as misguided as nearly everything else I had once believed about the people in the Cirque du Soleil.

"You should also talk to Alya," Olga adds. "You know Alya? She in the troupe. Hers very interesting story. I like her very much. She was in "O" but came because her boyfriend in *Saltimbanco*. She had to wait a year for an opening, to transfer! It is hard to have relationships in the Cirque. Also, you should see her body. She is amazing! She championship in fitness. And she very smart, and very warm person."

"That would be great."

"And the others, leave it to me."

But I've come with low expectations. The main thing, I realize, is not to offend Olga. There's always the next city.

We talk for another hour, my eyes drawn to the empty ash tray on the table.

Olga calls me late the next morning and invites me up for breakfast. She tells me to sit at the desk and serves me hard rolls, sliced ham, salami, orange juice and coffee. Her sister, Tanya, is busy tidying up. She's four years older than Olga, married, with three young children. She has a very pleasant, and even meek disposition, which cannot be completely accounted for by her lack of English or the strangeness of her new surroundings. Indeed, she seems different from Olga in every respect. Olga is short and very thin, Tanya is heavier and taller. Olga has sharp featured, Tanya's are soft and she has a round face. She also has blue eyes, while Olga's are brown. She speaks in a quiet voice, with a reserved smile and laugh. I will never hear her yell. Nor does she share Olga's sense of the extreme. She teaches seven-year-olds in the northern Siberian city of Novy Urengoi. She doesn't drink or smoke. She's even afraid of heights.

A couple days later Olga would ask me what I think of Tanya. And then she would confide, "Mark—my sister, I think she the person in world most like myself!"

It's Sunday and the Cirque has a matinee. Tanya has already seen the show, so I offer to show her the city. Where would she like to go?

Tanya unfolds a map and points to the museum at the Art Academy.

"She likes anything art and music," Olga explains.

"And what about you? Did you visit a single museum in Amsterdam or Barcelona?"

"Ah..."

"Mozart's house!" Tanya says, again pointing to the map.

"Isn't her English good? She learn just from books. She has no one to speak with. This her first time out of Russia."

"Ask her why she couldn't keep you from running away. When you were fourteen. She's your older sister, right?"

Olga speaks to Tanya in Russian and they both break out laughing, Tanya shaking her head vigorously at the idea.

I'm flattered that Olga entrusts her sister to my care. But it's an opportunity not without risk. Short of causing Olga to fall from the trapeze, I can't think of anything that would incur her wrath more than losing her sister in Vienna's dense historical district. But fortunately Tanya is both pleasant and responsible, and we communicate remarkably well considering that she forgot her dictionary.

At the Art Academy she looks at all the pictures. Can this really be Olga's sister? I ask about her childhood. It was a happy one. She tells me how Olga used to jump into the river from a high bank.

"It was dangerous," she says.

Their father was from northern Siberia and had come south because it was warmer. He had pledged himself to their mother but was drafted into the army, during which time he married someone else and had two daughters. Later he divorced and settled in Ishim with their mother, whom he finally did marry. Tanya and Olga would see their half-sisters over the years and remained friends. One of them had visited Olga in Spain.

Tanya's own husband was from the port city of Odessa, but they lived in Novy Urengoi because the money was good.

"It must be a very hard life," I say.

But Tanya doesn't complain. Indeed, the cloudless Viennese summer day seems lost on her. "I don't like the sun," she says.

I expect her to be tired, but she wants more. So we go to the Museum of Natural History and look at stuffed animals in mahogany cases. I ask if they have penguins where she lives. No penguins, but polar bears.

She's still not exhausted. Perhaps she shares Olga's energy, if nothing else. We walk across the plaza to the Museum of Fine Arts and stay until closing. Looking at Velazquez's portrait of the Infanta Margarita I ask Tanya's opinion of her sister's character, remarking that Olga insists she is just an ordinary person.

Tanya stares at me in surprise and smiles. "Olga ordinary!" she exclaims, as if I had just called the Infanta's dress plain. "Olga not ordinary! Oh no! Olga not ordinary!"

THE BLOOPER PARTY

Olga had asked us to meet in the Cirque commissary after the show. The Grand Chapiteau is only a five minute walk from the hotel. I've never entered through the security gate before. Tanya and I sign the guest book and are given passes. We can hear the music, although Olga told us they had to lower the decibels because of neighboring condominiums.

"We have to be very quiet in the artistic tent," she had said, "because the audience can hear everything!"

One of the troupe is sitting on a bench outside the tent, still in makeup, smoking a cigarette. He recognizes me and asks if I've come for the party.

"I thought every night was a party," I reply.

In the commissary tent two women are setting out chocolate bars and marshmallows on paper plates. A flyer on the bulletin board announces a "Bloopers Party" with wine, beer and roasted marshmallows. But just before the show ends it begins to pour. So the chairs are moved inside and the movie screen set up by the wall.

One beneficial effect of the party is that everyone is in attendance and it gives me a chance, on only my first full day, to take a visual survey of the performers, and also to show them I'm back.

And indeed, while I will always be an outsider here, I feel strangely at home. Several people say hello. The wire walker smiles. Olga offers me one of the chairs arranged in rows and only after I've sat down do I realize I'm seated beside the Olympian. We exchange smiles.

But Olga has second thoughts and leads Tanya and me to one of the tables in the rear. She points to a young girl sitting alone at the table, whom I have not seen before.

"Mark, talk to this pretty girl. Sit here, next to her. She the daughter of one of the troupe. I think you find her interesting."

In fact I find her extremely shy. She's lived in Montreal since she was three, but her parents are Russian. She's here for a month to visit her father. Her name is Victoria and she's fifteen.

I'd like to ask her what it's like to grow up in the circus, or rather divided between the circus and the real world, since her mother is a therapist, but I sense her shyness and defer to Tanya, who starts speaking to her in Russian.

The lights go down and Olga, who is still standing, pulls my sleeve. Amid the whistles and applause she provides a running commentary.

The video has no captions or narration and was produced specifically for this party, spliced together from the closed-circuit tapes of past shows. *Saltimbanco* begins dramatically when the white sheet covering the stage like a tent is mysteriously whisked away through the canopy over the band, like a napkin pulled through a ring, revealing the musicians. Every time I see the show I wonder how they pull it off—literally—night after night, because it's done so fast and it seems there must a thousand things the material could catch on. Well, sure enough, the video opens with the sheet getting tangled up and one of the clowns stumbling over it. Everyone roars with laughter.

"These are from many years ago," Olga informs me. "Different people."

Even so, I would think they wouldn't want to watch mistakes.

Next comes Bungee. The four flyers are supposed to fall in unison and then grab hands to form a ring as they rise. But, as the video shows, they don't always get it right. And mistakes at bungee can be particularly embarrassing, especially when a flyer loses momentum and just hangs in the air while the other three wait impatiently on their bars.

The previous juggler, a man, walks onstage juggling three balls and immediately gets into trouble. He loses them, then drops again, and he hasn't even stepped onto his platform. I wish I could see the current juggler's expression, but she's sitting somewhere up front.

The clowns clown around and fall, not always deliberately. The previous wire walker has a problem attaching her safety, so the clowns distract the audience with an impromptu dance. The following clip shows her climbing atop her unicycle on the high wire and then—falling.

The room fills with laughter. I can't believe it.

"I wish they would show my fall!" Olga whispers in my ear.

There's a brutal clip from the Chinese Poles. Two climbers are poised on separate poles, face down, preparing to slide.

"Look at that one," Olga points out. "He's lower."

And sure enough the man on the right is positioned too low and hits his head on the stage. They show it two, three times.

Maybe it makes the cast feel good to see their predecessors' mistakes. And it's harmless fun. No animals were harmed in the making of this video. But I can think of images I'd rather take home with me if I had to perform these same acts tomorrow.

The last time I planned to do something with Olga on her day off I wound up circumnavigating the Segrada Familia in Gaudi-like despair. So today I wake early with a feeling a slight trepidation.

I await a call from Tanya. She is supposed to join a Russian group for a tour at nine, and I'd told her I would take her to the meeting point, knowing Olga would want to sleep. But nine o'clock comes and goes and I assume she changed her plans.

Then at a quarter past Olga phones and invites me up. She offers me coffee as they clean up the room and dress. Tanya's eyes are red.

"I made my sister cry!" Olga confesses.

What happened, in a scene worthy of Dostoevsky, was that Olga wished to sleep, as I predicted, and didn't think the tour was important. When Tanya picked up the phone to call me Olga told her to let me sleep as well. "Who paid for the museums yesterday?" she asked, plunging her sister into a chasm of guilt.

As Dostoevsky might have written:

> And Olga all but flew into a rage.
> "But..." her sister cried, turning crimson, "it's paid for..."
> "Devil take it!" Olga interrupted haughtily and with vexation.
> "And if I don't go...they'll send me...back to Siberia!"
> Just at that moment Olga reached for the axe...

Well, I'd been up reading *Crime and Punishment* and hadn't gotten much sleep. I could only imagine what violent episodes lay in store as the three of us took a taxi into town.

"I can't believe I made my sister cry!" Olga says with a remorseful smile. "I terrible person."

"She makes our mother cry also!" Tanya remarks.

In light of this new information I realize I've held up remarkably well. Maybe I'm the only person Olga hasn't reduced to tears. Still, the week is young.

We go to Demel, the famous cafe across from the palace and the meeting spot for Tanya's tour. But we're late, so we go in for coffee and pastry. I tell Tanya I'll give her the tour myself, but she doesn't appear consoled. At least she and Olga are smiling at each other.

Despite her earlier outburst, I think it's to Olga's credit that she decided to join us, especially since she doesn't like museums. Or maybe she does. Once again Olga's behavior surprises me, for not only does she accompany us to the palace, and to the Lipizzaner Museum and St. Stephen's Cathedral, but she genuinely enjoys the experience and pays close attention.

As we walk through the furnished rooms of the palace I expect her to be bored, distracted, impatient, but her pace is slower than her sister's and she bombards me with questions.

"Who was the king?" "How big was the country?" "Did they fight Russia?" "Do they have king now?" "Why not?"

I point to a portrait of Sissy, the beloved empress of Franz Joseph, and tell Olga she was an exercise fanatic and had equipment installed in the palace. And, sure enough, in the next room are a pair of wooden rings hanging from the door frame. Olga smiles incredulously.

When we enter the grand waiting room, where supplicants hoping to gain an audience with the Emperor were brought, Olga gazes at the regal portraits and gilt ceilings and observes, "I think this room is to make people feel they very small."

Then, in the emperor's bedroom, she turns to me and inexplicably says, "I think you would make good king! Everybody would love you!"

Back outside they are drawn to the row of open carriages parked in front of the palace. Olga pets the horses and asks if they are expensive. I pay the driver for a forty minute ride and we hop on. I've never taken a carriage ride before and am surprised how smooth it is. Without asking permission Olga slithers onto the driver's box to pose for a picture. Tanya peers through the video camera Olga has lent her. I point out that carriage rides were not included in her Russian tour.

Olga asks the driver directions to a famous schnitzel restaurant, the one where the schnitzel hangs off the plate, and after our ride we walk there.

"What are you going to have?" Olga asks me, looking at the menu.

"Schnitzel, of course."

Olga beams. "You won't believe how big it is!" she exclaims. "How can anyone eat it all?"

She orders one to share with her sister, and they make short work of it. "Are you finished?" she then asks.

I have made a small hole in mine, leaving the perimeter. "Help yourself."

She takes my plate and devours the rest.

"I would like to open a restaurant," she announces. "For schnitzel. What you think? Do they have schnitzel restaurants where you live?"

"No."

"Do you think it would be popular?"

"Maybe, but it would have to offer more dishes. For people who don't like schnitzel."

"But I want it be just for schnitzel. It so good! That what make it special. I want have schnitzel restaurant in Australia. Do you think it will succeed?"

"The restaurant business is hard," I tell her, taking her seriously because I believe she is serious. "If you only serve schnitzel what are you going to do about the couple who go out to dinner and she's a vegetarian? Or a group of friends and one of them hates schnitzel? They won't go to your restaurant."

"Oh, I don't care about them. I think Melbourne needs a schnitzel restaurant!"

We go to the cathedral. Olga walks to one of the pews in front and sits down. She isn't praying, she isn't admiring the altar. I don't know what she's doing. When I sit next to her she turns to me and says, "What you want? Go look around."

Olga's family is Russian Orthodox, but I don't think they're very religious. In fact, I've been struck by the lack of outward signs of religion among the Cirque in general. No Biblical quotes on the bulletin board, no pamphlets, no prayer meetings, no acrobats crossing themselves before going onstage, no icons hanging on the tent walls. When Olga gazes up at the vertiginous ceiling of St. Stephen's Cathedral who know whether she's thinking of God, admiring the architecture, or fantasizing what it would be like to do a pirouette while swinging from the apse?

She notices a crowd descending into the crypt for the free tour. "Let's go there!" she says. "Is it possible?"

She and Tanya have never been in a crypt before, they've never seen human bones before. Olga is fascinated by the coffins. "Are people still inside?" she asks. "Why aren't there animals?"

She puts her fingers through the grating to stroke the casket of some cardinal. And then we come to skeletons in a dark chamber. "Oh my God!" she cries. "Are they criminals?"

"They don't bury criminals in cathedrals," I tell her.

We come to piles of bones, neatly stacked. Piles of skulls. Victims of plague from the Middle Ages.

"I can't believe it! Aren't you frightened?"

All the gulags in Siberia and Olga is shocked by an Austrian crypt!

The last time I was at St. Stephen's Cathedral I didn't have time to climb the tower. Three hundred and forty-three steps. Tanya's up for it. Olga's wearing sandals but scrambles up the winding stone staircase like a cherubim.

"Climbing great exercise," she calls down to us. "I never used to do but now I like. Good for your ass. Can you feel the muscles in your ass?"

She runs up the last hundred steps. When I reach the top I'm breathless and sweating. Curious, I take Olga's pulse. It's seventy at the most.

Tanya brings up the rear, gasping for air.

"We should do it three more times!" Olga says. "And after one week, two weeks, climbing three times every day, you will have such a strong ass!"

We return to the hotel only long enough to shower and change clothes before attending a concert of Mozart and Strauss at the Liechtenstein Palace. In the taxi Tanya sits in front and asks the driver to turn down the air-conditioning. I'm astonished. It's a hot day.

"How can you live in Siberia?" I wonder.

"She's no different than you or me," Olga explains. "They just wear more clothes!"

We pass the Prater and Olga looks hungrily at the steel arc of the bungee jump.

"Would you like to do it?" I ask her.

"Oh yes. But it too low. You can see the ground!"

We have half an hour before the show and Olga wants hot tea, so we look for a cafe.

"How is your stomach?" she asks me.

"My stomach?"

"Do you have pain? From the schnitzel? I have pain." And she bursts out laughing. "And to think I want open schnitzel restaurant!" And she laughs all the way to the cafe.

Again, I marvel at Olga's mercurial character. A few hours ago she was schnitzel's greatest champion and now she'll probably never eat it again!

The concert is not the sort of thing Olga would normally do. The Concertgeboew in Amsterdam is one of the world's greatest symphony halls, with free performances on Wednesday afternoons, but I doubt Olga even knew of its existence during her stay in Holland. No, she's here because of her sister, who loves Mozart.

"I tired, I sleep," Olga keeps threatening.

Nevertheless, we bought the most expensive tickets because she wanted to sit in the first row. "I want see their expressions," she explains, which oddly is the same thought I had after seeing her perform on the trapeze.

The concert is for tourists and Olga points out all the Russians in attendance, wearing suits and dresses. Olga outshines them all in her own inimical style. She is a cross between Isadora Duncun and Heidi. She hates shoes, makeup, jewelry, perfume. She rarely styles her hair. And yet she somehow manages to be extremely feminine and fashionable. Tonight she's wearing a creation made just for her, by Alya's mother and aunt, who are fashion designers. Alya's mother was so taken by Olga's performance that she gave her this gown, a diaphanous cream body suit with a second piece worn over the shoulders and harlequin-like spangles dangling from the waist. It isn't the sort of thing every woman could wear, but Olga looks like a fairy in it.

The concert is given by a quartet in the ballroom, with ballet dancers Olga informs me are Russian. She doesn't nod off at all but enjoys the music every bit as much as her sister. At one point she surreptitiously turns on the video camera, despite the prohibition against photography. When the rest of the audience politely applauds, Olga claps wildly and screams, "Woo, woo, woo!" drawing curious glances from the other Russians sitting in our row.

A first, I think, for the Liechtenstein Palace.

PRACTICE

The next morning a muscular woman approaches me in the lobby. She has long flowing blond hair and high cheekbones and is wearing a black tank top, which shows off her muscular torso.

"Hi, my name's Alya!" she says, extending her hand.

I'm so surprised she has approached me I fail to notice whether her handshake is firm or light. She's the fitness champion Olga had told me about, who had transferred from "O".

"I read your chapters on the Cirque. Olga gave me a copy. I don't know whether I like it or not, but I kept wanting to turn the pages, so I guess that's good, right? There are a couple mistakes, if you want to know. You mention the Cirque doesn't have ringmasters, but *Saltimbanco* has a character called 'Ringmaster.' And you talk about the artist killed in a car accident in Las Vegas. You say he was in "O", but he was in *Mystère*. I know because I knew him. I went to the funeral. It was very sad. They didn't cancel the show, but they dedicated it to him. It was very hard for everybody. His wife went back to Ukraine. At the funeral they had an open casket, and some of the mourners kissed him. I'd never seen a dead body before. And when my turn came I couldn't touch him. Well, good luck!"

Tanya and I follow Olga to the Grand Chapiteau. Olga rides her bike, the one she bought in Amsterdam.

"Do you notice anything missing?" she asks. "The dog you bought me, I kept it in the basket, remember? Well, I keep the bike parked on the street and someone stole it."

"They took the dog and left the bike?" I ask in disbelief.

"I very sad. Can you believe someone take my dog?"

We go to the commissary for lunch. Olga piles two plates high with food, but she doesn't join me on the patio. I see her arguing with her sister, and then Tanya walks off and sulks on a bench outside the artistic tent.

Olga sits across from me at my table on the patio, but without the food.

"I throw it in the rubbish!" she exclaims.

It's only Tuesday! Doubtless they will hug and cry when they part, but how to survive until that time?

"She won't let me do anything for her!" Olga complains. "It's Russian mentality. She won't eat anything. Even it's free. And she never let me pay for anything!"

"She took the carriage ride, didn't she? And went to the concert," I point out, sympathizing for once with Olga. "You just have to do it. Don't ask."

"Maybe you right."

"And you need to eat. Go on."

She goes back and gets a small salad.

"You're a good sister," I tell her. "I know it's hard for you."

"My family does not understand life here. It's Russian mentality. My sister, to get visa she has to buy tour package, with hotel. But I want her to stay my hotel. You know what she says first night? She thinks she has to go back to her hotel. She thinks it's a rule! They will make her leave Austria!"

She rises anxiously and walks over to where Tanya is sitting.

A muscular man sits across from me, greeting me in a Russian accent with a broad smile that reveals a gold tooth. He's Igor Issakov, Victoria's father. He's carrying a photo album and shows me a picture of his daughter when she was a small child.

"Is this her first time seeing you perform?"

"No, we were all together when I was in *Alegría*, in Mississippi a few years ago."

"Do you want her to join the circus?"

"I prefer her to go to college. The circus is a hard life."

"But you love it."

"Yes, I love it. But it's hard when you have a family. And you can't do it forever. Then what?"

I look through the album and realize what he did formerly. There's a handsome photo of him standing proudly in a Soviet army uniform.

"I was in special forces," he tells me. "We used to pretend to be the Americans in simulations. We had all American equipment."

I try to gaze at this affable Ukrainian through the lens of the Cold War, this gold-tooth smile the face of the enemy.

"Were you happy when the Wall fell?" I ask.

"No," he answers candidly. "I believed in the system. It was good to me. It was my country. I was prepared to die for it. Or kill for it," he adds ominously.

Next subject. I flip through the photos. A party with comrades, his house in Canada, his wife.

"Did this happen in the army?" I ask, pointing to a photo of him wearing a cast around his neck.

"No, in the show."

"This show?"

"It was a long time ago. I was the top man on the Russian Swing. You know at the end of the Russian Swing, we have a man standing on top of a pole held by another man? Well, I was on top and the flyer's foot hit my neck instead of my shoulder. So I broke it."

"You broke your neck?"

I'd talked myself into believing the Cirque wasn't dangerous. Driving a car or riding a bicycle, those were hazardous activities. But circus arts were performed in a controlled environment by seasoned professionals. I close the album and pushed it back across the table.

Olga returns, grinning, having made up for the moment with her sister. "You want come watch me practice?"

Every week Olga gets an hour in the big tent to practice the trapeze. She doesn't have to. If she would rather go to the movies no one is going to reprimand her. But like most of the performers she needs no external motivation. Dedication is one of the few common denominators among this cosmopolitan group. Without it they never would have risen to this level. Competitive athletes might be drilled like soldiers, but circus performers must perform the same exacting acts day after day, and if they don't possess a passion for what they do they will quickly burn out or make costly mistakes.

I proceed Olga onstage, walking out through the ramp. The tent is empty and the seats dark. The stage is lit by a handful of spotlights.

I walk to center stage and look up. The tent is not that high. Perhaps only thirty feet to the trapeze and forty-five to the aluminum ring from which the lights and rigging hang. But the space spreads out, giving little sense of scale.

"One day you have to try bungee!" Olga tells me.

I decide to try the seats in the front row. Tanya sits beside me. The trainer comes out and I watch with fascination as he lowers the trapeze to the stage.

The trapeze does not hang directly from the rafters but from a crane bar, about fifteen feet higher. Olga, wearing her black warm-up suit, helps the trainer connect the trapeze to the bar by two ropes with hooks on the ends. They work quickly but methodically.

I venture back onstage. This is the closest I wish to come to the trapeze. I ask if I can touch it and gently lift it off the wooden stage. I'm surprised how heavy it is and examine the cylindrical weights on each end. This makes it easier to swing, of course, and minimizes deviation. But it also poses a great risk to Olga if she falls, or if she dangles on the safety and it strikes her on the return.

Olga and the trainer go to one of the posts and together pull the trapeze into the air. Then Olga hops back onstage and stretches while the trainer walks to the other side and lowers the safety, which isn't attached to a harness but to an inelastic rubber ring, which Olga wiggles over her hips. At her signal she is pulled up and stands atop the bar, facing us.

I can't believe I'm here. When I first saw *Saltimbanco* years ago it was beyond my wildest wishes to imagine I would one day sit in the empty tent watching the trapezist practice. Olga has indeed made my dreams come true. After I decided to write the book my first wish was to watch the show backstage. Additionally I hoped to talk with the other performers. What was left? Only to watch Olga practice. But I dared not ask for that. I knew Olga didn't like people watching her practice. Alya told me when they were first training in Montreal Olga stopped practicing to demand the artistic director leave the tent. The artistic director!

So it was a great honor to sit here, and an even greater pleasure. Tanya would start fidgeting after a few minutes, but I could have watched for hours. Olga had even allowed me to bring my camera, and after returning home I would make a poster of her hanging from the trapeze by her armpits. A small black figure dangling solitary against a black background midway between the golden rigging above and the psychedelic stage. Studying her in this symmetrical image she appears to me not alienated by the vast space surrounding her, like an astronaut walking in space, or trapped like a goldfish in a bowl, but as another artifact of the circus, like the chairs or the lights, fixed and immutable.

She practices for a few minutes while the trapeze hangs stationary, dropping from a standing position to hang by her armpits, hanging by her hands, by her knees. Then she starts swinging, occasionally talking with the trainer. She doesn't seem pleased but she is relaxed. The one time I wish she would yell, for I cannot hear her comments! Then she hangs by her knees in the catcher's pose, with her feet wrapped around the rope. She swings several times, then says, "Next one," and executes a forward flip.

"No, that was not good," she says, although it looked fine to me.

"Your shoulders were a little late," the trainer observes.

Olga keeps swinging. "Next one."

When she reaches the apogee of her outward swing she's looking directly down at the stage. I inch forward and gaze up. Her face is tensed in concentration and she exhales rapidly through her mouth before swinging down for the flip.

She does several more, then practices a different maneuver. Watching this way is much more instructive than watching a performance because you know what is coming and can watch each maneuver several times in succession. But even so, the movements are so rapid it is difficult to fully appreciate their subtleties. Indeed, as with many top athletes, one is more impressed with her skill when watching a tape in slow motion.

Finally she does a backward somersault, catching the trapeze with her hands as it descends. It seems an act of great faith to let go of a bar in the air when you are going one way and it is going the other. It seems to defy physics. But she catches cleanly every time, and my awe is not diminished by repetition.

I want to applaud, but knowing Olga's disdain for praise I restrain myself.

"You want take pictures?" she asks, standing on the bar. And she strikes several poses before sliding down.

I step onstage. I want to hug her, squeeze her, tell her how honored I am that she has let me enter her life. But I merely smile.

The trapeze is unhooked and the crane bar is hoisted up, to await the night's performance.

During the show I take Tanya and Victoria to the Prater and we ride the Ferris wheel. Tanya doesn't want to go, she's afraid of heights, but we manage to persuade her. Once on she seems relaxed enough and marvels at the view. We stand by the windows as the large wooden compartment rises. Victoria, as might be expected, isn't afraid of anything—except answering my questions.

"Talk to the hand!" she responds, thrusting her palm in my face.

Later that night I go to the lobby bar. Olga is already back from the show.

"Where you been?" she asks. "You supposed to wait in lobby. People want talk with you. I say he'll be in lobby after show."

"I didn't know."

"But Alya don't want talk to you for book."

"Are you sure? She told me she did. She read the chapters."

"I know. Maybe she changed her mind. She told me it too personal."

"I see. But you understand I'm not going to write about the others the way I write about you."

"I think maybe I don't show the book. Maybe I wait. If people want talk to you, why show them book now?"

"It's your decision."

"Oxana will meet you tomorrow at two by the pool. Is it okay? And Elena at noon in the lobby."

Oxana is the wife and mother in the Adagio act. Elena is the Olympian. "That's great! Thanks a lot. Have you talked to the juggler?"

"Masha I think will talk to you Friday morning. But I not sure."

Just at that moment I see the juggler's mother walk past, alone. I've never seen her in the bar before. I nudge Olga. "Can I talk to her?"

Olga steps over and says a few words. The mother nods and smiles at me. I'm surprised by her smile. She hadn't smiled once when I watched the show backstage. But she's not a coach now, or a mother, but a lovely, well-dressed woman who might pass for her daughter's sister.

We sit next to each other on the sofa, away from the others. I'm surprised how relaxed and warm she is, not at all suspicious or reserved.

Olga asks me what I'd like to drink. I answer ginger ale. A moment later she calls from the bar, "You want gin and ale?"

Margarita and I laugh. I know her name already, and by the time Olga returns with the correct drinks I know her age, and the fact that she worked in the Moscow Circus for many years, and hates juggling.

"When I first saw Margarita I thought she was like this!" Olga says, pushing up the tip of her nose with her forefinger. "I was working in Australia and she came to the show because we had a juggler there. I think *Saltimbanco* was in Australia then. But after I talk to her I can see she such nice person!"

"Did you want your daughter to be in the circus?"

"Oh no. I never pushed her. It's a very hard life."

"Margarita had a very hard life," Olga attests. "Remember this was in communism."

"Did you travel?"

"Yes, but it wasn't like this. Not luxury hotels. We had to do everything for ourselves."

"What was your role in the show?"

"I did balancing. One of my acts was to climb up and down a pole balancing a vase on the end of a strip of clear plastic I held in my mouth. No one else did this!"

"I can't imagine anyone else doing that! Do you miss performing?"

"Yes, but it's too hard on the body."

"Do you miss the spotlight? The audience?"

"Of course."

"And your daughter, she's been with *Saltimbanco* for four years?"

"Yes, since she was fourteen."

"And you've traveled with her?"

"Of course she travel with her!" Olga says. "Why you ask such stupid questions? Masha only fourteen! Cirque have rule. Children must have...what you call?"

"Chaperone."

"Yes, chaperone. But now Masha eighteen. So what you do now?" Olga asks.

"Now that she's an adult," Margarita answers, "I think it's important to spend more time away from each other. So now between cities we go different ways."

"Do you have a home?" I ask.

"Yes. In Moscow."

"That's where your husband lives?"

It's a measure of Margarita's affability that I dare to ask such a personal question so soon after meeting her. I had expected our conversation to be formal and guarded, and surprise even myself how comfortable I feel in her presence. We're sitting only inches apart from each other on the sofa, and her body language is relaxed and open, not stiff as it had been backstage.

Margarita blushes. "I don't have a husband. I left him when Masha was a child."

"I'm sorry. I didn't know. Do you find it lonely on tour?"

"Well, I don't mind. I don't like bars and parties. I prefer quiet."

"What are your hobbies?"

"I like to sew," she says with a smile. "You know, when I was in the Moscow Circus we had to fix our own costumes. It was funny. Backstage would be all these glamorous women still in makeup who had just performed aerial acts or acrobatics or equestrian and now they were washing clothes and sewing!"

We all laugh.

We talk for about an hour before she excuses herself to go upstairs. I thank her and give her a hug and kiss, reflecting that one of the most difficult impulses to restrain is that of making assumptions about human personality.

Olga and I join a group of the troupe, who are drinking beer and smoking. I wondered how she would react to the temptation of being around so many smokers. Perhaps she would avoid them. But she hasn't

137

changed her habits at all. The anxiety and confusion of nicotine withdrawal have passed, and she doesn't even seem to notice the smoke.

The House Troupe do Russian Swing, Chinese Poles and Bungee, as well as performing other roles throughout the show, such as spotting Olga or playing tricks on audience members. There are six jumpers in the Russian Swing and twelve climbers on the Chinese poles. But there are only four spots in Bungee for jumping—not counting the two men who climb a rope ladder to the rafters and leap down at the end—so not everyone who wishes to participate has the opportunity.

Olga and I sit down just as one of the troupe is describing her experience of performing for the first time. It's interesting not only to hear her comments but also to observe the curiosity of her peers, who ask questions in excited voices.

"Were you nervous?" someone asks her.

"Totally! My heart was pounding, my palms were sweating! And that's when I was on the ground!"

"But it rocked, right?"

"Oh man, but it's so different from practice! I mean, it's the end of the show and everything's gotta be in unison. I was so afraid of letting you guys down."

"Oh, you were great!" someone else says. "I couldn't believe it was your first time."

"It was so bizarre. I'm so used to being a catcher onstage and watching you guys fly."

"And what about the meeting?"

The "meeting of four" is the last and most difficult maneuver, when the four jumpers dive off backwards from their trapezes and grab each other's hands as they spring up, like skydivers in free fall. They make it look easy, but synchronous jumps with four persons are never easy, and if they miss they don't get a second or third chance, as with the final jump in Russian Swing.

"I was so relieved when I caught your hand!" she admits. "I thought, 'Yes!'"

"What were you thinking?"

"Well you know, it's strange. After I attached the bungee and James let go and I flew up to the bar... Well, I looked around. And normally, when I'm doing something for the first or second or third time I don't see anything. I mean, I don't notice details. I'm so focused on what I have to do. But when I caught the bar I looked around. I looked at the audience, I looked at you, I looked at the stage. It was like I was up there forever. I even noticed the shadows. I looked at James' long shadow and thought, 'Cool, I've never seen that before.' Yeah, it was like I had been so nervous, but at that moment I was completely relaxed. Well, not relaxed, but pumped, just happy and content. I thought, 'Man, I can't believe I'm here!'"

My sentiments exactly.

I was twelve when the world fell in love with Olga Korbut. But she did more than awe and charm us, and win gold medals. She became in a fortnight one of the most influential athletes in history. She changed her sport, she popularized and glamorized women's athletics, and she created a paradigm for teen girl superstars from Nadia Comaneci to the thirteen-year-old Chinese gold medal diver Mingxia Fu, to Jennifer Capriati and Venus Williams. And she was Russian. The Soviet Union was a chilling world, a gerontocracy whose boxers couldn't dance, whose basketball players couldn't jump. And yet here was a fourteen-year-old who looked eleven, who from the depths of the Cold War smiled boldly at the free world. She won one individual gold medal and should have won a second, but a more impressive achievement was the glimpse she offered of undiscovered beauty behind the Iron Curtain.

Then Romanian Nadia Comaneci came along at the next games and stunned the world again, this time with perfection. Olga had been stylish and energetic, but Nadia was implacable. How do you explain so many tens in a sport which had never seen perfection? Maybe one or two, from a gifted veteran. But from a fifteen year old? In her first Olympics?

I remember looking at Nadia on the cover of *Sports Illustrated*. A girl of fifteen on the cover of a magazine usually given to boxers and quarterbacks. How had she become more important than all the runners and swimmers and weight lifters?

I realized at that time if I could have dinner with anyone in the world it would be her. And not just because she was talented and famous, but because she lived in such strange worlds—the closed world behind the

Iron Curtain, the fishbowl of the Olympics. How could she not be over-whelmed by it all with her imperfect knowledge of the outside world? What qualities were required to perform flawlessly, knowing a single mis-take could wipe out years of training, struggling alone on the balance beam, the parallel bars, the vault, the floor, with a hundred distractions, and the eyes of all the world watching, the critical gaze of your coach and teammates, the pride of your country?

Even then I dreamed of being a writer and traveling the world like Twain and Melville and Hemingway and meeting all kinds of people. But had I been a gambler I would have bet heavily against ever crossing paths with an Olympic gymnast from behind the Iron Curtain.

I haven't been waiting long in the lobby when Elena Grosheva arrives. She smiles and we shake hands, although we've met before. She asks if I want coffee and we go downstairs to the restaurant. Although it's noon, nobody's eating inside and we take a table by the window.

"For years I didn't drink coffee," she says, ordering latte.

Elena is about 5'4" with an athletic body, brilliant ice-blue eyes, styled blond hair with pointed bangs, a wide, pretty face, smooth tan skin. She's wearing sapphire ear rings, a small silver nose ring, a low-cut t-shirt and tight-fitting floral print jeans she just bought yesterday. She's twenty-three and appears to be glowing with health, although she'll tell me she's not so healthy. "I'm young up here," she'll say, pointing to her head, "but I have an old body." And she'll point to a faint scar on her right shoulder. "I had surgery here. Not for an injury but just from overuse. Gymnastics is terrible for the body."

I'm tempted to ask if she remembers telling my father not to walk on the mat when we watched the show backstage. Maybe she had been in a bad mood that night. Or maybe, like Margarita, she put on a different face during the show. I certainly had never seen her in a serious mood since then, and once had watched her laughing uncontrollably.

"I'm always laughing!" she confesses.

She tells me she would prefer if I ask her questions. Which is fine with me, I have scores. But for someone who claims not to know what to say, she talks like a hair stylist, and I hardly have to say another word. I sip on my orange juice and look into her wide eyes. She leans forward, giving me her undivided attention, talks animatedly, smiles, and I begin to suspect she's enjoying herself, as if this weren't an interview for a book but a conversation between friends.

I'm flattered and stunned. I feel her eyes so intently I dare not look away myself to ask the waiter for another orange juice. The spell is broken only by Olga, who enters the restaurant in her purple robe, laughing hysterically.

I had bought her a dog the evening before, to replace the one that was stolen. When you press its stomach it barks.

The restaurant is empty, but I don't think Olga would have been any less exuberant had all the tables been filled with diners wearing evening clothes. What a contrast she forms with Elena, the pair of them expanding the continuum of femininity. No sapphire ear rings for Olga. No lipstick, no bangs. She may own a pair of floral jeans, but at the moment she's wearing a bathrobe. A very stylish bathrobe, to be sure, and royal purple, but how many women, especially pretty women who are not beyond flirtation and coquetry, and performers nonetheless, knowing they are being scrutinized for a book, would appear in the restaurant of the Hilton at noon wearing only a bathrobe and laughing like a drunken sailor?

She lunges over to our table and thrusts out the dog for Elena to see.

"My sister, you know what she say this morning? She take my dog..." And we have to wait for another fit of laughter to pass. "And she say, 'Olechka, you like this dog!'"

And Olga presses the dog's stomach. "Ruff, ruff, ruff!"

Olga bends over in laughter. The dog barks and barks.

Finally, after we all catch our breath, Olga pulls up a chair and orders coffee. Elena continues her story, and Olga occasionally asks a question of her own, such as, "Which is harder, competition or circus?"

"Gymnastics training is harder on the body, but you only have a tournament a few times a year. In the Cirque you have to perform every day."

"Yes, it's true," Olga agrees. "But I think you need something special up here to compete," she says, tapping her temple. "I not competitive person. I don't like compare myself others. I like compete only with myself."

"In the Cirque du Soleil everyone is cheering for you," Elena adds. "No one is hoping you will fall."

When Olga had told me Elena would talk to me I assumed she would give me fifteen minutes or half an hour at most, and that we would probably be interrupted by friends or cell phones. I expected curt answers, reticence, distracting behaviors such as tapping her tea spoon or gazing out the window. But two hours have passed. Two hours of riveting conversation, during which she's done most of the talking, telling me her story with the enthusiasm you would expect from someone who's never told her story before. She hasn't looked at her watch once, or even out the window. And rises now only because Oxana Vintilova approaches. An embarrassment of riches.

THE QUIET OLYMPIAN

I looked at my old notes: it is strange, but Life is such a phenomenon that even would I like to understand it, I could not. But I will take this incomprehensible Life and enjoy it, or fight it, despite its complications. It shapes me however it wishes, pushes me, forgets about me and then suddenly recalls me, pets me, annoys me. But sometimes I also trouble Life, play with it, thinking it naive and will not understand. Or, better, I forget about it, tease it without caring for the consequences. We play like lovers. But Life is perfidious and knows how to control me. And, like a real lover, Life keeps me on a short leash, knows when to loosen or tighten it...

> —from the private notebook of Elena Grosheva

You might think it was a secret she had won a silver medal with the Russian gymnastics' team in the 1996 Olympics. She wears her Cirque jacket often enough, but nothing from Atlanta. Not a sweatshirt, not even a pin. And she doesn't find a way to insert the story into every conversation, the way many people do who have achieved far less lofty goals. Indeed, when she joined *Saltimbanco* even her fellow troupe members were ignorant of her past. It wasn't until they were riding back on the train one night after their show in Amsterdam that someone said he had heard she won an Olympic medal. Elena smiled in acknowledgement and everyone broke out in applause.

Perhaps her modesty was the wisest course. Vanity is not appreciated at the Cirque du Soleil and just because you made it to the Olympics doesn't mean you can make it here. The Cirque has its own unique demands, apart from its rigorous schedule. There are the costumes, the choreography, the teamwork. Some athletes don't like it. Others can't dance. The Cirque gives Olympians a ticket to Montreal and a chance to try out. But they have to prove themselves all over again.

Yaroslavl is a city of one-and-a-half million people, 150 miles east of Moscow, known for heavy machinery and petrochemical plants. And once a year, as in other cities across the country, coaches arrive in town to scout the grammar schools for future stars. In the Soviet Union Olympians were born and made. The Olympics were too important to national pride to be left to individual effort. They were a state enterprise like the space program or the steel industry. But while factories were infamous for their inefficiency and moon rockets blew up on the pad, the U.S.S.R. produced the most adorable athletes the world has ever seen.

If irony were a crop, the Soviet Union would never have had to import American grain. And perhaps the greatest irony of this communist juggernaut was that after preaching egalitarianism and smashing all expressions of individuality, it invested heavily in prodigies, sending them to elite schools, lavishing them with special treatment, raising them above the proletariat so they could shine on the balance beam or the ice rink or the dance floor, so that *Pravda* could proclaim with Orwellian logic that only a classless society could produce athletes and performers of the very first class.

So every year coaches scoured the country, bending legs for ballerinas and backs for gymnasts and feeling muscles for weight lifters and on and on. They didn't come to Ishim or Olga might have competed for a medal too, but they did visit the cities, from Vladisvostok to Odessa, and one day in 1985 they came to Yaroslavl.

Elena was six years old and without gymnastic pretensions. Her parents were not athletes and valued education more than sport. Her mother was employed by the police as a social worker who counseled troubled youth. Her father managed a large bread factory—don't call it a bakery. She would have been happy following either of them, but her legs were flexible and her back bent nicely and she could jump and do cartwheels and handstands.

Many prospective athletes were sent to specialized boarding schools. But there was a gymnastics school in Yaroslavl, so Elena was able to attend her regular school and live at home. She therefore spent more time with her family and lived a more normal life than many of her gifted peers.

She was six years old and dared not even think of the road ahead. She liked gymnastics and that was enough. She didn't dream about being a champion. The Soviet Union didn't encourage dreams. Many girls were dismissed after a year or two, injured or nervous or a few pounds over-weight. Washed up before puberty. The system let them go. There were always others to fill the tiny voids.

Elena knew this. She worked hard. She liked the work. She studied hard at school. She liked school. The Soviet Union suffered many social ills, but spoiled children was not one of them. Elena didn't need demanding coaches to motivate her. Like Olga, she drove herself.

But she didn't share Olga's sense of destiny. Olga knew her road, she saw its end. Olga didn't know how she would get there, but she knew she would reach the trapeze. But Elena didn't have to wait to reach her bar. She had somersaulted the vault before her seventh birthday. For her the process mattered more than the performance.

From seven o'clock until nine she trained in the gym. From ten until five she attended school, then back to the gym from six until eight. She commuted alone by train. It was safe in those days for a young girl to be out alone at night. Certainly safer than the balance beam.

Her idol wasn't Olga Korbut but Lyudmila Turishcheva. Korbut was always more popular in the West than in Russia, where she was viewed as the girl with the nice smile. But Turishcheva had won more medals, and there were a host of other champions, all of whom had won more gold than Olga Korbut.

The turning point in her career came in the 1994 Goodwill Games in St. Petersburg where, at age fifteen and the youngest member of the team, she scored a 9.825 on the bars with a double forward somersault landing, and won bronze in the individual all-around, ahead of Ukrainian Lilia Podkopayeva, who would win the all-around gold in Atlanta. This was an affirmation of all the long hours she'd spent before and after school repeating the same movements. For Elena the bronze individual and the gold they won as a team in the Goodwill Games was as important as the silver she would win in the Olympics. She had never really won anything before and faced the shameful prospect of being remembered as a disappointment. "The girl from Yaroslavl who had some talent but never made it." Instead of being admired by her community, as any high-school all-American would be respected regardless of her future success, Elena's neighbors would regard her with a hint of suspicion and malevolence. "All the money the system spent to train you and no medals!"

Atlanta was gleaming on the horizon and suddenly people began to take notice of the girl from Yaroslavl. She had developed a full twisting back somersault on the balance beam. No one else in the world did this move. She might take it to Atlanta and win gold. It was a risky maneuver. She only landed it clean fifty-percent of the time. But Elena liked risk. She would have gladly wagered eleven years of training on a single revolution in the air lasting only a heartbeat. But her coaches' hearts were not as strong and they made her take it out.

American athletes run and jump and somersault along a yellow brick road of fame and fortune and sinecures from alumni when their knees give out or a drug test is failed once too often. Soviet athletes, and the Russians and Ukrainians and Belarrusians that succeeded the fall of the U.S.S.R., ran waist deep through swamps, jumped barbed-wire fences, somersaulted over empty tables.

The dreams of Russian athletes didn't aspire to wealth and fame. Few ever became affluent, and what was fame when you lived in a communal flat in some remote province? Their dreams were dreams of expansion. To travel. To live in a better place. Quite modest by our standards. After all, the poorest Mexican can migrate to the capital or sneak across the border. But in the Soviet Union citizens were required to carry internal passports. Imagine. You couldn't buy a train ticket without one. And certain citizens, such as residents of collective farms, weren't given internal passports. They weren't paid with money but with a percentage of their own crops. They couldn't buy anything, they couldn't go anywhere. If you were unfortunate enough to grow up in such a place one of the few ways out was to be an athlete. And if you grew up in a town or city like Ishim or Yaroslavl and you did possess a passport, you could only travel to towns and cities of a similar status. Moscow and St. Petersburg were off limits. Unless, like Elena, you made the national team. And if you were fortunate enough to grow up in Moscow or St. Petersburg and you wanted to travel abroad, you had to give the state some reason to send you abroad, such as making the Olympic team.

Even then, you didn't see much of the world. There wasn't time. And there was no money. In the eighties the best female basketball player in the world was Uliana Semenova. The Soviet Union let her play for a Barcelona club team, but her paycheck was sent to Moscow. The government took so much that she didn't even have money for food.

Elena's career bridged the Wall, but the fall of communism was neither a hardship nor a liberation. The gymnastics arena admitted little light from the outside world. Although few Russians traveled more widely than Elena, all she saw was the beam, the floor, the vault, the bars. Her liberation would come later, when she joined *Saltimbanco*.

Ironically, it was her father who prospered under Yeltsin. Many of the factories in Yaroslavl, which had been struggling under communism, collapsed in its wake. Mr. Groshev applied for the directorship of a small fuel plant and turned it around, an achievement for which he won an award.

In Russian business, as in sport, there are different levels of mastery, awarded by the state. Nothing, not even her silver medal, would give Elena more pride than to be joined by her father at the pinnacle.

Of course she almost didn't make it to Atlanta. But recent performances on the beam and parallel bars got her in. There was no time to celebrate. An injured foot plagued her, and in a preliminary event in Atlanta only seven months before the Games, she broke it.

She returned to Russia and hobbled in a cast for three months. But she trained on her own and, in August 1996, returned to Atlanta.

She was disappointed the host country didn't stay in the Village. The food was good but the rooms were small and the crowds were bad. They cheered so much the gymnasts sometimes couldn't hear the music for the floor exercise. But she wasn't nervous. After all, she hadn't know until the last minute whether she would make it back on the team. There wasn't time to be nervous.

Twelve nations are represented in the gymnastics competition and each country has seven members. There are six medal events: team, individual all-around and individual in the four apparati—bar, beam, vault and floor. Naturally, all eighty-four girls can't compete in the individuals, so there is a qualifying round. Elena qualified in both vault and floor, an excellent result for her first Olympics, especially considering her recent injury. She didn't medal but placed a respectable seventh in the vault. As for the floor, she possessed the artistry and charm that might have gained her a medal, but had to withdraw.

In the team competition both the United States and Romania were particularly strong that year and the Russian coach didn't predict gold. But when they stood first after the compulsory round his expectations rose. The U.S., however, was more solid in the final round and took gold. Had Elena been told before the games her country would win silver she would have been elated. But now they were disappointed, heartbroken. Their coach, normally so sullen, had to wipe away their tears as he led them up to the podium's second step.

So what did she do next, this seventeen-year-old with a silver medal? Her foot had completely healed, she was in the best shape of her life. Sydney was only four years away. She would not even be old enough to order a vodka martini when she celebrated on the wharf in Sydney Harbor.

But only a year after Atlanta, after a disappointing showing at the World Championships in Lasanne, she quit. She was burnt out. Her body felt perfect but her mind was tired. Or hungry. Her parents had always told her there was more to life than sport.

So she flew home to Yaroslavl and enrolled in the university. And then she went to St. Petersburg to train in aerobics. And then the Cirque called.

She went to Montreal for two months to audition. It was her first extended stay in the West. She could relax, smile, laugh. Perhaps the reason she laughs so much now is that now nobody tells her she has to stop laughing. She replaced a pregnant acrobat in *Alegría* on Fast Track, a trampoline act, then returned to Russia to have shoulder surgery. After rehab she was invited back to Montreal. *Saltimbanco* had been revived, and Elena was shown the Russian swing and informed that she was to be the final leaper, the one who lands on the man atop the pole. After all these years she would have to learn a new somersault.

ADAGIO

Elena rises from her chair, Oxana occupies another. We were to meet by the pool but this will do. Olga orders latte all round. I have to go to the bathroom but it's going to have to wait, for Oxana Vintilova has four stories to tell.

She is thirty-four and has a striking face, large boned, with crisp blond hair you don't see onstage because she wears a skin-tight blue hood. Her body is well sculpted. You'd never know from looking at her she has two children. But her maternalism reveals itself in her smile, in her eyes. Adagio is about family.

"Where is your pen?" she asks. "Aren't you going to write what I say?"

"I thought it would be more natural if we just talked," I answer.

"I think you should take notes," she says. "How are you going to remember anything?"

"He have very good memory!" Olga remarks, putting a finger to her temple.

As with Elena, I assume Oxana will only talk to me for a few minutes. After all, they have a show today. But she gives me all afternoon.

At first glance the Vintilovs appeared to be the quintessential circus family. Husband and wife performed together, and their six-year-old son, Maxsim, was part of their act as well, having replaced twelve-year-old Dasha, who had outgrown the role but still participated in *Saltimbanco* as a cavalier. Years of performing together had not driven them apart, as such proximity does to many American families. Years on the road had not made them tired of touring or of one another. *Saltimbanco* remained as fresh for them as when they first joined the show. And Dasha, despite her years of experience and diminished role, never looked bored backstage, but trained as hard as anyone. She had even asked Olga to teach her trapeze.

But the Vintilovs were not a circus family in the manner of multi-generational acts in the early American circus. The American circus was a hard life, but for all the risks in the ring, it provided more security than the world outside. Children were integrated into the acts, ageing performers were given jobs backstage. Many were immigrants from Mexico or Europe, gypsies of the big top. For circus families at the beginning of the last century, or during the Depression or the war, what other road could they follow?

But both Dasha and Maxsim were bi-lingual and cosmopolitan. Their parents took them on trips during holidays, so they could see life beyond the tent. Dasha liked to read. Maxsim was into computers. Rather than being stunted and one-dimensional as were many child performers, unable to deal with the outside world, they appeared mature beyond their years.

As for Andriy and Oxana, he was a competitive acrobat more interested in winning the world championship than performing onstage, and she never liked the circus. It wasn't athletic enough for her. Too many tricks, not enough fitness. And even now, as much as she loved the show, she doesn't foresee staying with the Cirque after she retires. She would be happy coaching acrobatics or aerobics.

She was born in Kiev, in the Ukraine, to a mother who was a top gymnastics coach. At that time coaches would teach their girls how to flip by holding their backs and guiding them. Oxana's mother believed this was a crutch that didn't inspire confidence. Instead she broke movements down into segments. This way her students were able to learn more rapidly and independently.

But she couldn't create a formula to coach her own daughter. Oxana rebelled, her mother lost patience. So Oxana tried other sports.

Aside from the more popular sport gymnastics there was rhythm gymnastics, which involved throwing and catching ribbons and balls in a choreographed routine and eventually became an Olympic event. There was aerobics, which involved cardiovascular exercises set to music. And there was sport acrobatics, which focused more on strength and balance and involved two or more persons. Adagio was a creative form of sport acrobatics, as were Hand-to-Hand, performed by the Polish twins, and Russian Swing.

As a child, Oxana tried each of these sports for two years and settled on acrobatics. She liked the combination or strength and artistry and, at thirteen, was talented enough to gain entrance to a special academy. Before then she had lived a normal life, attending her neighborhood school. Her mother traveled often but Oxana and her father stayed in Kiev, in a small communal flat.

At thirteen, however, her prospects brightened. Acrobatics didn't receive the state support of Olympic sports, but there were still prestigious national and international competitions, and as a member of her school she would be permitted to travel and perhaps follow her mother into coaching.

She developed a pairs act with a boy, much like ice skating. Oxana was the flyer, and she carefully choreographed their movements to music. She preferred this to gymnastics because their act lasted two-and-a-half minutes, almost twice as long as floor exercises.

They were good enough to compete, but only the top acts in the U.S.S.R. were permitted to travel to competitions abroad. Oxana would have welcomed the fall of the Soviet Union if for no other reason than she would have been able to compete for the Ukraine, an advantage two younger compatriots, Oxana Baiyol and Lilia Podkopayeva, used in the 90s to win gold medals in their respective sports. Ironically, when the Wall did fall it was more a hardship for her than a blessing because her state funding was cut.

Fortunately she saw life beyond the competition. So when she entered the university it was with a view to take advantage of the opportunity acrobatics had given her to broaden her horizons.

Andriy Vintilov was more single-minded. So narrow was his view that Oxana only occupied it when reflected off the mirrors in the weight room. Andriy had come to Ukraine from the military city of Sebastapol on the Russian Black Sea not to find a wife or start a family or improve the condition of his life, although he certainly wanted these things in time. But what he wanted now was to win the world acrobatics championship.

Of course he asked Oxana out. Their paths often crossed in the gym, and she was pretty and he was strong and handsome, with a soft smile that almost made her forget his iron biceps. But then she would find him doing bench presses at the hour appointed for their date.

"Why do you ask me out when it's obvious you would rather lift weights?" she would reproach him.

And he would reply, "Just give me another half hour."

And the half hour was always an hour or two hours, but she always waited and he always came. It was good practice for the long months they would spend apart from each other, across the world, after they were married.

Dasha was born shortly after the collapse of the Soviet Union. But the jubilation over Ukraine's independence was soon shrouded by economic depression, uncertainty over the future and the latest revelations about the disaster at Chernobyl. Oxana didn't want her daughter growing up in such an environment, but they had no money.

She wanted him to get a job. He had been following his dream, competing as part of a four-man acrobatic team. And now that the Soviet Union had fallen there was no money for his sport. But Andriy saw this as his big chance. His group would now be able to compete for Ukraine. Preliminary rounds would be a breeze. They could concentrate their energy for the meet itself.

He asked Oxana for one more year. Then he would get a job. Oxana agreed, and he won the world championship.

Some people burn out after achieving a dream costing many years of struggle. Others fall into a depression or submit to excesses their former disciplined life never allowed. But Andriy never burned out, he just burned, and after winning the world acrobatics he not only kept his word and got a job with the Moscow State Circus, but plunged himself into the circus ring with the same enthusiasm and dedication he had given the weight room.

Of course, there were weights enough in the circus. And Andriy was still an acrobat, although now he was throwing around a nine-year-old girl, the daughter of a friend. But he was no longer being judged, at least not in the same way. There were no scores, no trophies, only smiles and applause. But Andriy found this world to his liking and channeled his competitive fire into expanding his abilities and moving his career forward.

In the days when Andriy was still competing, Oxana supported the family by sewing. It seemed there was a lot of sewing being done in the former Soviet Union by talented athletes and performers. She also cared for her father and brother, who shared their flat, and often felt like the mother of four.

Unfortunately, now that Andriy had a job he was home less than ever. In her youth Oxana had to adjust to a mother who was often away. Now it was her husband. Moscow wasn't terribly far, but then he got an offer to tour Japan for six months. The Moscow Circus spent many months abroad because the money was better, and Andriy couldn't say no.

But now that Dasha was walking there was no reason Oxana couldn't get back into shape. She got an offer to be an assistant coach in Bratislava for two months and jumped at the chance. Her family could use the money and she could once again express her creativity through the medium of the human body. And with Andriy across the world, what were a few hundred miles further?

She was a great success and two months turned into two years. She introduced fresh choreography, which the girls loved, borrowing generously from classical music, pop and jazz. The head coach was a tough woman of forty-six, of the old Eastern European school. Oxana learned a great deal from her about discipline and form, but capitalism was apparently absent from the fraulein's book of virtues, for their first class of seven rigorously selected girls was almost immediately reduced to three.

In the meantime Andriy was traveling with the circus between Russia and Japan. He was in Tokyo one night when a friend took him along to see another circus, also touring the country. Andriy had never heard of

Saltimbanco or the Cirque du Soleil, and became entranced by the show, as so many of us have. But unlike the rest of us, who simply hope we can get though to the end without the wandering spotlight shining our way, Andriy saw a place for himself on their unconventional stage. Over the next few weeks he attended the performance again and again.

He contacted Montreal about working for the Cirque. They asked him to send a videotape. The only tapes were back in Kiev. Oxana, who was home now, sent the tapes by train to Moscow, where a friend took them to the airport and persuaded a Japanese businessman to carry them on his flight. Eventually they made their way to the desk of Cirque founder and CEO Guy Laliberté, a logistical feat worthy of the circus.

Laliberté wanted the act, renamed "Banque," for a new show being developed called *Quidam*. But instead of four men he wanted fifteen.

So by this circuitous route husband and wife and daughter were finally reunited for good on a neutral continent. But they wouldn't perform together. The act was for men only, and Oxana had no aspirations for the circus. Besides, she wanted to have another child.

After training in Montreal they toured North America with the show. This was a new lifestyle for Oxana, but it was nice to have her family together, and after their struggles of the last few years and the economic and environmental problems in Ukraine, the rigors of touring seemed quite bearable.

But Andriy remembered his act with the nine-year old girl. Dasha was approaching that age. She loved the circus and was talented and flexible. Oxana wasn't yet thinking of her daughter's career, but she knew being pretty wasn't enough and wanted her daughter to have a foundation upon which she could build an independent future. Andriy kept thinking of Adagio in *Saltimbanco*. His family would be a perfect replacement for the family that had performed it before. Unfortunately, after a six year run on three continents, the show had been retired.

Then one day they heard a rumor *Saltimbanco* was going to be revived. It was just a rumor, but for Russians rumors are often more credible than what they read in their newspapers, and the Vintilovs decided this rumor was worth their day off. So for the next few months every Monday the three of them practiced in secret. And when the rumor was confirmed, they were ready, finally, to step onstage together.

Adagio is about family, of course. And during the act the three members are in close physical contact with one another. How different from the Vintilovs real history! By the time Dasha had grown too old for the role and their son, Maxsim, was old enough to take over, Oxana and Andriy had been married fourteen years, having spent much of that time continents apart, having lived through the fall of the U.S.S.R., having struggled, amid their acrobatic dreams, just to put food on the table and spend a few precious days in the same flat. That they finally came back together from such distant outposts, and found balance in an unbalanced world, must be considered their greatest accomplishment, not just as husband and wife, but as acrobats.

After two hours Oxana finally looks at her watch. She is surprised by the time. Unfortunately, she's only gotten to the wedding, and there's so much more I want to know. But to my surprise she doesn't say goodbye. She keeps talking as I follow her and Olga to the Grand Chapiteau.

Olga has agreed to give Dasha a lesson today and they've reserved an hour above the stage. Again, nobody seems to be in charge. We simply walk into the tent and Olga raises the trapeze. I find this informality a continual surprise, but it speaks to the discipline and cohesion of the cast. Fishermen don't need curfews, and Icelanders don't need traffic cops.

Oxana and I sit in the fifth row, on the side. Olga stands on the opposite side holding the safety and calling instructions to Dasha in a surprisingly soft voice. There is no one else.

Knowing what I do now about Russian training methods, I expect shouts and tears. But I can't even hear Olga's comments, and Dasha looks like a child enjoying recess on the playground, and her mother continues with her family's story, only glancing occasionally at her daughter and withholding comment.

She's remarkably laid back for a woman watching her child practice trapeze, and I feel this must reflect on Olga, who, in addition to providing instruction, is holding the safety. Indeed, the first time Dasha misses the bar and falls, her mother doesn't react at all and turns her eyes back to me. Nor does Dasha even utter a gasp, or Olga yell, as one might expect her to. Not that Dasha actually falls. She hangs in the air for a moment before grabbing the bar again. She'll lose her grip a couple more times when trying pirouettes, but never plunge below the bar. Still, it's the first time in all my life I've ever seen anyone fall from the trapeze.

Andriy enters the tent and sits on the other side of me as though we're old friends. His wife asks him about Max, in English, and they talk across me for a moment before he offers me his firm hand and formally introduces himself. Like his wife, he smiles generously, which surprises me, and elaborates on his wife's story.

"You must see *Quidam*," he says, occasionally glancing at his daughter, but otherwise giving his full attention to me. "It's touring the U.S. now."

I ask him if his competitive instincts are frustrated now that he is in show business.

"Not at all. In competition you train for seven months for one day. Here you must perform every day, so it's a different challenge," he replies, echoing what Elena had answered to the same question.

"But don't you get tired of repeating your act?"

"But it is never two times the same. There is always something better or worse, something to work on."

"The moment you are perfect you are dead!" Oxana adds.

"It's true I'm no longer judged in the same way," Andriy admits. "But every audience member is a judge. My goal every night is to please at least one person."

"Many people have been moved by our act," Oxana says proudly. "They have told us it is an inspiration to family unity."

As the Vintilovs themselves are an inspiration.

Oxana looks at her watch and says she has to go warm up Max. I follow them back into the artistic tent, where the youngest member of the family is patiently waiting.

Maxsim is both playful and mature, with light brown hair and wide cheeks. His supple limbs aren't just a product of athletic parents. His mother stretches him before and after every show.

"What happens when he's sick?" I ask, for his role extends beyond Adagio. He curls up on the stage when Dreamer sleeps and sits in the chair that spins around to reveal Eddie, the mime, identically dressed. It isn't as though another cast member could substitute for him, and aren't children his age plagued with colds and infections?

"There's another boy we use," Oxana replies. "He performs on matinee days, so Max doesn't have to do two shows. But Max doesn't get sick."

"Really?"

"Dasha, when she had the role, only missed two shows in three years!" And she laughs, recalling something, and moves closer to me.

"Max and I were riding the tram here in Vienna a few days ago," she tells me in a softer voice. "And he looked at me very seriously and said, 'Mom, I think I made the right decision to replace Dasha in *Saltimbanco*!'"

THE DANUBE DECATHLON

Olga has arranged for me to play tennis with a Dutch woman who works in logistics, but it pours an hour before our court time, the only rain of the week. So I accompany Tanya, who wants to walk along the Danube, and we pick up Victoria, the shy fifteen-year-old, along the way.

Of course now the sun is shining again, but the damage has been done to the courts. Still, feeling the need for more than a leisurely walk, I challenge them to a race. Tanya isn't interested. She's busy listening to her Walkman and defoliating the bushes that separate the pool from the promenade. But Victoria rises to the challenge.

I give her a head start, but when she sees she's going to lose she revises the finish line.

"To the hotel door!" she announces, and leaps like a gazelle onto the stone wall, then over a hedge of thorn bushes.

I foolishly follow but get tangled in the bushes, my legs scratched by thorns, and fall. I'm lucky I haven't sprained an ankle.

Victoria stands at the back entrance, laughing, ignoring the curious diners on the patio.

I walk carefully back to the promenade, picking out the thorns. That was fun. But Victoria is only just beginning. She leaps back onto the wall and walks it like a balance beam.

"Come on!"

"There are people eating! I don't want to fall into someone's tortellini!"

"Can't you do it?"

I accept the challenge but I can't catch her. She jumps down and sprints over to the embankment, where concrete posts about three feet high and a foot in diameter are spaced at regular intervals.

She climbs onto the nearest one and motions for me to take the next. "See who can stand on one leg the longest," she says. "You have to bend it all the way back. Arms at your side."

The clouds have passed and the sun is beginning to set. The Danube is peaceful here, if not blue. There's no traffic on the water and nothing but vegetation on the opposite bank. In the distance the skyscrapers of Vienna's suburban UNESCO City seem like a mirage. In the other direction a sleek cable bridge spans the Danube's quarter-mile width. Because the river is dammed the water is fairly still and settles right against the bank, a few feet away.

In the city's long history many have surely admired the Danube at sunset, but probably not standing on one leg, fending off cramps. I finally give in.

"Other leg!"

She wins this one too. But I manage to tie on the log, a long log sitting on the grass beside the promenade. Victoria hops its length, and I disappoint her by not falling.

She looks around for a moment, then pulls some berries from a bush and puts them in my hand.

"Set this on the ground. Then crush them with a pirouette."

I do my best, but she shakes her head.

"You didn't extend your knee. You did a jazz pirouette, not ballet."

"You studied ballet?"

She steps behind a stone bench, grabs the top edge with her hands and lifts her feet off the ground, balancing with her head facing the seat.

"I'm not going to experiment on a stone bench," I tell her.

We continue our interrupted walk along the promenade. Tanya is not far behind, still engrossed in her music. But except for an occasional cyclist and a group of fishermen on the bank ahead, we have it all to ourselves.

Victoria runs to a lamp post. "Chinese Poles!" And she prepares to climb. But then she thinks better of it and steps away. "I don't want to break it," she says.

She spies concrete steps built into the short embankment, leading down to the water's edge. "You take that ledge and I'll take this," she commands, stepping onto the left concrete rail at the top of the steps. "Whoever gets closest to the water wins. Be careful at the bottom where it's wet—that's slippery."

I have no intention of going that far down. "I'm not jumping in after you if you fall in," I warn her.

"I'm a good swimmer."

And she gracefully steps down to the water's edge and climbs back up.

"I win again!"

I had assumed, when I first began spending time with the Cirque, that I would encounter a lot of Type A personalities, endlessly playing games and trying to outdo one another. As performers, seeking the spotlight when out of it. As athletes, seeking victories after the game.

Instead they drink coffee and beer, talk and play music, go dancing and lounge by the pool. Olga continually insists she is not a competitive person. She nearly won a judo championship in her youth, she beat hundreds for a place in the prestigious Moscow Circus School. But she's not a competitive person.

So I'm surprised to find that the greatest expression of competitiveness I've witnessed during my time with the Cirque comes not from Olga or from Alya, the acrobat and fitness champ, or the Vintilovs, or Elena Grosheva, but from a fifteen-year-old who has spent little time with the circus, who seems at first glance a typical teenage girl, who reads Judy Blume, wears heels to the Jacuzzi, and would like to be a fashion designer.

She spots a metal playground jeep on springs, a ride that children can sit in and tilt by shifting their weight. Victoria thinks for a moment, then cries, "To the car!"

And she runs to the jeep.

She instructs me to stand in the driver's compartment, while she straddles the edges of the hollow hood, her back to me.

"You've got to try to make me fall off. Count backwards from thirty. Whoever stays on longer wins."

She's about four feet off the ground. "You could get hurt," I tell her.

"I'll fall inside," she replies, jumping harmlessly into the space where the engine should be.

She stands tall and confident, with her arms outstretched, but I can tilt the jeep not only side to side but forward and back, and she falls in two seconds. But she falls as promised and isn't hurt.

"Your turn!"

I carefully test my balance. At least with a mechanical bull you have something to hold on to and there isn't a maniacal teenager standing behind you wishing to cause you bodily harm. But I manage to stay on a few seconds longer than she and gain my first victory.

She runs to the posts along the embankment. She climbs up on one leg, squats almost to her heel and balances with the other leg outstretched.

I concede the event.

"Can you do cartwheels?" she then asks.

"Theoretically."

"You see that pole?" she says, pointing to a lamp post fifty yards away. "Cartwheels to there!"

"You've got to be kidding!"

"I'll give you a head start."

Maybe, maybe, I could string a few ugly cartwheels together on nice spongy mats. But on pavement? I try two just to save face but already I have abrasions on my hands.

Victoria then whirls down the promenade like the spokes of a bicycle tire. Her back straight, her legs high, she cartwheels to the lamp post without pausing once.

"I'm winning seven to one, with one tie," she announces.

"I liked you better when you were shy!"

What I need is an event of brute strength. Perhaps arm wrestling. But even here I'm outmatched by this circus child.

"Can you do roundhouse kicks?" she asks instead.

And she starts kicking me.

"Karate fight!"

And she punches me on my arm, then leaps back and menaces me with an attacking stance.

"You took karate? What color is your belt?"

"Black, I think."

"You think!"

Most of us live in the world of classrooms and offices, where work and play are strictly segregated. A lucky few breathe the rarefied air of the circus. And an even smaller number, like Victoria, grow up in both worlds. I had hoped she would enlighten me as to how she reconciled these disparate environments, but she ignored my questions and probably couldn't have articulated her feelings even had she wanted to.

But by the time we return to the hotel and take the elevator up to the penthouse Jacuzzi, where she will splash me as I try to soothe my wounds, I have my answer.

Who better suited to straddle two worlds than the daughter of an acrobat?

FIVE THOUSAND EYES

Later that night Olga invites me to join her as she makes the rounds of several rooms. In the first are four crew members, as well as Marie-Claude Lecroix, the Canadian who performs boleadoros. They're sitting in a circle, drinking and smoking, talking about nothing in particular. I sit next to Marie-Claude, who always seems to be smiling, even when she's complaining about her treatment in Barcelona.

One doesn't often think of Canadians as the object of discrimination, but boleadoros is as Latin as the tango, and Marie-Claude says the Spanish didn't take her seriously. The Catalan press, for instance, only wished to interview her Argentinian partner. I assure her I have no such compunction. In fact I'm more interested in how someone from Quebec took up the boleadoras. Marie-Claude replies that she once had an Argentinian boyfriend, but our conversation is interrupted by Olga, who wants to leave.

We proceed to the room of one of the wardrobe staff. The furniture has been rearranged, the bed pushed into the corner, and a map of Vienna is taped to the wall. Five women sit on the bed and the floor watching *Sex and the City* on DVD. I have never seen Olga watch television and after ten minutes she asks if I want to go.

We return to her room only long enough for her to make a call. "Alya wants me to try some clothes. You can come if you want."

Tanya is getting ready for bed. "When do you leave?" she asks.

"Tomorrow afternoon."

"Tomorrow!" she cries with a sense of regret. "I won't see you again!"

I give her a hug good night, and perhaps farewell. It's easy to tell people you'll meet again, but when they live in Northern Siberia the sentiment sounds unconvincing.

I find myself once again in a room full of women. Four to be exact, not counting Olga. There is Alya and her blond aunt, visiting from France. There is Susan Daly, the singer, and, lounging on the bed, her schoolhood friend visiting from England.

Judging by the hundreds of CDs covering the tables I assume this is Susan's room. Also, she is the one trying on clothes. The white diaphanous creation Olga had worn to the concert.

There are two singers in *Saltimbanco*, and they alternate shows. The other is from Germany. Susan is from London, the only British member of the cast. She's also one of only two black artists, the other being the American who plays the ringmaster. She's forty-two, but looks younger, with very short hair, large eyes and a clear, striking voice.

But I don't have a chance to ask any questions.

"Wait in the hall," Olga says. "We have to change."

"You can change in the bathroom," Alya suggests.

"Okay. Sit over there," Olga tells me, pointing to a chair.

I sit quietly while Susan models the white outfit, and then a dark green body suit that Olga also owns, with hollow loops ringing the waist. I feel bored and then chastise myself for my impatience. What has the Cirque done to me? I'm taken to a room with five women, then a room with four women, and both times I can't wait to leave!

After the fitting is over Alya introduces me to her aunt. She and Alya's mother design their own fashions. Everything is custom made, hand knit in Ukraine, where her mother still lives. Alya tells me that when her mother saw Olga perform in Amsterdam she was so taken with her act she gave her these clothes.

I take this opportunity to tell the aunt how much I like her work, and to ask what else she and her sister design, and if they design for men as well.

She shows me a catalogue of photographs, and I'm very impressed. There are body suits, pants, dresses, skirts, jackets, vests, sweaters. I haven't seen anything quite like them. They're as creative as the Cirque costumes, richly textured with oversized buttons and patches, like mixed-media collages, but also revealing in places, with gaping openings between the stitches or rings and holes in the fabric.

"These designs are also for men," Alya's aunt says, turning to a page of cardigan sweaters and jackets.

"They're very nice. Only in these colors?"

"No, whatever colors you like."

We settle on a color range, for the sweaters are multi-colored, and she warns me it won't be ready for several weeks. I tell her I plan to come to Brussels and she assures me it will be ready by then.

"Did you buy something?" Olga asks.

"I have to keep up with you!"

As we're saying good night, the singer turns to me and says, "I think I'm supposed to talk to you."

This is news to me, but I'm delighted.

"Tomorrow after the show?" she asks.

But I'm leaving tomorrow. And I have an appointment with the juggler at noon. Yes, Olga overcame Maria's resistance. Or maybe her mother found me sufficiently charming—or innocuous.

"I'll be in Brussels. Maybe we can talk then?"

"Love to!"

Life is getting easier.

Alya follows Olga and me up to Olga's room and plugs in her laptop. I think she's excited by my enthusiasm for her mother and aunt's fashions, for she shows us their web site.

The catalogue is very high-tech and professional, more than you might expect from a cottage industry in Kiev. I'm particularly impressed with the models.

"She was Miss Ukraine," Alya points out, as I examine the tall blonde wearing a pants suit that Miss Peele would have approved of. "She was runner up in Miss Universe!"

Maybe my next book should be about the post-Soviet fashion world?

Alya then shows us her digital photo album from her last vacation, camping with her husband in Spain and France. One photo depicts a tent near a gorge and Alya confesses how frightened she was to spend the night there.

"We were completely alone!" she says. "If we screamed no one would hear us!"

If I had her or her husband's physique I can't imagine anything making me scream. "I think you were the largest mammals in the country," I remark.

Though, in truth, despite her shoulders and biceps, which she highlights by wearing tank tops, Alya is very feminine. She's shorter than one might expect, has extremely long blond hair, wears makeup and, naturally, stylish clothes. This contrast between her femininity and physique makes her appearance all the more striking.

And, as if to affirm my unspoken observations, Alya relates the story of her first encounter with Olga.

"I was training in Montreal for *Saltimbanco*," she says. "And I heard there was a new trapeze act. So I went into the dressing room where Olga was sitting to introduce myself. Well, you know how sometimes Olga's body isn't large enough to contain her emotions? She turned around and looked at me and just gasped! I was so embarrassed!"

"She so beautiful!" Olga explains. "I couldn't believe it!"

"Of course we're friends now, but I didn't know her then," Alya says. "One day she was practicing on the trapeze and she refused to continue until one of the men watching her left. It was the artistic director! Can you imagine? Telling the artistic director to leave his own stage? There were some other artists there also training for *Saltimbanco*. We looked at each other and said, 'She's gonna work with us?'"

The next morning I'm awakened by a call from Alya. She and her aunt want to come down and measure me. What service! I don't bother to dress, except to throw on some jeans. I should be more self-conscious, exposing my chest to a fitness champ.

Maria, or Masha, the juggler, meets me in the lobby precisely at noon and, after so many glances and nods in Amsterdam and Barcelona, we finally shake hands. We go outside to the patio and sit by the ledge overlooking the river. The same ledge Victoria and I had walked across yesterday as part of our contest. It's another cloudless day. Maria wears mirrored sunglasses, although she sits with her back to the sun. Her last name in the program is Markova but she prefers to go by Choodu. I suspect that's her mother's maiden name, but I don't ask.

Her long brown hair is pulled back and she's wearing a white t-shirt cut above the navel and low-cut embroidered jeans. She's prettier in person than onstage, where her natural beauty is hidden behind a blue suit and top hat.

I can tell at once she's a very serious and introspective person, although she smiles easily enough and looks directly at me through her glasses. She orders café au lait, but nothing to eat. Like Elena and Oxana, she will give me two hours, interrupted only once by her cell phone, which she then turns off.

I ask if she sees herself in Dasha, having grown up with a circus mother and joined *Saltimbanco* at fourteen.

"Not at all," she replies. "Dasha is a girl. I was a boy. I played with boys, I hated dolls. If someone gave me a Barbie I would twist the arms and legs into the shape of a gun and pretend it was a weapon!"

"But you don't look like a boy now," I shrewdly observe. "What about men?"

"I don't want a boyfriend right now. I tried dating last year, so I've tried it. But men are a distraction, they don't make you a better person, they put bags under your eyes! First in my life is the show. Then my mother. Then my friends. Men are fourth."

She rattles off this hierarchy of attention as though she's said it before, but to whom? Men? I ask how she deals with the inevitable come-ons she must receive from guys in the cast, in the crew, on the road.

"I try to be nice," she replies. "I don't want to hurt anybody. But people understand. And if anyone tries to hurt me my mother would kill them!" she adds with a laugh. "She's a lion!"

Masha seems leonine enough herself, especially for eighteen. Although she looks and dresses like a normal teenager, she speaks and carries herself like someone much older. Her manner, although polite, gives one the sense she won't tolerate anyone wasting her time.

I tell her I was struck not merely by her juggling but by her other movements onstage. As though she had a background in ballet or theater.

"My mother taught me how to move. How to smile." And she flashes a smile on cue. "She told me it's not enough just to juggle eight balls. You have to know how to act in the complement—when you are waiting for the next ball to be thrown to you or looking into the audience. I used to put my hand out like this," she says, holding her hand out to receive an imaginary ball from one of the characters. "My mom said you have to use your fingers." And she again holds out her hand, but this time pronating the wrist and spreading her fingers.

"Do you practice every day?"

"I used to. But now my mom makes me put away the balls between cities."

"You've been in *Saltimbanco* since you were fourteen. Do you still need to practice a lot?"

"Oh, of course. Sometimes I envy the acrobats when I see them resting and I know I have to practice. When I began my career I would practice ten hours a day! Five hours—eat, wash, soosh, soosh—five hours!"

"Do you want to spend your whole life in the circus?"

"No. I'd like to go to school and become a lawyer."

"Where?"

"In Moscow, of course. It's my home. Or maybe if I have the chance I'd like to be an actress."

"You're acting now, aren't you?"

"No. In the show I have a costume, true, but I never act. I only show what is inside myself."

"Speaking of costumes, I noticed when I was backstage the way you laid everything out. Someone told me you have a specific routine, that you're superstitious."

"It's true I have a routine, but not because I'm superstitious. I think a performer must have respect for the costume. I don't want anything to be dirty or wrinkled and I only wear it when I go onstage. I never sit in my costume. The balls must be clean too, of course. And kept in the box when I'm not practicing. It's not superstition but a sign of respect. My mom used to tell me the balls were my bread, because with the balls I make money and the money buys food."

Olga appears on the patio and pulls up a chair. She asks Masha if she feels a rush after the show. "I myself always feel a rush!" she volunteers.

"I can't sleep for hours!"

"Oh yes," Masha replies. "I always have a lot of energy after I come off, especially if the audience was good."

"What do you think about when you are performing?" I ask.

"Nothing."

"But you're aware of the audience?

"Sure. I always try to make a connection with them. They pay to watch us perform. We owe them our best effort. When I go onstage five thousand eyes are watching me. When I look back at them I may see that one-third of the audience is happy, one-third is not happy, and one-third is neutral. My job is to bring them together."

Afterward I ask her for a photo. I wasn't going to ask, but change my mind at the last moment. I'm sure she'll decline, but there's no harm asking.

To my surprise she agrees. She even takes off her glasses and smiles as Olga photographs us with the Danube behind. A minute later I find her inside paying for her coffee. I don't let her, of course, but I'm impressed that she didn't even charge the price of a café au lait for her time.

I finish packing, check out, and go up to Olga's room to say goodbye. Tanya has gone into the city with Victoria, so it's just the two of us. She asks if I want a video and gives me a promotional tape she had made in Australia. We talk for a few minutes, then I kiss her goodbye. As I'm opening the door to leave she calls out with a grin, "May all your dreams come true!"

My time here has far exceeded my conservative expectations. But my experience has also been illuminating. I had spent these days tumbling with the Cirque, with hardly an hour to myself, not as a spectator—I didn't even see the show this trip—but as a friend. The best way to learn a language is by immersion, by speaking nothing else. And that is what I have done in Vienna, speaking the rarefied language of the Cirque. And I've begun to get a sense of the special camaraderie among the cast and crew of the Cirque du Soleil, insulating and claustrophobic, solicitous and supportive. I know I'll always be an outsider, but Olga and the others have made me feel I belong.

And leaving the Cirque is like leaving Tahiti. A distant paradise you may never see again. And I know, as I begin to reconsider my life at home, a world without Olga and Masha and Alya, a world without Olympic gymnasts and families of acrobats, without commissary tents and all-night parties and hotel lobbies always populated with familiar faces—I know that very soon there will come a time when I won't have Vienna or Brussels to look forward to, when I won't be coming back.

JUGGLING

At six she was homeless. But unlike Olga, who ran away on her own, Maria Choodu followed her mother. But where? It was not a question of running away to join the circus. Her mother, Margarita, was already an acrobat with the Moscow State Circus. But she wanted to escape a bad marriage. So she took her only child and left. At least Olga had a train ticket when she left home. All Margarita and her daughter had were a few modest possessions packed hurriedly into trunks.

So this first step on their road to the Cirque du Soleil did not take them very far. In fact, only to the courtyard of their massive apartment complex on the outskirts of Moscow, where Margarita plopped down their trunks in the snow and sat there with her daughter, wondering where to go.

Neither cried. Or spoke. What was there to say? Or cry about? A failed marriage? A lost home? A passerby might have seen two frail females in need of rescue. But they were sturdier than the trunks they sat on. Margarita possessed talent and discipline. She had a thriving career and was still young. Her daughter was a boy in disguise, who beat her male cousins in soccer and basketball and suppressed the tears when she fell.

For the mother it was a liberating moment, but she hadn't rehearsed it the way she practiced her acrobatics. So they sat on their trunks while she thought of her next move. They would not go as far as Olga. Just a few Metro stops to another anonymous suburb. But for the daughter it was the defining moment in her young life. As she sat silently in the snow awaiting her mother's decision she vowed she would never again let life catch her off balance.

The next defining moment in her life came that same year when she watched a juggler practice backstage at the Moscow State Circus. He was juggling twelve rings and Maria stared in fascination, wondering how he did it. Over the next few weeks she watched him every day in practice, sitting quietly, patiently, not asking questions, just gazing with her big dark eyes.

She began juggling herself, with golf balls. It so happened the old woman with whom they shared their new flat, in a building for circus performers, had once juggled umbrellas. Maria continued to play soccer as well, and when she was eight her mother told her to make a choice.

"Better to be excellent in one thing than good in two," she advised.

Maria chose juggling. Even though it was an activity dominated by men, the circus held more possibilities for her future than soccer and better suited her patient, self-reliant nature. Her mother concealed her dismay. She found juggling boring and didn't want Maria to grow up in the circus. It was a hard life, far less glamorous than the theater or ballet, circumscribed by a claustrophobic social life, modest state apartments and squalid hotels, coaches who never said a kind word, injury and early retirement.

The Moscow, or Bolshoi, State Circus was the most prestigious in Russia and housed in a large round concrete building. There were not three rings, like the American circus, but only one, with a practice ring backstage. Maria developed her act in front of a mirror but her mother would not allow her on the practice stage. It was dangerous, since the space was shared with acrobats and bears and a stray ball could have cata-strophic consequences.

Finally, after one year her mother allowed her to touch the practice stage. Just to touch it. Maria was surprised how soft it was. It had to be soft for the equestrian acts.

At last, at eleven, she was allowed to perform. She wasn't nervous juggling in front of people—she had been around the circus for so long it seemed natural to take her place onstage. She started by throwing a baton, then worked up from three balls while doing the splits, and finished in the darkness juggling six glowing balls.

She was instantly popular and soon her mother assumed her new role as coach. At age twelve Maria won a prize at Monte Carlo and at fourteen the Cirque du Soleil invited them to Montreal.

Maria had seen a video of *Saltimbanco* when she was nine and immediately wanted to be in it. But by the time the Cirque called she had forgotten the name of the show and wasn't certain what sort of routine they wanted her to perform. She was therefore astonished when she and her mother arrived at the training facility and the artistic director led her to the familiar juggler's stand which Miguel Herrera had climbed thousands of times and which she would now climb as well. She approached it like an altar and examined the narrow platform at the top of four otherwise ordinary steps, covered with scratches from Herrera's heel marks or errant balls, the pinnacle of her young life.

Only fourteen. At the same age Olga had left home, Maria Choodu had found hers.

RUNNING AWAY FROM THE CIRQUE

Novelists often talk about their characters resisting manipulation, going their own way. And it's true. I myself have created characters who stubbornly refuse to follow the plot. But in real life they really do go their own way. And sometimes they don't come back.

My life has been cursed by false security. Every time I think the world is in order and what I wish for within my grasp the ground cracks and I find myself standing not on solid land but on an ice sheet crackling into a thousand shards. And wherever I turn, everything I want is drifting inexorably away.

It happened with Vika. Like an earthquake, without warning. And now, perhaps, with Olga. We spoke almost daily her last week in Vienna. I think she was lonely after her sister's departure and burnt out from performing. She also complained about personality conflicts and insomnia.

"Mark," she whispered. "Trapeze take all your life. I want normal life. I has to go for that. How many books been written about girl in trapeze who dead in trapeze? One day I just take my clothes and go!"

But the next night her voice would be buoyant and hopeful. "Oh Mark, I had best show! What you doing tonight? You watch porno?" And she would laugh like a little girl.

So I thought her complaints were just the typical reactions of an overworked performer at the end of a run who, except for her boyfriend, didn't have anyone in whom to confide her anguish.

I well knew she was capable of running away. But during her career she had always been highly professional. Her contract with the Cirque would expire in only a few months, after London, and she had never broken a contract before. Besides, we were planning to meet in Las Vegas to see "O" and *Mystère*. Why would someone disillusioned with the Cirque travel half the world to see two of its shows? And why, when we were considering itineraries, would she tell me the date she needed to be in Brussels?

Cast members only get about one week between cities. Although I wanted her to come to America, I didn't encourage her. It was a lot of travel time and money for three days in Vegas. I kept expecting her to change her mind, but each day the plan solidified further, until, on Wednesday, she asked me to reserve a flight.

She wanted to leave from Amsterdam, so I called the travel agency that got me out on Singapore Air when my standby ticket failed. But when I phoned her Thursday night I knew something was wrong.

"So, how your book coming?"

I thought there would be plenty of time to talk about the book in Las Vegas.

"How it gonna end?"

"I don't know."

"Mark, for one week I can't sleep! I up and down. One night I have best show. Next day I feel no energy. I crying all the time. I call artistic director in Montreal. I say I need these days off. He says okay, I can be cavalier. But I need to be away from circus completely. Do you understand? I give what I have inside. I feel good I work good. I feel bad I work bad."

"If you can't perform you shouldn't perform. But you only have three days before the break. Can't you just do the cavalier?"

"All my life I been doing trapeze. But I want normal life. I want children. You know how many girls grow up in circus never know anything else? One day she will have to face this real life and how she gonna do it? It will be so hard! Tomorrow I take my clothes and go!"

Well, it wasn't the best time to talk about Las Vegas. But I e-mailed her the flight information and planned to phone her the following night.

Then on Friday, before phoning Olga, I called Marie-Claude Lacroix, the boleodoro dancer. She had agreed to talk to me, but before I could ask her any questions she said, "Do you know Olga's left?"

"She really left?"

"Yesterday she came to the artistic tent and said she had resigned. It was quite a shock. The Russian swing broke too, so in the second act we had no Solo Trapeze and no Russian Swing!"

"Did she say goodbye to you? Tell you where she was going?"

"No."

Marie-Claude was one of the people closest to Olga, so I could imagine Olga's state. I called the front desk and they told me she had checked out at 3:50 that afternoon. I pictured her carrying her own luggage to the train station. Then where?

I assumed she went to Amsterdam, to her boyfriend's. But she could have gone to Australia. She could have gone to Russia. There was only one place I could be certain she hadn't gone. Las Vegas.

She had once given me Arthur's number in Amsterdam, but I don't call, or e-mail. I decide to wait a few days. I'm disappointed about Las Vegas, of course, but I still plan to go to Brussels. And I intend to see Olga again, wherever she is. But I never thought she would leave the Cirque before I did, and I regret the prospect of never seeing her perform again, or joking with her in the artistic tent, or sitting in her hotel room with a glass of wine after the bar has closed.

But what I most regret is that a woman who ran away to join the circus, who dedicated her whole life to the art of the trapeze, would end her career by running away. She had told me all along of her plans for retirement and that she probably wouldn't renew her contract. That she felt she was growing old, that she needed knee surgery, that she wanted to marry and have twins and start her own school for trapeze.

She only had a few months left. Then she could take a bow and leave the stage with dignity and her friends and colleagues in the Cirque with endearing kisses. She was the most determined and dedicated of woman, and I thought it highly regrettable that anyone might think her a quitter.

Of course, Olga didn't care what others thought. Except perhaps for a twelve-year-old girl. It's a quirk of Olga's character that, like a magnet, none of her extreme qualities exists without an opposite pole.

To my relief she phoned me a few days later, from Amsterdam. She sounded bright and cheerful, she was sleeping again, and running every day to stay in shape. Her decision was firm, and I didn't question it, or inquire about the details. I figured she needed my support, and as I listened she volunteered more and more information.

I assumed she had just burnt out or had a breakdown. How else account for such a precipitate departure? But normal rules of behavior don't apply to Olga, and her oscillations on the ground were never as predictable as they were in the air.

She had been giving Dasha Vintilova trapeze lessons. It wasn't part of her job. She did it because she wanted to, and because they wanted her to. The session I attended appeared a model of harmony. But Olga, as I knew by now, was a rigorously non-competitive person. It seemed incongruous to me that a non and even anti-competive person could rise to the highest level in a discipline with so few professional opportunities. And at first I wondered if her dismissal of compliments and refusal to appraise herself or compare herself to others wasn't merely an artist's affectation. But I gradually came to realize this was a deeply ingrained quality of hers. She had become the best because she had natural talents, a vigorous work ethic and an uncompromising devotion to her dream. Perhaps the greatest proof of her disdain for medals and rankings was that she had turned down, more than once, invitations to the festival in Monte Carlo, the most prestigious competition in the circus arts.

Of course, the Vintilovs were very competitive, and, like many in the Cirque du Soleil, came from competitive backgrounds. Naturally their daughter was competitive as well, and she began to compete with Olga.

And Olga couldn't deal with it.

"Of course, it not her fault. It's the parents. But they competitive people. They know no other way. But I not competitive person."

And then there was an incident before the show.

"You know I have low practice trapeze in artistic tent. Well, Dasha can use this any time she wants. But thirty minutes before my act I need my space, you understand? I has to focus. And one night in that time Dasha was in my space. I say, 'You can go there any time you like, but not those thirty minutes!'"

I waited to hear how the situation escalated into a final break. But it seemed to me more simmering than boiling. Easily resolvable. But people with great strengths often harbor great weaknesses. Elephants panic at mice, and trapezists, apparently, at little girls.

"What you think?" she asked.

But this was not the time for logic, or even conversation. I gave her my support and asked few questions. I knew as well as anyone that Olga could be difficult and unfair. But I'd met few people more warmhearted and giving, and thought it cruelly unfortunate that, whatever the facts, she was suffering for an act of generosity.

Her mood remained bright when we spoke again a few days later. She was running ten kilometers a day, but she had also started smoking again. She wasn't concerned about her relationship with the Cirque. She had e-mailed the artistic director to explain why she resigned and to tie up some loose ends. He phoned to tell her she was fired.

"How he can fire me when I resign? I don't think he likes me because in Montreal I ask him leave stage when I practicing!"

But she didn't seem concerned. She asked my thoughts about starting a trapeze school, and I offered to help in any way I could. I didn't ask how I would manage in Brussels without her, but she brought the subject up herself.

"People will talk with you, no problem. Where you stay?"

"With the Cirque I hope."

"You know, couples who both in show get two rooms, but usually just use one. Maybe I can get you free room."

"Maybe I can have yours!" I tease.

The next night I broach the subject of rapprochement. I accepted that she wasn't returning, but thought it prudent for her future to appease Cirque management, as well as the friends she'd left behind. Her life was complicated enough and she might need their support if she started her school.

But the truth is she was never good at saying goodbye. You'd talk on the phone for an hour and then she'd abruptly say, "Okay. Goodbye." Or you'd be chatting all night in her hotel room and she'd say, "I talk too much. I need sleep." Or you're at a party and you look up and she's gone.

And now she confesses part of her motivation for leaving the Cirque as she did. "When you change life you must make complete break. If I not make complete break how can I go? I will hear voice— "Olga—trapeze waiting you!"

But the next time we talk it's not to speak about circus school, or twins. She had asked me earlier if I knew how to have twins, and I'd undoubtedly made the day of some fertility clinic nurse when I e-mailed Olga's strange request. Multiple births can be an unintended consequence of invitro-fertilization. But to use the procedure on a fertile woman for the sole purpose of increasing her chances of having twins was an alternative probably never explored in the annals of reproductive science. In any case, American clinics wouldn't do it, she would have to pay thousands of euros if she could find a European clinic to consent, and even then her chances of giving birth to twins would be less than one in four.

But before I could report the results of my research, she informed me, in an uncharacteristically casual tone, that she was going to Brussels.

The artistic director had called again and, apparently forgetting that he had fired her, asked if she could come back for Brussels. The duo trapeze twins weren't ready. The Cirque asked *Saltimbanco*'s original solo trapezist, Shana Carroll, to step back in, but she could only work a week. At the end of the day the Cirque wanted Olga back. She would miss the first week, but she would be in Belgium when I was there, just like old times. And she would stay on for Madrid and London.

Maybe that's why she was given to running away, why she said her goodbyes so abruptly, or not at all. Because when cornered, she found it so hard to say no. And because she heard that voice— "Olga, trapeze waiting you."

She could have asked for more money. She didn't. She didn't ask for anything. She took her clothes and went.

SINGING

Her e-mail says "Diva," but Susan Daly's temperament is more like an airline pilot's—pleasant and reserved, laconic and in control. You don't even know she's on board until you've touched down, and then you wish you'd had a chance to get to know her better.

Not that a better acquaintance would allow you to uncover all her secrets. Some people are intriguing because they're unusual. But Susan is intriguing because she appears so ordinary. A youthful looking forty-one with large, searching eyes, soft lips and closely cropped hair who dresses unpretentiously in earth-toned slacks or skirts, she could be a lawyer or a teacher or a broker or a mother or a waitress—she could be almost anything but a singer.

The only clue to her profession is her voice itself, soothing and clear, well-suited to communicating the latest developments at Downing Street on the BBC or reading bedtime stories to children, or to enliven with meaning the confabulated language of the Cirque du Soleil.

The deepest mysteries about her she cannot answer: how such an unprepossessing person managed to succeed in the cutthroat world of show business, and what drove her to the stage? To the second question she can only claim ignorance. To the first she answers "hard work," but the theaters of London's West End are littered with the corpses of hard workers. When she dismisses any suggestion of natural talent, insisting she has an average voice and just works very hard, you know she really believes this, that she's not feigning modesty. After all, few encouraged her, and she remembers when she was a child the mother of a friend told her she couldn't sing. But Susan wasn't particularly offended. She had no intention of a singing career. She wanted to be a dancer.

The fact that her West Indian parents had no interest in the arts, that her friends, her neighbors, her working-class community in Tottenham North London were not lightning rods to the Royal Ballet Company, was a detail she chose to ignore. Still, there was one friend of her mother's who suggested she enroll in ballet school when she was four. Susan didn't have to be prodded. Other children are traumatized by their overbearing parents' unhealthy preoccupation with culture and as adults can't enter a room containing a piano without shivering at the memory of practicing scales beneath the caustic gaze of Miss Horowitz. But Susan's idea of paradise was rehearsing *Swan Lake* while her neighbors wasted their lives skipping rope and chasing boys.

You think her perseverance must be due to the encouragement of a teacher, but Susan insists she was never teacher's pet. She studied ballet and jazz, and won some awards for tap. But had she quit no teacher would have knocked at her door, begging her back. Some performers are so driven they cannot be ignored, but Susan's determination was of a quieter sort and she was happy to be left alone.

Her influences are equally impossible to explain. She grew up with the Beatles and Motown, but even when she was the lead singer in a pop band decades later she had no ambition to be a pop star. She loved to watch old Hollywood black-and-white movies on television and idolized Deanna Durbin. Not Marlene Dietrich. Not Judy Garland. Deanna Durbin. My mother's favorite also.

Imagine this child of West Indian parents singing "Spring Will Be a Little Late This Year," on the streets of Tottenham! How did she survive?

Her quiet determination led to her acceptance into the Corona School for Performing Arts when she was fifteen. However, her parents wouldn't let her attend because it was too far away. If Susan was bitter she didn't show it. She didn't argue, and her rebellion was more subtle than that of other teenagers. Instead she applied to a ballet school in Covent Garden.

She knew by now she couldn't be a ballet dancer. She didn't have the body for it. But she thought the school would be good training for the West End. However, the school didn't allow its students to audition for outside shows. Those who weren't good enough for the stage were supposed to become teachers. But Susan still dreamed of dancing, so she eventually left.

She auditioned for *Bubbling Brown Sugar*, a black musical that had come to the West End from Broadway. It wasn't a pretty story—the audition, not the musical. But Susan's long lonely road stood her in good stead. One lousy audition wasn't going to send her packing. She would audition five times, over many months. She would hang out at the theater and come to know the people in the show. Susan loves cats, and one can imagine her at this point in her life a stray herself, waiting to be let in the door.

For the fourth audition she had to sing as well as dance, but she hadn't prepared a number. So the night before she went over to a friend's and settled on a song from *Dr. Zhivago*. She had never sung it before, and when the time came for her audition she forgot the words completely. She stood on the bare stage, by now a familiar presence to the casting personnel, and improvised until the music stopped.

Not many people would come back for a fifth audition after such a humiliating fourth. It wasn't as though she was making progress, as though the director were consoling her with assurances that next time she was bound to get in. Not even a cat would come back after such a scalding. But Susan came back.

And...

They said no. Maybe they said nyet. Maybe they offered her a cup of tea. She danced her heart out. Just as in all the Hollywood musicals she'd grown up on. But she didn't get the part in the end. Or did she?

Someone in casting suggested she return in the afternoon for the singing audition. The singing audition? Was he mad? But she came. With another song this time, words committed indelibly to memory. And she got the part!

Well, it wasn't the lead. It was the backup chorus. Still, it was a major show in the West End. How did she celebrate this exhaustive confirmation of her youthful aspirations? The end of a road that began at age four, the first rung on her professional ladder? Did she get drunk on champagne with her girlfriends? Or go to the pub with the gang and chug warm beer until her eyes glazed over? Maybe her parents took her to a fancy restaurant?

But the truth is, when you haven't been pushed along your road, when you're not part of a team, the celebration is no less sweet but it is more private, a turning inward. So she didn't mark the occasion in any special way at all. Perhaps in any case she had no energy left after all those auditions.

Many people handle failure better than they handle success. Good fortune often leads to excess, and we're more likely to believe the good lies people tell about us than the bad lies. But Susan, as in Kipling's poem "If," was dismissive of both imposters. When you credit your gains to hard work you know they can vanish if you relax your discipline. Besides, she had never succumbed to peer pressure, always choosing her own friends, never belonging to groups. And she didn't drink or smoke or take drugs or sleep around or crash sports cars into telephone poles. How did she survive?

She followed *Bubbling Brown Sugar* with a role in Porgy and Bess, for which she only had to audition once. Then she traveled the world singing lead on Princess Cruise Lines. She loved this role because the show included songs from all the countries in which Princess called. So there were Russian folk songs, Tahitian ballads, Italian arias. After a couple years on the high seas she settled in Germany and sang with a pop band.

Her introduction to the Cirque came during a visit to Las Vegas, when she saw *Mystère*. Later she saw *Saltimbanco* in London and thought, "I can sing this show!" The music of the Cirque fascinated her and she felt it would be a great challenge, not just because of the language but because of the multitude of musical styles, like singing ten different shows.

She sent a tape to her friend in *Mystère* and was invited to the next Cirque audition in London. Registration was at ten, but the audition wasn't until two, so she went home for lunch. She was feeling much more comfortable with auditions by now.

She got on well with the casting people, relaxing and laughing. But then a rare thing happened. They were videotaping the audition and at one point, while singing from *Saltimbanco*, the woman asked Susan to look into her eyes. Susan suddenly began to cry, and cried the whole song.

She still cries at times. During the show she lets her emotions go. She's been singing it for four years, alternating with Nicole Sieger, from Germany. She never improvises and is content to roam in the background. She likes to move, she's still a dancer, and the singer in *Saltimbanco* isn't confined to a balcony, as in *Mystère* and "O". She even gets to wander onstage from time to time and gaze up at the acts. But she knows her role is a supportive one. "I'm here for them," she says.

Sometimes she'll climb atop the canopy made of aluminum rings that hovers above the band and sing from there. But she's no acrobat. A balletic leap is the limit of her flight. Yet once, on a whim, she tried the bungee. It was during a practice session and they let her go up. When she grabbed the bar she couldn't pull herself onto the trapeze. But she couldn't let go either. She clung to the bar like Deanna Durbin might have clung to a window ledge while trying to elude a romantic villain. Her spotter shouted to her to let go. But she couldn't. Letting go was the one discipline she'd never trained for.

BOLEADOROS

Many in the Cirque received formal dance training in their youth. Not Marie-Claude Lacroix, one of the two boleadoros dancers. We've just seen how Susan Daly stretched at the altar of the ballet bar. But Marie-Claude didn't even want to be a dancer. She didn't even want to be in show business. Her dream was to live an ordinary life, and she studied to become a psychologist. She was painfully shy. She didn't audition for plays in school. She didn't even audition for the Cirque. The Cirque came to her. She's had a serendipitous life. Perhaps that's why she's always smiling.

And she is always smiling. Backstage before going on, dining in the commissary tent after the show. Even while performing, if you can make out her features behind the ricocheting bolos, you can see she's enjoying herself. Still, the performing arts are filled with mercurial personalities who are pleasant as cherubim when everything's right with the world. How does she handle calamity?

The boleodoros is a vanishing dance and few in the audience are qualified to criticize her performance. It isn't like juggling, where dropping a ball constitutes a distinct failure. But there are perils in the dance even more potentially embarrassing and, though not as dangerous as the other acts, even harmful. The bolos are thin ropes three feet long with one inch Teflon balls on the ends, wound around the last three fingers. Sometimes the balls hit a metal strip in the round wooden platform and bounce erratically, striking the dancer in the leg or knee. Sometimes the ropes become entangled. Once, she recalls, she lost one of the bolos completely. It severed from the three-inch connector around her fingers and the rope and ball came to rest behind her. One of the Masques adroitly flung it back to her, but because of the severed connector it was three inches shorter than the right bolo. So she had to whip the left bolo faster to keep time. "I prefer to laugh," she says. "I am not a perfectionist. My whole world is not collapsing."

Still, that was years ago. Maybe time has ameliorated the trauma. But then she confesses to a more recent miscue. "Ten days ago the bolas got entangled! I was really surprised. It hadn't happened for such a long time! I think of it like a virus. You recover as quickly as possible."

She didn't storm off the stage in tears. She didn't sulk in the artistic tent. "I do four hundred shows a year. I do bolos because I love it. I am not a perfectionist," she repeats.

"If you are happy you lead by example," she says. "Where I'm from, near Quebec city, people are pretty happy. They laugh a lot."

One of the Russian performers had admitted to being disconcerted by Americans. Russians, like the French, only smile when they have a reason to smile, and she was suspicious of all these smiling Americans always wishing her a nice day. One may be forgiven for thinking the same of Marie-Claude. Her smile is so prominent a feature you wonder if it's just another mask, as artificial as the columns of masks hanging in the artistic tent. And when you discover that it isn't, that her contentment is as genuine as Susan's unpretentious earnestness, you wonder how she made it this far and marvel that her nature has remained uncorrupted.

Neither Susan nor she seem to possess any significant quantity of angst—that quality so crucial to the artistic temperament. At least Susan is quietly driven. But if it weren't for Marie-Claude's pale skin and French-Canadian features, you might be forgiven for thinking she had grown up in a Buddhist monastery. The fire is on the outside, on her costume. Inside she just glows.

Of course, even angels have inner demons, and Marie-Claude's demon was shyness. As a child she never dreamed about performing. She never imagined that she could walk on a stage. Even now she remains a very private person, avoiding groups. "In big groups there is so much politics," she complains.

If she had become a psychologist perhaps she could have specialized in helping people overcome their shyness. The moment of decision for her came in high school when she had to make a presentation. She was extremely nervous in the days leading up to the event. But she decided, finally, to attack her demon head on. She talked to her classmates and learned that they too were nervous. She tried exercises, such as holding a pen and letting it act as a magnet for her stress. She told herself not to try to please everyone. She didn't overcome her shyness in a week, but over years, step by step.

"I think you will be more happy with who you are if you challenge yourself," she believes. "Ask yourself, what you are hiding? Ask if there is anything in your life you would like to feel more comfortable with."

Still, it's one thing to make a speech in front of your classmates, quite another to dance before 2,500 people eight to ten times a week. Until she was sixteen her only exposure to rhythm was playing the clarinet in music class. Others come to the Cirque by a road. It may be a long road, stretching from the depths of Siberia. But Marie-Claude had no such route connecting past and future. Rather a chasm dividing them.

The bridge was an Argentinian who spoke neither French nor English. Marie-Claude's best friend had asked her to go to an arts festival. Marie-Claude said no. The friend insisted. Among the acts were two Argentinian guys doing boleadoros. Marie-Claude was bored. Her girlfriend led her backstage and introduced them. Marie-Claude didn't know a word of Spanish.

Nevertheless, one of the men managed to extend an invitation to her by phone through a friend who spoke English. He was living in Montreal, playing festivals and doing odd jobs. Marie-Claude was only sixteen, but she had a strong, independent character, and her parents couldn't prevent her from becoming involved with a foreigner in his mid-twenties. They would stay together for seven years, but not marry. He taught her the bolos.

The bolos were used by Indians in battle and later by gauchos to rope cattle. The dance originated in Argentina as an expression of machismo. Unlike other Latin dances, the bolos keep the dancers apart. Watching Marie-Claude and Adriana in *Saltimbanco*, they seem less partners than adversaries, challenging each other from their separate platforms like gun-fighters shooting holes in quarters.

There weren't many good teachers of the boleadoros when Marie-Claude learned the dance, and fewer female performers. Spain had the flamenco, and tango dominated in Argentina. Adriana, a native of Argentina, left because of the dance's waning popularity. Many Argentine's thought it old-fashioned, a relic of their Indian rather than European heritage.

Cirque scouts went four or five times to Argentina, searching for experienced dancers. They came back disappointed. It was then they found Marie-Claude in their own backyard. She and her boyfriend had been performing together at festivals, and she had even appeared on television. She loved the dance but never contemplated it as a career. She was devoting most of her time to studying psychology at the University of Montreal. But she found academic life boring and too competitive. More emphasis was placed on test results than actual learning. And Marie-Claude had always valued the destination less than the journey.

When the Cirque called it was like a pair of wings falling from the sky.

The act had originated with others, of course, and the first part is performed in unison. But Marie-Claude's solo belongs to her. She could have copied her predecessor, or strung together a series of moves studied from other dancers. "But I wanted to create something that is me," she explains. Her performance is subtly affected by her energy, but with so many shows there's little room for variation. She never improvises. She only improvised the dance once, and that was not in *Saltimbanco*, but while visiting an Indian temple in Kuala Lumpur. A renown guru had also come to visit, and Marie-Claude took this as a sign to perform. With the aid of a percussionist she improvised the boleadoros for the first time in her life.

Like Susan, Marie-Claude has been with *Saltimbanco* for four years. First in Australia, then, after a seven month break, in Japan, and now in Europe. But London will be her last city. She has plans for the future but, with Russian-like superstition, she won't say what they are. You have the feeling, however, that she will succeed in whatever she tries and that, like the Cheshire Cat, her smile will punctuate the fading dance.

You only regret the loss to the world of psychology. She has a lot to teach us all about not getting tangled up.

BUNGEE

In a few months Sandra Feusi will stop to smell the roses or, we should say, the edelweiss, since she's from Switzerland. Like Marie-Claude, Sandra and her husband are calling it quits after four years in *Saltimbanco*. London will be the final city on their international road, after which they'll tour New Zealand—ironically, the home of modern bungee jumping.

The bungee began as a rite of passage among certain African and Polynesian tribes. Adolescent boys would climb to the top of a wooden platform and dive off with water-logged bamboo vines tied to their ankles. If the vine was measured correctly no harm was done. But once was enough.

Then, a thousand years later, members of the Oxford Dangerous Sports Club dove off a suspension bridge and the act was commercialized in 1988 both in New Zealand and the United States using latex cords. Another step in the march of civilization and further proof that one tribe's fear is another's obsession.

But Sandra isn't bringing her bungee cord. She doesn't even plan to ski, and New Zealand is famous for heli-skiing. But when thrills are your life six days a week all you seek is a warm fire. So she looks forward to leisurely hikes from one spa to another, and long facials to scrub away the circus paint.

She and Sam met in San Francisco, and after New Zealand they plan to move back to California and perform a two-person Chinese poles, which they've been developing in their spare time.

Sam's originally from Massachusetts and is one of the few performers with neither a circus or athletic background. He studied English at
Oberlin College in Ohio and only became an acrobat after traveling to
England on a playwrighting grant. He had never thought about the circus. He dimly recalls his family taking him to Ringling Brothers when
he was three. He got lost and his mother found him looking up at the
elephant.

But in London he got a job as stage manager for a production that
included an acrobatic troupe and became intrigued. Tall and muscular,
he thought he could perform and began training. It was harder than it
looked, but he relished the challenge. Hardest was balancing, which he
found counterintuitive. Often when he felt the need to move, those were
the times he must remain still, especially in group formations, like pyra-
mids.

He never did write that play.

Sandra grew up in a small town near Zurich and began skiing at two. At
eight she began training three times a week. She was a racer and loved the
speed and competition. She didn't smell the flowers, or enjoy the radiant
sky. She never looked up at the pristine peaks, only down at the course.
"I ate lunch on the ski lifts," she says.

But her family kept her from being one-dimensional, and the values
she inherited from her parents eventually led her to turn away from the
slopes. "I quit because I realized life was passing by me. I started losing
passion and, to top it off, my father was diagnosed with cancer."

Now that she was living at a slower pace and dealing with harsher
realities, her life as a skier seemed to belong to someone else. For a time
she was a nurse's aid at an elder care center. Then one day she auditioned
for the renowned Dimitri School, a professional physical theater academy
that awarded degrees. It was not her first exposure to the performing arts.
She had danced and acted in plays since the age of five, but when she
turned thirteen had focused more on sports.

As with many young adults who have trained rigorously as children in
a narrow discipline and have now stopped, Sandra liked the freedom of
experiment and the thrill of not knowing where her life would lead. She
was open to impulse. While visiting a friend in California, she decided

to stay.

The Pickle Family Circus in San Francisco was one of the new breed of small circuses that had cropped up in America. They had their own school as well, and after training there Sandra joined the circus as an acrobat. She also worked for other companies, including Make a Circus, taught at the San Francisco School of Circus Arts and performed with dance troupes in the Bay Area.

It was here that she met Sam, whose own course had slalomed back to America, but to the opposite coast from where he started.

And then one day Sandra decided to send their tape to the Cirque. Sam didn't think they were ready, but they were both accepted, and their travels resumed, allegro.

They've been with *Saltimbanco* four years, performing Chinese Poles, Russian Swing and Bungee. They don't consider matinees a burden, because the second show is easier. "We're already warmed up," Sandra explains. "After the first show we take a power nap. It's no problem."

The troupe also has training twice a week. For Bungee troupe members alternate, but Sandra and Sam always perform Chinese Poles and Russian Swing. "There is no such thing as days off other than Mondays!" Sandra says.

When *Saltimbanco* was first staged there were sixteen performers in the troupe. Then the number was increased to twenty-one, and now it's thirty. Even so, many troupe members have chronic aches that never seem to get enough time to heal. Jean-Paul Boun, the oldest member, has been struggling with a bad back for half a year. And he doesn't perform Bungee.

"Acrobats think Bungee's easy," Sam says. "It's so graceful and light, its demands are deceiving. But you see, there's no rest. It's continuous choreography."

It's also terrifying. The four trapeze bars aligned in facing pairs that serve as their base may only be twenty-two feet from the stage, but in bungee altitude is your friend. Jumping from a bridge may appear more dangerous, but recreational jumpers don't descend to within four feet of the ground. So in this respect *Saltimbanco*'s version of bungee has more in common with the ancient rite-of-passage than with its contemporrary thrill-seeking counterpart.

And, thrilling as it is, the overwhelming impression to viewers is one of graceful harmony—an aerial ballet. The act seems to take place almost in slow motion, perhaps because the flyers can control their descent by pulling on the two thick nylon cords harnessed at their waist. There are many examples of teamwork in the show, in Russian Swing, in Chinese Poles. But the most inspirational is the formation that marks the finale in Bungee. The four flyers in their white skin-tight lotus costumes stand facing each other on their trapezes and begin to swing. They release together and rotate in a double layout, arms outstretched, and grasp hands in midair as they rise back up, forming a ring.

Sandra and Sam have been reaching out in midair for four years. Now it's time to let go.

BRUSSELS

It's a good thing I've visited Belgium before, because I'm not going to see much of it now. Not that the Cirque's hotel is located outside the center, as in Barcelona and Vienna. The Renaissance Brussels is only a mile from the Grand Place, one of the great squares in the world, but I'll only take a peek at it one afternoon while walking to a cafe with Olga and Arthur. The Parc de Bruxelles with the Palais Royal and Musée Royaux des Beaux-Arts at one end and Parlement at the other is even closer, but I will only hurry through with my luggage on my way to another hotel. The Parc du Cinquantenaire with its automobile and military museums is closer still, but I would have remained ignorant of this fact if I hadn't looked at a map. As for the fashionable Avenue Louise, which separates the lower from the upper town, I only chance upon it because Arthur and I get lost one day while running errands for Olga.

Brussels for me becomes the stately lobbies of the Renaissance and Marriott hotels, the Intermezzo bar and Symphony restaurant, and the now familiar interior of the Grand Chapiteau. For, like the bureaucrats who patronize the Renaissance because it is conveniently located across the street from the gleaming headquarters of the European Union, I have come to Brussels on business.

True to her word, Olga has asked about a spare room. I don't know what to expect, but when I give my name to the desk clerk she hands me a key.

There are two mountain bikes locked together beside the bed. Alya's and Nico's. She may not wish to talk to me for the book, but she trusts me with their spare room.

It's Sunday, which means the second show finishes early. By the time

I go downstairs some of the performers have already arrived. I order an orange juice at the bar and take a table by the lobby and watch for Olga.

One of the troupe, with whom I've never really talked, waves to me. He orders a beer and sits at my table. After lighting a cigarette he tells me he's read the first chapters of my book. He doesn't tell me what he thinks, and I don't ask. He's sitting here, isn't he?

I ask about Olga instead. He tells me he understands why she left, but regretted her sudden departure. "We're a team," he says.

I ask if he's angry, but he's not. He's glad she's back in the show. And then he leans forward and looks at me intently. "She's the best I've ever seen!"

Olga arrives soon after. I don't know what to expect. Not that one ever knows what to expect from Miss Sidorova. She ran away from this life a few weeks ago, and now she's back. I have resolved to be supportive, not to say the wrong thing. In fact to say as little as possible.

She seems happy to see me, that's a good start. And she's in a bright mood, as if she had never left. We go up to Alya's room, which adjoins my own, and Alya asks me to try on the sweater I had ordered from her aunt.

"What do you think?" she asks, carefully unwrapping it from cellophane.

I hold the sweater up. A rock-and-roll cardigan made from uniquely styled patches of wool, some with black fringe, others with silver thread, one or two with knobs of lilac yarn. A work of art.

"Beautiful! What do you think, Olga?"

"Yes, it very nice."

"Try it on," Alya says. "I want to make sure it fits."

As I pull it over the sweater I'm wearing I express my gratitude for the use of her extra room. She replies that I'm welcome to stay, but that Nico might have guests visiting Wednesday.

"What do you think?" I ask, modeling the sweater for Olga.

She leans her head to one side.

"Wait!"

I go next door, and put on a black shirt underneath it.

"Oh yes!" Olga exclaims. "You look so handsome! You look like movie star!"

I hand Alya a folder containing a few pages—the scene with her aunt in Vienna.

"If you object I won't use your name," I tell her. I also hand Olga the complete manuscript to date.

She's impressed by the number of pages. Alya too takes an interest. "Can I borrow it?" she asks.

I wear my new creation down to the bar, where Olga unburdens herself for an hour and a half. I'm reluctant to ask too many questions, but then I don't have to. She tells me more than I want to know about her problems with the Vintilovs. But she arouses my curiosity when she tells me about her trapeze.

She has her own trapeze. Made to her specifications in Australia. When she went to Montreal to train for *Saltimbanco*, she took it with her.

"What do you mean you took it with you?" I wonder. "You shipped it?"

"No, I took it. With my luggage."

Imagine this wisp of a woman walking through Terminal *D* with a trapeze!

"What are you talking about? How do you carry a trapeze?"

But it turns out a trapeze is quite portable. I had always thought of them as part of the rigging. But as I had seen during Olga's practice, the trapeze, which consists of a metal bar with ropes on either side, is attached by hooks to a crane bar. After the performance it is lowered and removed for storage.

Well, it turns out when Olga left she didn't just take her clothes. She took her trapeze! She left the trapeze that hung in the artistic tent, but she took her own.

But when the tent was raised in Brussels the second trapeze was missing. And when Olga came to Brussels someone informed her that it had been stolen, insinuating that Olga had stolen it.

"I say, 'So? It not my problem. You think I steal trapeze? I take trapeze that mine. Other trapeze, Cirque trapeze, I not take. If someone stole other trapeze, it not my problem!'

"And you know what? Other trapeze not stolen. They found it later, packed with other equipment. Why people bother me with these things?"

She stamps out her cigarette. "So, there's a party tonight. You want go?"

A block away is the Luxembourg Square, and the Cirque has hired out an Irish bar for the night. It's a chance to say hello to some of the cast, but the music is too loud for conversation. After a while a group of us decide to go to a disco. Olga takes her wine glass. If you ever have Olga over to your house, use the paper cups, because she always leaves with a drink in her hand. However, the taxi driver won't start the engine until she spills out the wine.

I had told Olga I'd like to spend her day off together, but it's very difficult to make plans in advance with her. Originally she intended to take the train to Amsterdam. But it turns out Arthur has rented a car and is coming down Monday after work for a few days. So there's really no reason for her to go. Yet Sunday night she decides to go anyway.

Monday morning I leave the profiles I've written so far—on the Vintilovs, the Issakovs, Elena, and Masha—with the concierge. I neither ask for nor expect responses but do it as a courtesy.

As Olga and I are on our way out we see Alya, who tells me in an apologetic tone that she will need the spare room Wednesday after all. She then says she's read the scene with her and her aunt and points out a couple errors. But she likes it and will be happy to talk to me later in the week.

"I so glad!" Olga says. "Alya so smart, such good person. And she been in "O". From the beginning. They made a cast of her body for the costume!"

We take a taxi to the Gare du Midi, or South Station. Olga urges the driver to hurry, we have less than half an hour. By the time we get to the ticket window we only have ten minutes, and there's a woman at the counter and another in front of us.

Then a third woman asks the woman in front of us if she can cut in because her train is leaving in five minutes. The woman in line agrees without consulting us. I can't believe it. But what can we do?

Well, what Olga does is cut in front of both of them! "Excuse me," she says, "our train is leaving in five minutes."

The counter opens up and Olga turns to the clerk. I stand a few feet away, trying not to make eye contact. I expect a quick transaction, but the next thing I know the clerk is calling me.

"What is your age?" the clerk asks.

My age? I've never been asked my age at a train station.

Olga has her purse out, her Australian student ID card on the counter. She's trying to get the student discount! For me too!

I put down a hundred euro note, take the full fare tickets and pull her away. "Our train's about to leave and you're trying to get a student discount! You're twenty-eight years old! And I haven't been a student since I was fifteen!"

"Can you believe that woman cut in front of us?" she says.

I shake my head. Sometimes I think the trapeze is the least dangerous thing she does.

We run to the platform and check the computer screen. There's our train, listed third from the top. Three minutes to spare.

One train comes, a second. The third is not for Amsterdam, however. I keep my eye on the adjoining track.

Olga pulls my arm. "Mark, look, it gone!"

And indeed, our train is no longer listed on the screen. Olga begins asking people on the platform, but no one seems to know. A few minutes later she asks me if we could have missed it. But I don't see how.

"Maybe it was track eleven instead of ten."

"But I was watching."

"What should we do?"

We rush up the escalator to the information booth and are told to take another train to the Gare du Nord—the North Station. We can catch the Amsterdam train there. Olga is full of questions as we run to another platform.

"We missed it," she says.

"I don't see how."

When we reach the Gare du Nord we see the Amsterdam train listed and we have forty minutes to spare. "This doesn't make sense. It's a different train," I tell her.

But I would have left it at that. It's a credit to Olga's curiosity that she has the tenacity to solve the mystery. One would think someone with as complicated a life as Olga would not give the matter the slightest attention. Instead she trots to the information booth.

The clerk underestimates her intelligence and tells her our train leaves in forty minutes.

"I know this," Olga repeats. "But we were just at the Gare Midi and the train did not come. It was on the computer and then it was off."

"It was cancelled," the clerk explains.

Olga and I smile at each other. Cancelled!

"But I didn't hear announcement," she says.

"It would have been in French. But there wasn't any notice on the monitor, so who knows? At least we're not waiting for the Siberian Express!"

We take seats across from each other by the window in a nearly empty carriage. I'm already exhausted and we haven't even left Brussels! The good news is that I have three hours of Olga's undivided attention. And she can't run away. Or can she?

As we're leaving the city I finally ask her why we're going to Amsterdam. Simon, who is in charge of the VIP tent, had invited her and Arthur to a dinner party at his parents' house outside Antwerp. But that didn't seem to be a priority for Olga. Was it worth running from platform to platform for a few hours with her boyfriend, whom she would be seeing that night anyway? It was a quaint romantic thought. But then, why bring me?

"I need go bank," Olga explains.

"You're going to another country just to go to the bank?" I haven't the heart to tell her the banks will be closed by the time we arrive.

"And I want update my resume. There's a woman in Amsterdam who made for me before."

"Your resume? Let me see. Maybe I can help."

But instead of a standard printed resume, Olga pulls a spiral-bound portfolio out of her bag, eight pages long, with color photos and purple borders. It ends with her work at the National Institute of Circus Arts in Melbourne.

"I need put about the Cirque. And some of the quotes and photos I want change."

I read it with interest, although most of the pictures and text I've already seen on her web site. I decided not to ask why she wants it, as she's retiring.

"I need it to show people for what I do next," she says, as if reading my mind. "For example, if I want start school. But I also want for myself."

This makes more sense to me. Certainly everyone in the business already knows who she is, and a page of text seems adequate to the task of recruiting students for her school.

"I could do this for you," I offer.

"You think?"

"Tell me what you want."

We talk about her resume for a few minutes. Then I ask if I can borrow it. She tells me I can have it. She has more.

"I want a hundred. But I pay for everything," she says.

"Well, I'll send my additions and changes to you to proof first."

"I need it soon."

"Of course."

So now she won't be going to the bank or the graphic designer. Why are we on this train?

"What you want talk about?" she asks.

We haven't really talked about her past much since I saw her in Vienna. Planning the trip to Vegas took priority, and then her sudden departure. She needed to talk about her present problems, not her distant past.

"Tell me about the Moscow Circus School," I ask.

"You know, this is why I decide to go Amsterdam," she reveals. "On the train will be better to talk."

So that's the reason! I couldn't be more flattered, or grateful.

"But don't ask so many stupid questions. I has to think more when you ask questions. It easier you just let me talk."

And talk she does, as I relax in my seat, glimpsing out of the corner of my eye not the road from Brussels to Amsterdam, but from Siberia to Moscow.

THE MOSCOW CIRCUS SCHOOL

Olga had first seen the circus in Omsk, the home of her grandmother. But the end of Olga's yellow brick road was Moscow, to the west, and Omsk was east. It didn't matter that Omsk was only a few hours by train from her home in Ishim. Considering how far southern Siberia was from the capital, a few more hours made little difference. Certainly the advantage of having her grandmother nearby, and perhaps being able to live with her, would have more than justified her traveling in the wrong direction. But Olga didn't think that way. For her the move was more symbolic than practical. She had trained her dog to climb steps, one at a time, in one direction. And that's how she would climb her stairway to the trapeze. So after earning enough roubles by selling candy for the price of a train ticket, she traveled west, to Tyumen.

Tyumen was comparable in size to Omsk. A city of about half a million, know for oil and natural gas production, it too had a small circus school.

And that's about as much as Olga knew as she and her dog arrived in the city. She didn't even have a map. She searched for a residential street that looked clean and safe, but not too prosperous, and began knocking on doors. She introduced herself as a student looking for a place to sleep. Knowing how unabashed Olga is now, constantly asking strangers in public for directions or other information, one can more plausibly imagine this fourteen-year-old girl just arrived in a strange city knocking on people's doors and requesting a spot on the floor to lay her head.

"I was lucky," she would say, looking back. "Everyone always nice to me. No man ever touch me, no one steal my clothes. I was never afraid. I just didn't think about it! I was thinking only of trapeze."

One woman offered to let her stay, but wouldn't take the dog. So Olga found an abandoned building and left her dog there. She brought him food every day and, unlike her, he never ran away. But she didn't like being separated and after a few nights moved on.

She found another woman not far away who was willing to lodge them both. In exchange Olga would tutor her two young daughters. Who ever heard of a teenage runaway earning her keep as a tutor?

But Olga even enrolled herself in school, forging her grandmother's signature to get in. And then she applied to the circus school.

All large cities in Russia have a resident circus with an affiliated school. But the provincial schools are often small and unsophisticated. The circus arts aren't like gymnastics, where scouts channel talented prospects to the center. Circus performers in the provinces don't have the same opportunities for good coaching and quality facilities as gymnasts do and are likely to spend their professional lives in their home town circus.

So Olga didn't have the chance to perform trapeze in Tyumen. But she got to perform. With her faithful dog. She wore a doctor's jacket and her dog was dressed in school clothes. Lassie, unlike Olga, didn't want to study, and feigned illness. She limped through Olga's legs and fell to the ground. She rolled in pain. She played dead. Olga listened to her heart, then motioned for the dog to sit on a chair. Lassie wouldn't move. But Olga caught her out when she waved a hoop. The dog jumped through it. Olga raised it higher, ran in circles with it. Before long the two were performing acrobatics together.

This was Olga's first performance, before a small audience in the Tyumen Circus. The act, at age fourteen, was her own creation.

But her aspirations lay higher. Although being accepted into the Tyumen circus school was a dream, it was only part of her dream. She realized she could only learn so much there. She may not have been competitive, but that doesn't mean she wasn't ambitious. And as soon as she felt she had learned all the Tyumen circus school could teach her, she moved on.

The next big city west on the road to Moscow was Yekaterinburg—formerly Sverdlovsk. This was a giant step up from Tyumen. No longer in Siberia but the capital of the province of Sverdlovskaya at the foot of the Ural mountains, Yekaterinburg was famous as the home of Boris Yeltsin and infamous as the city where Czar Nicholas and his family were executed by the Red Army. When Olga arrived the population had grown to a million and a half inhabitants, and there was a subway system, palatial government buildings, high rise apartment blocks, restaurants and movie theaters. Of course she had never seen anything like it.

And rising in the center of town was a futuristic round building with a sloping metal roof, adorned with rocket wing spires. It might have been a headquarters for the space program or an avant garde church. But it was the Yekaterinburg Circus.

Olga ran to it. She didn't even know what it was. But there were tears in her eyes. "Olga, what happening with you?" she asked herself. "You're quite strange."

The coaches laughed at this barefoot waif from Siberia. How did she get here? Hitch-hiking, making soup from rubbish. She told them none of that, however. She explained she had just moved to the city with her grandmother. And her shoes? Had she left them in Siberia? "Who performed trapeze wearing shoes?" she asked.

They gave her an audition and accepted her. But the trapeze would have to wait. Instead she would train in acrobatics like everyone else.

Olga found a place to stay, as she had in Tyumen, but she and her dog would soon have an apartment, for she wrote her mother and told her where she was. Olga's parents were astonished. They knew she had moved to Tyumen but didn't believe she would go any further. Her mother took the next train out. She intended to bring her daughter home with her. Olga had tried her wings and now it was time to fly home. But Olga hadn't even touched a trapeze yet. How could she quit now? So her mother rented her an apartment, gave her some money, and returned to Siberia alone.

Olga enrolled in an academic school, as she had in Tyumen, but she also enrolled in other circus schools. Beside the main school where the professional circus performed, there were a few smaller studios. Afraid she might be missing something, she attended all of them. And if that weren't enough to guarantee her a trapeze of her own, she trained inde-

pendently as well. All the apartment blocks of that time ▓
around courtyards, and these courtyards had playgrounds. Olga ▓
pass through several of these on her way to school each morning. S▓
would stop on each playground and do chin-ups and monkey bars a▓
climb the poles.

She still didn't dream about Moscow. In fact she wasn't even thinking
about performing professionally. She believed that to be in the circus you
had to be from a circus family. She just wanted to fly on the trapeze. But
one day she learned that anyone could audition for the Moscow Circus
School and informed her mother she was leaving Yekaterinburg.

Again her mother took the train out. This time she accompanied
Olga to the capital and found a place for them to stay. She assumed Olga
would not be accepted. Then she would return to earth and, perhaps, to
Ishim.

Auditions for the Moscow Circus School were only held twice a year
and were extremely competitive. Olga found herself on the same floor
with gymnasts, dancers, acrobats and aerialists, all older than she and
many already members of established circuses.

The audition was rigorous and took place over several days. The first
stages dealt with posture, balance, movement, flexibility. Each day the
number of participants was halved, until Olga found herself in the final
group of twenty.

The panel of judges asked her what she aspired to perform.

"Trapeze!"

They frowned. Some of her rivals laughed. After all, everyone wanted
trapeze. It was the most glamorous act. And she was just sixteen years old,
with no formal training in gymnastics or dance. Her two years in provincial circus schools was hardly worth noting to these staid Muscovites.

She wasn't expected to audition on trapeze. But for her final test she
was asked to approach beneath it, as she might in a show.

Olga decided to be daring. She would do an impromptu dance, then
run out to the middle of the stage and finish dramatically by leaping into
the splits. A dozen years later she remembers the moment perfectly and
cites it as the reason she dislikes competition. She jumped too hard and
stumbled upon landing. Behind her, she could hear her rivals' laughter.

... in her eyes as the participants were called into
... didn't mention which line was in and which out.
...en she was placed in the line opposite a girl who
...omising. She assumed she had been selected after
...e tears of joy.

...ntinental journey, her two years eating from rub-
...self, were nothing compared to the crossroads at
which she now stood. Or rather the crossroads she crossed, then crossed
back. For when everything seemed decided and two groups of ten stood
in neat proud and despairing rows, the judges conferred for a few anxious moments, and then a male judge called Olga's name and pointed
ominously at the other line.

Olga crept across. Two thousand miles had not seemed further. Only
years later would this former judge tell her, after a few vodkas, that Olga
had been rejected by the others, but that he had argued vociferously for
her because he glimpsed something indefinable in her eyes.

The girl Olga thought was unimpressive turned out to be the daughter of a coach.

Despite the perils or aerial acts, it was the clowns who suffered most
at the Moscow Circus School. One hanged himself in the communal
shower in the co-ed dormitory where Olga lived. Another threw himself
off the roof, but miraculously survived. Broken hearts no doubt. But
Olga claims innocence in these matters, naive as she was herself. She'd
never had a boyfriend and repelled all advances. She wasn't as gregarious or confident as she is now, she couldn't be accused of flirting or
seduction. If she was afraid of men as a twenty-eight-year-old woman in
Amsterdam, as a sixteen-year-old girl in Moscow, she had been terrified.
Unlike most girls her age, she didn't have romantic fantasies or dreams of
family. She knew that if she wanted to remain in control of her destiny,
she had to remain alone.

Lassie served as companion, and she made a few friends. She also had
security now, a place to live, a stipend. And her parents were proud of
her, and perhaps a bit relieved, thinking that despite the distance between
them she had at least reached the end of her road. The Wall hadn't yet
fallen. She couldn't go farther west, could she?

There wasn't much trapeze the first year. The core curriculum included all the circus arts, and Olga studied acrobatics, juggling, even the high wire. The acrobatics coaches were impressed with her strength and balance and wanted her to stay on the ground. But Olga would not be dissuaded and during the second year took to the air.

Olga is proud to have studied with three of the best aerial coaches in the world, all from the Moscow Circus School. One currently teaches trapeze at Cirque du Soleil headquarters in Montreal. Another teaches in Florida. The third remains with the Moscow, or Bolshoi, Circus, and it is this man, Gennady Totoukhov, that Olga refers to when she speaks of her coach.

"This man born me," she told me that night in the Park Plaza bar in Amsterdam. "Everything I know about trapeze, I know because him!"

Gennady had been a trapezist himself for many years, at one time working in the Moscow Circus as part of a three-man single trapeze act. During this act they would hold each other in an inverse column, Gennady in the middle. They worked without safeties or a net. Once he fell and broke his back.

Like most aerialists, his was a life of pinnacles and steep descents. But the deepest tragedy came in the water, when his son died in a boating accident. He was the same age as Olga, seventeen. Olga observed her coach's hair turning white. But he worked harder than ever.

One night he invited her for dinner, and his wife confided that her husband was training Olga from morning until night because it took his mind away. "You give him something," she said.

Gennady had a daughter as well, coincidentally named Olga. But she didn't go into the circus. Instead she studied ballet from the age of four and became a dancer in the Bolshoi.

The first time Olga saw her coach, she knew he was the coach she wanted. She chose him as much as he chose her, and her loyalty was astonishing. When Gennady took a job with Ringling Brothers for a year, Olga was assigned another coach. But instead she went to the director and insisted on waiting. So she practiced acrobatics and ballet until Gennady returned.

Knowing her recalcitrance, one might think they had a tempestuous relationship. But Olga trusted Gennady completely. She never argued, she never ran away. Flying on the trapeze redeemed all the struggles of her long journey from Siberia, and she treated her coach with a deference her parents could only have wished for. After a frustrating day, she wrote in her Trapeze Diary, "Olga, why don't you listen to his words? Don't think. Just do what he says."

She liked him because he explained the physics of the trapeze. Why it swings the way it does. In what direction her body will fall if she lets go at a particular point in its arc. She liked him because he returned her trust and dedication. He believed in her ability and potential. He trained other aerialists at this time, but Olga was his only trapezist. She liked him because he too enjoyed the trapeze for its own sake and didn't push Olga to turn professional before she was ready. And she liked him because he was completely original. He had a vision for the future of the trapeze and enjoyed creating new acts. Some of the moves he taught Olga, such as the standing pirouette, were his alone.

She specialized in solo trapeze and Gennady never pressured her to do anything else. Later, she would receive offers from troupes, including the Flying Cranes, the most innovative flying trapeze group at the time. But she wanted to be independent. Someone who was so partial to a particular coach and even a particular trapeze couldn't be expected to adjust to different partners.

Unlike her fellow students, she wasn't thinking about her future. Her dream wasn't to perform in front of an adoring audience but to fly, and she only cared to be watched by the protective eyes of her coach. She was a real life Peter Pan. Although for those who have had the pleasure to meet her and watch her fly, Peter Pan might seem the less extraordinary creature.

Maybe her reluctance to turn professional was merely prudence. During her five years in the school she did occasionally perform publicly. And these weren't small shows for family and friends but major events. In her second year she performed an aerial act in the circus's Christmas season ice show, held in the Olympic arena. Her act was on a rope, not a trapeze, suspended above the ice. She performed four shows a day, and had to walk across the ice to make her entrance and exit. Her antipathy for shoes gave her chills, but it wasn't walking barefoot on the ice day after day that weakened her to the point that one evening she found herself unable to move. She was taken to the hospital by ambulance. The doctor who attended her was drunk and asked when she had had sex. Olga insisted she was a virgin, but the doctor informed her she had a miscarriage. Later she was diagnosed by another doctor as having an ovarian cyst. She spent six months in the hospital.

During her first year she had suffered stomach problems, not from aerial somersaults but from eating from too many rubbish bins during her days in Tyumen. The pain was so bad she was sent to a clinic in the Ukraine. But she didn't have any serious injuries on the trapeze. She was a fearless student and trusted her coach completely. Unfortunately she couldn't trust her equipment.

Solo trapezists never used nets. Olga doesn't speculate why. But she points out that originally they didn't use safeties either, because the soloists of those days didn't fly off the bar. The first safeties, the ones Olga trained with, weren't cords but wires 3.5 millimeters thick, attached from the trapezist's belt to the bar itself. In their later evolution, when they were held by the coach, they were still harder to control and more dangerous than cords. One time during a fall the wire wrapped itself around Olga's neck.

But the most spectacular accident was caused by the apparatus holding the trapeze. Olga let go while swinging to do a somersault, and while tumbling saw something fly beneath her to the stage. It was the trapeze! She dangled in mid-air, saved by the safety, which fortunately was of the variety not attached to the bar. Had there been jugglers or acrobats practicing below, as there often were, they might have been killed.

This happened to Olga twice! But not even a falling trapeze could keep her from re-ascending.

When Olga joined *Saltimbanco* she looked forward to seeing other circuses in Europe and observing how the art and science of trapeze had progressed in the ten years since she began training. The equipment was certainly safer, but as for the art she was surprised to discover little that her coach hadn't anticipated, or transcended, all those years ago in the Moscow Circus School.

SOLO TRAPEZE

On the outskirts of Amsterdam Olga finishes her tale. Naturally I want more, but she's tired, the spell is broken. However, a moment later she starts speaking again, thrust back into the present by the familiar gabled houses of Holland. She talks about running away, running back, the Cirque management, the Vintilovs.

I nod supportively. I don't say anything. Then I lower my guard. Olga's outburst in Barcelona seems a distant memory, and we've gotten along famously since—more or less. I have to strain my memory to recall the last time she raised her voice to me.

I ask: "Did you start teaching Dasha because she asked or because you thought she had talent?"

I know the Vintilovs had asked Olga to teach their daughter, but I was curious to know whether Olga did it simply as a favor or because she saw Dasha as a possible protégé.

It's an innocent enough question, isn't it? But Olga glares at me. "I don't want talk you anymore! Goodbye!"

And she takes back the resume, stuffs it in her bag and leaves the carriage!

The train is pulling into Amsterdam Centraal Station. I can see the street where Arthur's hotel is located from my window.

I curse myself for my importunity. But what did I say? What did I say? There's a line in Jonathan Franzen's novel, *The Corrections*, in which he describes a frail elderly couple's chronic anxiety as an alarm bell that keeps ringing throughout their house, that's been ringing for years. Well, I might describe Olga as being afflicted with a siren that goes off intermittently, like the fire drills we used to have at school. Who knows what triggers these unnerving episodes, but I know it wasn't my innocent question.

Maybe it's the time of month. Maybe it's a disturbance in the arc of an invisible trapeze.

I decide I'm not going to follow her. I'm done with following her. But she's waiting on the platform, and as we walk to the Amsterdam Renaissance she continues her rant, without apology or explanation. I don't say a word as we cross tram tracks and skirt cyclists. But when we enter Arthur's bar she transforms in an instant back into the Olga I love, like an actress playing both heroine and villain.

Arthur appears from behind the counter and we all smile at one another. He's about Olga's age, thin, with blue eyes, short auburn hair and angular features. He could pass for Russian but he's Dutch and, like most Dutch, speaks English fluently. He smiles often, has a broad sense of humor, is personable and extremely easy-going.

"So, how was your trip?" he asks innocently enough.

It's a rare sunny, windless day in Amsterdam and we sit on the patio and order lunch. Arthur serves us, then pulls up a chair.

Somewhere between the Heineken and celery soup I find myself back in possession of the resume. The three of us discuss what should be added and changed. Then Olga asks me about her proposed school and I suggest it would be easier to attach herself to an existing institution or a resort hotel to avoid start-up costs and overhead.

She seems interested in my ideas, but after a few minutes she says she's tired of talking about business. I return to my soup. A minute later she says, "So why you stop talking about school?"

Arthur laughs. "Olga, you told him to stop talking business!"

But Olga seems oblivious.

Arthur has to stop at his apartment before we drive back to Belgium. I imagine they'll just be a minute, so I don't think twice when Olga asks me to wait in the car.

"You can't come in," she adds. "There are narcotics everywhere!"

Then she says I can come up but that I should wait so they can hide the narcotics. I assume they're going to have sex, but she's back in a minute.

"You want come inside?"

Arthur lives on the top floor, in a spacious flat by Amsterdam standards. Seventies retro, decorated with his sister's fantasy paintings on the sloping walls, a queen-sized mattress on the floor, a plush red sofa, a long-necked arcing floor lamp, bookshelves stuffed with history and literature in English and Dutch. The narcotics may be hidden but the marijuana is in plain sight. Arthur and Olga share a joint, legal of course in Amsterdam. But I decline.

"You never smoke?"

"Not since I was fifteen."

"What age you start smoke marijuana?"

"Twelve."

"Twelve! That's young!"

"But I didn't run away till I was thirty," I tease her.

I notice Arthur is cooking something on the stove. Olga and I had just eaten, and I thought we were going to a dinner party. But I don't say anything.

I sit on the sofa and look through a New Age magazine featuring Arthur's sister's paintings. Then Olga sits beside me and shows me photo albums from Arthur's childhood. I'm not sure if she's brought the albums over for me to see or whether she's looking at them herself for the first time. It turns out he comes from an affluent family and attended the same private school as the Prince, whose recent marriage to an Argentinian woman made world headlines. He's been to the U.S. seven times, and there are many pictures from Disney World. His brother's still in college, studying history. But Arthur disdained the corporate world, selling second-hand clothes at festivals throughout Europe and now working at the Renaissance bar. He saw what the rat race had done to his father, a lawyer and accountant, and didn't want any part of it.

"I remember being in the lobby of a hotel with my father," he would reveal to me later. "The phone at the front desk rang and he jumped!"

Olga puts the albums away and looks at me with a whimsical expression. "You want see my trapeze?"

What does she mean?

She points to a large canvas bag lying beside the mattress. She unfolds it to reveal her trapeze.

I stare in amazement, as though she's a high priestess uncovering a relic.

She lets me hold it, like a pirate letting a confederate rifle through his treasure. The metal bar is covered with white tape. The lower extremity of the rope is also taped. I don't uncoil the rope but imagine it's about ten feet long.

I grip the bar tightly, then loosely with my fingertips. I raise it off the floor and am once again surprised by its weight. But it's perfectly balanced.

"When I did show on Gold Coast in Australia I no like their trapeze. So I had my own made. You know how hard it is find someone make trapeze? Then when Cirque hire me I took it to Montreal. I say I has to use my own trapeze. They said they could make one just like it, but nicer design. You see here there are scratches, and the metal is plain," she says, pointing to the cylindrical weights on either side of the taped bar. "They make with little carvings, very nice. But this trapeze special to me. It like person to me."

Arthur takes his time eating, and Olga eats as well. They don't seem in any hurry to go to the dinner party, and I wonder if our plans have changed. But shortly after sunset we pile back into the car and drive to Antwerp. When we reach the house, however, there are no cars in the driveway and the windows are dark. We don't even knock on the door, for fear of waking our would-be hosts.

But by now Olga is hungry again. She had spotted a Chinese restaurant on the way. Surprisingly, it's still open. I recall our late night fiasco in Barcelona, when she hoped to find a Chinese restaurant at two o'clock in the morning. Her face is beaming with contentment. I wonder if she even remembers leaving me on the train. If she wants to run out now she'll have to climb over Arthur.

She orders shrimp with vegetables and devours it.

The following afternoon we all drive to the Grand Chapiteau. This is Olga's practice day, but she's not going to fly. Rather she's practicing her new choreography, which she is quite excited about and wants us to see. She also thinks it's a good idea for me to be in the tent so those who weren't at the party Sunday night can see I'm here.

First we have lunch in the commissary tent. Arthur is very friendly with everyone and well liked, but he doesn't care for the circus and won't watch Olga perform.

"Once was enough," he says with a nervous smile.

He doesn't even like to go backstage. "I don't belong there."

"I don't belong there either."

"Yes you do. You're writing a book. I just feel I'm in the way."

We sit down at a table with Jean-Paul Boun, the Cambodian acrobat. The Cirque's sole injunction was that I not conduct interviews on the grounds. But I can't help it if people start talking to me. Besides, I'm sure they meant formal interview with pens and note pads like the one Dasha will give later to a Belgian journalist. Still, Olga will monitor me like a KGB agent, and every time she spots me talking too long with someone in the commissary tent will say, "You can't talk here!"

Another curiosity to add to the long list of curiosities swirling about this woman. She leaves the circus. She cuts in lines. She steals wine glasses. And yet a Mother Superior couldn't have done a more conscientious job of enforcing the Grand Chapiteau interview ban.

The troupe isn't practicing today, so I ask Jean-Paul why he's here so early.

He points to his plate. "I was hungry!"

I was hoping to hear something about dedication and team spirit. But I take his point. Even with discounts, hotel food can be expensive. Olga is always taking food home from the commissary. And not just food—bottles of wine, silverware, glasses. Where do all those glasses go? I dare not ask.

Jean-Paul also tells me he's getting therapy for his back. I assume it's a recent injury, but he tells me it's been bothering him for months.

"If I hurt my leg or arm, it's no problem. But my back is half my body! What can I do?"

Olga takes us into the artistic tent. Arthur follows reluctantly and stands by the wardrobe racks. Olga introduces us to the choreographer, who has flown out from Montreal. Then they begin practicing on the mats.

After a few minutes Arthur returns to the commissary. I make myself comfortable on one of the sofas and watch.

The artistic tent is quiet, but not without activity. Next to Olga, Alya is practicing on tissue, a yard-wide strip of red nylon that hangs from the rafters and which artists can use to climb up and swing on and wrap themselves in. It's a beautiful act and I remember Alya telling me she was learning it not because she likes aerial acts—she's afraid of heights—but because it demands great strength and she considers it a challenge.

There isn't a tissue act in *Saltimbanco*, but one of the features of the Cirque is that artists can work independently on new acts. And these acts might then serve as replacements.

I also notice a cube hanging above the mats. I had seen the cube performed in *Mystère*. It's also an aerial apparatus in which the artist performs slow maneuvers while hanging on to aluminum tubes soldered in the shape of a cube. Elena had mentioned wanting to try it, so I suppose it was ordered for her.

Alya swings on the tissue, low to the ground, over and over. She doesn't have a coach and I am the only one watching her. It looks like fun, at least when you're only six feet off the ground, but her face is tense with concentration, as though she's lifting weights. And perhaps the demands of tissue are just as great.

The artistic tent is a great advantage to me, as an observer. But I can understand how the open space might make performers uncomfortable. Olga, for one, doesn't like people watching her practice. And if you're working on something new, as Alya is, you can't develop your routine in private. Everyone can see your mistakes. She would mention this to me later in the week, not because I had been watching her, but because she was contrasting *Saltimbanco*'s environment with that of "O", where there are three practice spaces instead of one, and more privacy.

While I'm watching, Dasha comes over to the other sofa with a male journalist and they talk for half an hour in French. She's wearing jeans and a tight top and has her sunglasses pulled up on her head. Before her problems with the Vintilovs, Olga had told me about the twelve-year-old's transformation from a child into a young woman.

"When I first come to Cirque I say to Dasha, 'Dasha, you so pretty!'

And she put her head down. Now I say, 'Dasha, you so pretty!' and she lifts her head and smiles!"

I can see a change in her myself, in just the last five months. She seems not only more stylish and mature, but more confident. I attribute these changes not only to the passing of time, but to Olga's training. It must have seemed unfair to her to have outgrown the role now played by her brother. She seems to be enjoying the interview, and I can understand why. Once her face was plastered on billboards and magazines, and now the only place for her in the show is as a cavalier. But learning the trapeze has given her a new dream. Olga has mentioned that she may soon go to Montreal to train full time. So perhaps one day she'll return to the show with her own aerial act.

I'm surprised that her parents aren't present, that they trust their daughter enough, and the Cirque enough, to let her talk to reporters unchaperoned. But then they're apparently willing to let her move to Montreal. But that's one of the ironies of the modern circus family—that sometimes the circus demands intense intimacy and other times painful separation.

Thinking about circus children, I wonder how Victoria is doing. I had hoped to see her again. Olga had told me that she decided at the end of the summer to stay with her father and train for a possible career with the Cirque. When Olga told me how talented she was and that she could definitely be a performer I felt less embarrassed for having lost so many of our decathlon events. But just a few days before my arrival her father sent her back to Canada, considering her academic education more important than perfecting cartwheels.

On our way out Arthur points to the Circus School. He's admiring the logistics of the tent. "They have everything here—a restaurant, showers, air-conditioning and heating, electricity. There's even a school!"

The school is housed in an aluminum building smaller than a cargo container and sits alone not far from the commissary. There are some drawings in crayon on the door, one of which says, "LEARNING ABOUT EUROPE." I'd like to peek inside, but it's locked. I knew, of course, that the children had to be tutored, but I didn't realize they had their own school house.

Olga has an hour before she has to be back for the show, so we drive into the center of Brussels and drink coffee and beer at an outdoor cafe. Olga talks excitedly about her new choreography.

"I really like it," she says. "Except it really hard to learn choreography upside down! I hanging from bar and she says put your arm this way and I put my arm that way!"

Olga says I can watch the show backstage if there's room. Only four guests are allowed in the artistic tent. But Arthur won't be one of them. He drops us back at the site and returns to the hotel.

There are only two other guests tonight. One of them, a thin dark-haired girl of seventeen or eighteen, is sitting on the sofa. I sit on the other sofa and watch the tent come alive.

I certainly hadn't expected to watch the show backstage again. The first time had been the night show after the matinee, so this evening's atmosphere is somewhat different, with cast members arriving and warming up. Some come over to say hello.

"So I see you're back with the circus!" Marie-Claude, the boleadoros dancer, says with a smile.

"So is Olga," I reply.

Andriy Vintilov, wearing a winter cap, gives me a firm handshake. As does Igor Issakov.

Olga walks over with an illustrated hardcover book in Russian. "Remember I tell you I trained in circus school in Yekaterinburg? This book about that circus."

I look at the cover, which shows the futuristic building she had described, with its metal spires.

Olga goes to the other sofa and speaks to the girl for a minute. Then she motions her to sit with me. "Mark, talk this pretty girl. She girlfriend of Marian, from Romania!"

We look at Olga's book together. She's very shy and at first appearance might be any high school senior who wants to study languages in college. But I discover she knows Marian because she too was a gymnast, in fact a member of the Romanian national rhythmic gymnastics team. But injuries forced her to retire before the Olympics and she doesn't wish to go back.

Marian Malita joins us, already in makeup. When his girlfriend tells him I'm a writer he smiles and says he'd like to talk to me. "I have a good story!" he says. It turns out he was a top member of the Romanian gymnastics team, destined for the 2000 Olympics, but in 1999 he and two teammates ran away to Orlando during a meet in Virginia. A decade earlier the incident would have made international headlines, but with the Cold War over, they weren't defecting. It was an embarrassment to their country and to their hosts, of course, but they had committed no crime. Marian simply wanted to see more of America and relax a little. He'd been training and competing since the age of six. Eventually he traveled to Las Vegas and discovered the Cirque du Soleil through a friend who worked in *Mystère*.

I don't see Maxsim anywhere. Normally his mother would be stretching him or he would be running around the mats. But he can't perform all the shows due to Belgian child labor laws and they don't have a replacement, so Adagio is skipped tonight and one of the smaller female acrobats plays his part elsewhere. I'm beginning to realize it's the lucky spectator who gets to see all the acts, as I did the first time I watched the show.

Olga doesn't come back to the sofas or make eye contact with me. I watch Masha practice. She starts with one ball, throwing it in a high arc from one hand to the other. Slowly, patiently, for two or three minutes. Then she throws two balls, then three. She has the patience to be a golfer, I think. Or a writer. Her mother watches without comment as she adds balls. Then she practices bouncing them. Every day. Sometimes twice a day. As monotonous as an assembly line. But then no one applauds you on an assembly line, and the costume isn't as colorful.

She puts on her carefully folded aquamarine jacket at the last moment, grabs her baton and walks out. I watch her on the monitor. She drops a ball and returns shaking her head, but her mother is conciliatory. Masha begins practicing again.

I avert my eyes. She had dropped a ball the first time I had watched backstage. She probably hasn't dropped one since then and if she makes the connection I'll be banished forever.

A pale woman with dark curly hair, casually dressed in jeans and a sweat-shirt, perhaps in her late twenties, is sitting alone on the other sofa. She arrived late and the greetings she receives from other cast members tells me she's with the Cirque.

But it's she who speaks to me first. I tell her I'm with Olga and hesitate whether to reveal more. But she seems pleasant enough, so after talking for a few minutes about the show I confess my real reason for being here.

She seems interested and asks all the customary questions before I can ask the customary questions of her. This turns out to be her first time backstage, and she isn't as familiar with the cast as I had first supposed. She works in the Amsterdam office and is in charge of benefits. She's an anthropologist by training and came to the Cirque from Oxfam. She explains that in every city of the European tour, the Cirque does a benefit for Oxfam. They give Oxfam the tickets for one show and the famine relief agency disposes of them to patrons. I think they might have a still greater impact if they sent the Cirque kitchen from one African nation to another.

Olga doesn't appear to be warming up as much as last time. She doesn't do the one-handed chin ups and seems to be keeping to herself. I watch the monitor when she goes on and feel relieved when she catches everything cleanly.

Indeed, her mood is exuberant and she runs off beaming. She raves to a cast member standing nearby. "Oh, tonight I feel it so good! It was so nice!" But she doesn't speak to me or even look at me as she passes to her dressing table.

I'm actually heartened by this. I had thought that her aloofness during my visit backstage in Barcelona was due to my unexpected presence. But I now see that this is standard procedure. She had told me that friends and family make her nervous and this is merely her way of maintaining concentration. Which means she wasn't angry at me then, or later that night when we went back to my hotel. Something happened the following day, but I'll fly on the trapeze before I dig up that corpse.

When the show is finished she comes over and chats with Marion's girlfriend and me about the Yekaterinburg circus book. Oxana, who hadn't greeted me, comes over and gives me a big hug and asks about the book and when she can buy copies. I tell her it may be a while but that I'll give her all the copies she wants. She thanks me for the chapter but says she hasn't had a chance to read it. She then apologizes for not being able to talk more, but there are some visitors wearing Belgian Olympic jackets and she's wanted for a photo.

As Olga and I walk out I notice an aluminum crate in the hallway. In stenciled letters are the words:

OLGA SIDOROVA
TRAPEZE

THE MIME BREAKS HIS SILENCE

The mime, whose character in the show is called "Eddie," was one of the cast members furthest from my radar in Amsterdam, Barcelona and Vienna. He wasn't present at the hotel parties I attended, I never saw him in the bar, except one night in Barcelona when he was playing the piano, and when I watched the show backstage he literally ran to and from his dressing cubicle as though his performance couldn't exhaust his energy. He didn't interact with the other artists except to play paddle ball with Maxsim. So when Olga asked me in Brussels who I wanted to talk to, the imposing name of Jesko von den Steinen incautiously fell from my lips. After all, why would a mime want to talk to anybody about anything, let alone explore his passion for silence with an uncredentialed stranger?

But my social secretary asked anyway and Wednesday night, while I was talking with Susan Daly in a back corner in the hotel bar, Jesko found me and asked if I wanted to join him at another bar for a drink. It seemed not too long ago that no one would talk to me, that I packed my tennis racquet for Vienna to stave off loneliness. Fortunately, he was good enough to reschedule for Friday night after the show.

The lobby of the Renaissance Brussels is intimate and elegant. A tall, round marble table bearing a large floral centerpiece dominates the room, surrounded by plush crimson chairs and a royal blue sofa against the rear wall.

I made the sofa my office at the Renaissance, now that I no longer had a room here. I could stow my bag unobtrusively under the long table and read and write and observe everyone's coming and going without putting myself in anyone's way.

I am waiting there Friday night. Olga is among the first to arrive, dressed in jeans and a white top. I never ask about the show anymore, after her petulant reaction the first two times I questioned her backstage. But tonight she leans forward and says breathlessly that she had a great show. Such a performance as she has only experienced two or three times in the last few years. However, she doesn't elaborate, and before I can ask for details, Jesko arrives riding a scooter and asks me in an apologetic tone if I could wait a few minutes while he phones his father to wish him happy birthday. Olga takes the scooter and rides a lap around the expensive carpet.

The differences between the onstage persona and the offstage person are often dramatic in the Cirque du Soleil. One could say this of any troupe, but I think the differences are more striking in the Cirque than in other performing arts because the acts and characters are so fantastic and the artists themselves so dissimilar and diverse. Nearly everyone I've met has surprised me in some way, whether it's been Masha Choodu's demur smile, Oxana Vintilova's amiability, Alya Titarenko's understated intelligence and femininity, or Olga's—well, anything about Olga. But I think no one presents as irreconcilable a contrast as Jesko von den Steinen.

Start with the name. The aristocratic Von. But his character in the show doesn't even have a last name, and the most prosaic of first names— Eddie. Eddie is a nerd's nerd. His face made up with white paint, lipstick, arching eyebrows. He wears a red baseball cap with the brim turned up, a white shirt with a bow tie, and baggy black shorts with white stripes and suspenders. The only hint that the two are the same person is Jesko's boyish looks. But Jesko is sophisticated and serious, with short curly blond hair, soft blue eyes, a prominent forehead. He wears narrow black-framed glasses, dark clothes and two-toned brown shoes. Okay, he has a scooter, but his appearance seems more indebted to *GQ* than to clown school.

And where Eddie wouldn't know what to do with a girl, except perhaps throw her an imaginary baseball, Jesko is reputed to be a lady's man.

"Jesko, how many girlfriends you have?" Olga would ask at dinner. And he talks. How he talks.

He suggests going to the African quarter, about a ten minute walk from the hotel. Olga plies him with questions the whole way. Where he's from, where he studied, what he wants to do after the Cirque. I trail superfluously, enjoying the crisp night air.

We take a sidewalk table at a crowded bar that's still serving food. None of us is very hungry, so we decide to share an order of pasta. Jesko explains the menu to Olga. She doesn't like tomatoes, so he suggests the pesto.

"What is pesto?"

"It's a sauce made from basil, garlic and olive oil."

A most thorough answer for a mime. It turns out his mother was a maitre' d in Berlin. But Jesko's family left Germany for British Columbia when he was six, which explains why he speaks English like a native.

Olga declines the pesto and finally chooses the carbanarro. She drinks tea, Jesko and I beer. You have to drink beer in Belgium. Jesko tells us about a beer he drank the other night. It was 7.5 percent and he stumbled home.

But who stumbles better than a mime? Indeed, one of the first things I notice about Jesko is the beauty of his gestures. His slightest movements are crisp and well-defined. Everything from his walk to his handshake to the way he holds a glass appears choreographed, and when he uses a finger to illustrate a point by outlining some imaginary shape, it's a wonder to observe.

"Laughter is the easiest way to change someone's mind," he says, but he himself hardly laughs at all. At least on this night. His voice is quiet but confident, his eyes soft but insistent. He believes in the primacy of play, but serious play.

"My act is play," he grants. "But the audience laughs because I behave seriously. When I take someone onstage, I'm inviting them to believe. When we shoot imaginary arrows we act as though they're real arrows. When we hear a lion roar we don't laugh, we jump. That's why the audience laughs, because we don't."

Jesko doesn't know where his urge to perform stems from. He was an extroverted child but not a class clown. His father was a taxi driver.

His only connection to show business was a grandfather who performed in the famous Berlin cabarets of the thirties.

Like Olga, he left home at fourteen. He claims his youth wasn't a troubled one but that he wished to be independent. He maintained ties with his parents, and a younger brother and sister, and didn't abandon his studies. He worked in restaurants and slept in a friend's apartment.

When he was seventeen he lied about his age to gain admission to a theater school in Northern California. While there Marcel Marceau came to give a workshop.

"He's fucking amazing!" Jesko exclaims. "He has Parkinson's now, he's an old man. But he gets onstage and it's all there!"

And Jesko does his impression of Marceau's famous glass box.

"It's pure magic!"

He then attended a circus school in Canada. "I once had a teacher who said a good performer needs three things. The body of an acrobat to articulate movements, so if I want to do a back flip I can. The mind of an actor to understand the difference between sitting slumped or with your arms crossed." And Jesko acts this out to make his point. "And the heart of a poet."

Over the course of the long night, he would define art in several ways. "The essence of art is sensitivity," he would remark casually. And, later, in a more forceful tone, "All art provokes. All art is political—meaning it has a point of view. I like my work to be perpendicular, not parallel. Unexpected. What you say or see is opposite. Do you know the *Cherry Orchard*? You're a writer, you know Chekhov. Well, everything in that play is expressed by the characters saying or doing the opposite. There's a scene in Chaplin. Which film was it? He's sitting alone at a table and he's just read a letter from his wife, who's leaving him. His back is turned to us and he's trembling uncontrollably. Well, he must be sobbing. But then he turns around and he's shaking a tumbler!"

But my favorite of his definitions is when he calls art "creative communication." I consider this particularly relevant coming from a mime. After all, much of modern art doesn't communicate at all. Obscurity has become a language all it's own. But a mime can't afford incomprehension. If he can't paint a clear picture of a lavatory, the audience isn't going to see the imaginary toilet, or understand that the water is overflowing and the door jammed, and therefore laugh when the invisible filth rises above his bobbing head.

I ask why he agreed to talk to me. I haven't asked this question of the others. But my initial conversations had been with Russians and I knew they consented out of respect for Olga. But I hadn't had any contact with Jesko before Brussels and he said yes immediately. I was curious why.

"Narcissism," he replies.

But perhaps the answer lies nearer to something he would say later about the importance of giving. Maybe he agreed because he was asked. Or because Olga asked. But I would tell him by night's end that he wasn't at all narcissistic, but quite the opposite— empathetic. I drew this conclusion not merely from my brief observations, but from his art itself. An actor or writer or musician can be narcissistic. But not a mime. Because a mime, as much as any psychologist, makes his living by understanding others.

Some spectators think the audience member he brings onstage for an excruciatingly long routine must be a plant. I know better. But I don't know how he selects them. Do they have a choice? Does he ask them?

"No, I don't speak. First I look for eye contact. Are they looking down at their lap or meeting my eyes? If they're making eye contact I take their hand."

And he takes my hand, gently.

"How are they holding it? Are they trembling? Pulling away? Then I go to someone else. But if they stare and hold my hand like this—" And he grips my hand tightly, "I also move on, because they're dominating. They're not going to take direction. But if it's like this..." And he shakes my hand, which is neither dominant nor submissive but mirroring his own, "Then I take them onstage."

"But it doesn't always work," I say. "Once I saw a man go through the first steps in the routine, but when you lay down onstage he would only sit. So you led him back to his seat and took someone else."

"Yes, that happens. But not often."

"When it does happen, does it bother you? Are you angry afterwards?"

"No, I don't worry about it."

"Are you nervous before show?" Olga asks.

"Yes."

"How you prepare for show?"

"It depends on my mood. If I need to focus I take more time."

"Of all artists, you have most contact with audience," she points out.

"In my act I have to concentrate on three things. The volunteer, the audience's reaction, and my own sense of how it's going. I also have to taken into account cultural differences. For example, the Spanish are very literary. They understand everything. The Japanese are compliant. They'll follow directions because that's what's expected of them. But we performed in Singapore and the Chinese are the opposite. They'll resist to save face! And the Belgians, they're wonderful. I had a man the other night, and you know where I pretend to take out a handkerchief and wipe my forehead? Well, instead of doing that he takes out a cigarette! Fucking amazing!"

"When I was watching the show backstage the other night you came off and said to those of us sitting on the sofas, 'Did you see that woman in the front? She couldn't stop laughing!' Well, of course we couldn't hear her, but I noticed you improvised with her. Did her laughing disturb you?"

"No, I loved it. It was great."

"If you were in the audience at a show, would you want to be selected?"

"No. It's not good when you're a performer to participate."

"But I'm talking about anything. I once attended a tango performance in Paris and at the end the dancers came into the audience and one chose me to dance with her."

"Oh, Jesko would love that!" Olga teases.

"Well, it depends if I trust the performer," Jesko reconsiders. "Some artists are cruel. People are afraid of being humiliated. I want to support them. I want to play by taking a scene seriously, not by making fun of someone."

"But how do you support them when you can't speak?"

"I watch them," he answers. "If they're nervous I stand closer or touch them. Sometimes I'll put my hand on their shoulder or waist and keep it there. I want them to trust me, to understand that we're creating something together."

He tried to enroll in ballet school when he was twenty-one. He didn't want to be a dancer, his build was unsuitable, but he saw ballet as a way to refine his theatrical training. "Ballet is the basis for Occidental beauty," he claims. "All Western movement can be traced to ballet. But they didn't want me. Finally they accepted me on this condition: I had to train with the small boys in the morning and the older ones in the afternoon, and if I missed once I was out!"

Eventually he landed a casting agent and went to Germany to work in a cabaret, as his grandfather had done. He also played galas throughout Europe. Then the Cirque called and he joined *Saltimbanco* in Japan.

I ask what the psychedelic chair means, since Eddie first appears in the revolving chair, which serves as Maxsim's exit after Adagio. No one I've talked to has a theory for the chair.

"It's just a chair," he responds. "Maybe it's a throne," he then muses. "It represents a transition."

I ask him how he interprets the subtext of the show, and he asks me if I'm familiar with the six chakras. Chakras are Hindu energy points. The first is near the anus, the second near the genitals, the third the navel, the fourth the heart, the fifth the neck and the sixth in the head between the eyebrows. That's why some Hindus wear a mark on that spot. Beyond the sixth chakra is Brahma, often represented by a lotus.

"It's been explained to me that *Saltimbanco* represents the six chakras," Jesko informs us, articulating an explanation that isn't alluded to in the program. In Adagio the wife and husband represent Gaia and Eros, the creation of the world. The child is the most important character. He symbolizes the future. Then come the lizards in Chinese Poles, the first chakra. The clowns wearing white masks are citizens—the audience. The juggler and wire walker are humans, the second chakra. The boleadoros represent bodily passions, the gut, the third chakra. The Russian Swing are baroques, distinct personalities yet still at the mercy of animal instincts.

"Then in the second act the trapeze—" with a nod toward Olga, "is the beginning of the aerial stage that culminates in Bungee. An evolution away from the earth. Eddie represents the fourth, fifth and sixth chakras, heart and intellect. Then comes death. Hand-to-Hand represents Superman. And it ends with Bungee, or Brahama. You'll notice there are lotuses on their white costumes."

I hadn't noticed. And I hadn't heard any of this before. I don't remark that he takes the three best chakras for himself. It's an intriguing framework, though. But is it accurate? Does it matter?

"Dragone must not have considered it important for the audience to understand this symbolism when he wrote the show," I observe. "If a spectator didn't buy the program he wouldn't even know about worms and baroques."

"If you buy a watch you don't need to know what's inside unless you're a watchmaker," Jesko replies.

Olga remains silent during this discussion, neither agreeing nor disagreeing, perhaps not following Jesko's terminology. But then she asks what he intends to do after the Cirque.

"I'd like to have a one-man show," he answers immediately.

"Mime?" I ask.

"Yes. I don't like modern spoken theater. I love Shakespeare. Shakespeare's fucking amazing."

"Have you seen 'Snow Show?'"

This was a one-man performance starring Slava, a famous Russian clown who had appeared in *Alegría*.

"No. But I wouldn't do that kind of show. Slava is very temperamental. Russian clowns are different. Tragic. In Russia there are white clowns and red clowns. A white clown is powerful and takes himself seriously. The red clown makes fun of him. Eddie is a combination."

Do people in audience ever touch you?" Olga asks after last call.

"You mean move me? All the time. A few nights ago there was an old man in front. He had been in a war. After the show he was standing bent, clapping awkwardly, with effort. I just cried."

We stay until closing and then walk back to the hotel. It's two-thirty in the morning. The bar at the Renaissance is dark, the lobby empty.

Jesko pauses by the elevators. "Do you want to sit down?"

"Sure," I say.

We pull up the nearest chairs. It's very quiet. Even the front desk is deserted.

Olga smiles and says, "Jesko, you like talk! In show you ever want talk?" And she laughs and laughs.

Jesko smiles politely.

"But I tired. I need sleep," Olga goes on. "Good night!"

And she departs, leaving us alone.

I could not have imagined, watching the show in Amsterdam, that one night in a quiet corner of Brussels I would share an empty stage with the mime. In Amsterdam I had watched his act with trepidation, fearing he might choose me.

But I had chosen him!

We talk for another hour, about Becket and Shakespeare and Duchamp. I ask him, since he mentioned Chaplin, if he watches a lot of silent films.

"Of course. I love Chaplin, Keaton, Jacques Tati."

"What about stand-up comedy?"

He frowns. "Most of it's terrible." But then he pauses. "Some of it's good," he adds. "I saw George Carlin on TV not long ago. He was talking about public golf courses. He had researched or read somewhere the square footage of all the public golf courses in the U.S. And then he compared that to the square footage of all the public housing. Fucking amazing! No one likes to hear someone preaching on a soapbox, but we'll pay if you can make us laugh."

"But you don't consider yourself a comedian," I say. "What are you?"

He grins. "One of my teachers called me a non-verbal humanist! For me, the essence of performing isn't making people laugh but making them feel. Making them think."

"And what is the essence of being human?"

"Giving."

Strange answer for a narcissist!

"You die alone," he says.

I ask him to imagine that, for some reason, he could no longer perform. Would a fulfilled life still be possible?

"What does it mean, fulfilled?" he wonders. And then, "That's a loaded question."

He stares up, as if looking at the walls of one of his glass boxes. And finally, after many hours of candid conversation, magisterial monologues, desultory diatribes, the mime falls silent.

TWINS

The next day I have to change hotels. But first I have lunch at the Symphony restaurant with James Clowney. He plays the Ringmaster, although his role has little in common with the ringmaster of traditional circuses. He wears a leonine yellow costume, with a forest green cape and pointed cap, and carries a gold staff—the only clue to his power. But he does not address the audience or introduce the acts, and his presence is as much comical as authoritative.

In person he is more physically impressive than many of the members of the troupe, who have smaller gymnast's physiques. James looks like he could play football, and indeed he once played tight end.

He's wearing a black turtleneck and orders shrimp salad and ginger ale. Hardly a football player's lunch. But then this is Brussels. I tell him he's the first American I've talked to in the cast and contrast the American attitude toward publicity with the Russian. But he too dislikes interviews, not for reasons of privacy—James relishes talking to people—but because of the time.

"A lot of times you have to wait," he explains. "You have to hang around while other people are interviewed or they take pictures. And it's always on your time, not Cirque time."

"But you do a lot of interviews," I point out, having seen his photo in Spanish and Austrian magazines. "Is it part of your contract?"

"No, I could get out of them if I wanted. But I always say yes. I feel it's part of my job. Especially since I'm the Ringmaster. I don't do a lot in the show, but there's a responsibility that comes with the role."

I ask if he's tired of people asking about his name, and he is. But I will ask as well. And yes, Clowney is his real name. And he was teased for it and wanted to change it when he was a kid, but now he thinks of it as a name like Johnson or Smith. He doesn't consider it destiny.

I mention that my father had observed him backstage and remarked that he seemed the most social of the cast. Some kept to themselves, others had a group. But James roamed throughout the artistic tent joking and playing with everyone.

He replies that he enjoys people, and has no difficulty relating to different cultures. I ask if there is anyone he cannot reach, but he shakes his head.

"What about Wang?" I wonder, referring to the wire walker, who speaks little English.

"Oh, I like Wang. We get along fine."

"But how do you communicate? What do you say to her?"

"Well, she loves Chinese chess. You may have noticed the Chinese playing it backstage. It's kinda like chess but some of the pieces move differently. So I learned to play. She's very aggressive."

Well, why wouldn't a wire walker take risks on a board game?

"And what about Olga?"

He breaks into a big smile. "I love Olga. Olga, she's special!"

"What did you think about her leaving?"

I expect him to grow serious, maybe to lean forward and whisper some criticism. But his smile persists. "I think it was great!"

"You do?"

"She stood up to management. She didn't give a damn about being sued or anything. She did what she needed to do. That takes courage!"

"So you understood?"

"Look, I spot her during the fixed part of her act. So I'm always looking up at her. And I love to watch her because you can tell she's having a good time. But in Vienna I could see she wasn't smiling anymore. So you have to understand, if she's not having fun anymore doing what she loves, something serious must be wrong. And look, they asked her back, right? She didn't crawl back. They needed her. She could have held out for more money. She didn't. All these performers and athletes in the world you always hear about holding out for more money. Olga doesn't give a damn about money. For her it's about doing what she loves."

I turn the conversation to him and we talk about his childhood and his role in the show. As with the others I've talked to, he surprises me with his time and attention. No cell phone calls, no interruptions, no glances at his watch. And when the check comes he'll tear it out of my hand.

"But you said you hate interviews," I remind him.

"We were just talking," he answers.

I not only have to leave my room, I have to leave the hotel, which I discover is full. Arthur comes to the rescue. Because he works at a Renaissance, which is owned by Marriott, he can get me a discounted rate at the brand new Marriott, about a mile and a half away. And by brand new I mean brand new. It just opened yesterday.

I check in and then return to the Renaissance to meet a Belgian friend of mine who has come from the city of Ghent to have dinner with me. I would have taken her to the show, but she has to catch a train home. So we find a brasserie around the corner and then return to the hotel.

Arthur is nowhere to be found. Running errands no doubt. But I spot Simon sitting alone in the bar and we join him. After talking about his parents' party—the one we missed—he and Liesbeth chat about life in Belgium.

"Too bad you didn't go to the show," he then says. "The King and Queen are there tonight!"

"The King and Queen of Belgium?"

Simon is in charge of the VIP operations, which includes the best seats and a separate tent where food and champagne are served.

"Why aren't you there?" I ask.

"It's my night off."

"But don't you want to be there?"

"Oh, I've seen enough of that sort of thing."

Arthur appears and, after introductions are made, offers to drive Liesbeth back to Ghent so that she might stay longer. But I feel I've imposed enough on him already. So I take her by taxi to the train station, say a rushed goodbye, and return in time for my appointment with Susan Daly.

The next day Olga doesn't say much about the King and Queen. They came back to the artistic tent. She got to greet them. "They were nice," she says.

She has much more to say about the twins, the sixteen-year-old Ukrainian girls, who are supposed to arrive any day. Olga is excited not just because she loves twins but, more importantly, because they will perform half the shows.

I had assumed they had performed in a show before, but Olga tells me they have not. They come from gymnastics, she tells me, and had been training for eighteen months before one of them sustained an injury, delaying their arrival six months.

I have coffee with Alya in the bar and she tells me about her career in fitness. Then Arthur and I take Olga to the Grand Chapiteau and have lunch in the commissary tent. But today I accompany him on errands, walking for miles in the eastern suburbs.

He takes an inordinately long time in a drugstore, and he finally calls me over to a rack of personal care items. Olga needs tweezers, and Arthur asks me which among three pairs he should choose. Perhaps no other incident I've witnessed captures the effect of Olga's imperious demeanor better than the sight of this autonomous Dutchman deliberating before a row of tweezers as though they were keys in an automobile sweepstakes. In the end he buys all three.

The following day he leaves, and I'm sad to see him go. When Olga first told me she had a boyfriend I was jealous of course. I cherished the intimacy of our relationship and assumed that now she would have less time for me. It would be reasonable too for Arthur to regard me with suspicion and urge her to put our friendship on a more formal footing. But my primary concern was that he wasn't good enough for her. That he would limit and drain her, like the men she had known before. But now that I've met him and observed them together, I've come to draw quite different conclusions, and I now wonder whether Olga is good enough for him!

That night Olga and I have dinner with Jesko. The twins still haven't arrived. They're flying from Montreal, but Olga doesn't know when. I had seen their photos in the program, so I knew who they were even when I saw the show in Amsterdam. Indeed, when I first attended *Saltimbanco* in 1996 the trapezists had been Canadian twins, and I have never forgotten their performance.

I hadn't expected to meet these twins. Not until coming to Brussels when Olga raised my hopes with her constant, "Twins come tomorrow!" So I'm a bit disappointed now.

Olga never refers to them by name—Ruslana and Taisiya Bazaliy. "Can you tell them apart?" I ask her.

"I never separate twins!" she replies.

It's only fitting that on Saturday, my final day, I watch the show again. I haven't seen it from the audience since I went with my father in Barcelona. The arrival of a Brazilian friend of mine, whom I had met while on vacation in the Amazon, and her German husband serves as a convenient excuse to go, and Olga once again generously offers to get us tickets. It's evidence of the Cirque's global presence that my friend had seen *Quidam* on television in Manaus. So when I offered to take her she was almost as excited as when she finds a tarantula during a midnight walk. Afterward she would say that the show seemed to last ten minutes. And she would remark to me that Olga had a very strong character. This from a woman whose pets used to be boa constrictors.

And for me the show is no less magical. Once again I'm struck by how fresh it seems. But tonight I notice details I haven't seen before. I keep in mind Jesko's interpretation, and as I watch the various acts I recall their being described to me by the performers themselves. And I recognize faces. Not everyone. With all the masks and makeup it's sometimes difficult even to tell the men from the women. But in Chinese Poles and Russian Swing and Bungee the troupe of acrobats no longer appear to me as strange creatures with whom I share nothing in common but as acquaintances and friends with whom I share a great deal.

And when I watch Elena Grosheva mount the Russian swing for the final leap, and she catapults over the shoulders of her catcher and flails back to the stage, saved from serious injury by the safety, I don't simply gasp or wonder if she'll land the next attempt. I wonder if she's hurt her shoulder, if she'll storm off angry, if she'll pout in the artistic tent.

And when Olga emerges I point her out to my friend with pride, as if I've known her all my life. And I remember, as she ascends to the trapeze, what she said about learning choreography upside down. And I watch her flawless performance with a practiced eye.

At the end of the show some of the troupe, still in costume, run into the audience and quickly shake hands with spectators before the entire cast runs through the central aisle and back onstage for a group bow. I'm sitting on the aisle and the character who extends his arm to me is Igor Issakov. As I shake his hand his eyes grow wide with recognition and he breaks the language barrier.

"Hello!"

After the show we go back to the commissary tent and eat, while waiting for Olga. My friend looks up and says, "There are the twins."

And there they are! Standing alone by the door. One is wearing a Beverly Hills t-shirt. They have long shimmering blond hair, wide, pretty faces, and seem as inseparable as Olga claimed. I'm surprised how small they are. I've seen a lot of twins before, but I've never been so mesmerized by the sight. Perhaps I've been influenced by Olga's anticipation. But then I realize a quite different explanation lies at the heart of my excitement. It's not because they're twins that I gaze at them so fervidly. It's because of what they do. And I remember at the Paradiso, when Olga told me she did trapeze, how I stared at her, trying to imagine her swinging through the air.

They're sitting at a table now, still alone, not eating. So I walk over and say hello. I ask if they've just arrived and they smile in unison and nod. Perhaps if Olga were here we could chat for a few minutes, but in any case they must be tired. I shake the hand of the one wearing the Beverly Hills shirt. "I'm a friend of Olga's," I say.

I take leave of my Brazilian friend and her husband and accompany Olga back to the Renaissance. It's my last night, but I still have work to do. Elena joins us in the lobby. She's brought the chapter with her and starts by telling me she likes the writing and that her criticism has nothing to do with my observations. In fact she would welcome more observations, even if they are negative. And the first part she likes very much. But she wishes I would take out the gymnastics.

Where is my beer? Olga is smoking a cigarette and I'm tempted to light up myself. Take out the gymnastics!

But I listen to her patiently, and she talks at length, always looking at me with her ice blue eyes.

"I don't feel that's who I really am. Yes, it was a large part of my life, but I've grown since then. It's very difficult to put your past inside. In my mind, in my heart, I'm a different person. The Cirque gives me another language."

"What about the Olympics?" I ask, having downplayed her experience in Atlanta because it hadn't seemed of paramount importance to her.

She looks through the pages, which are marked with her own hand-written notes. "Yes, that's okay."

I breathe a little easier.

"I'm like an artist. I want people to take me like I am. People either like me or hate me, that's okay."

"That's not true," Olga cuts in. "I don't like you or not like you," she says with a shocking shrug.

Elena seems not to mind and turns her eyes back to me. "When I stopped gymnastics I said thank you to everyone. I take good side. Many things in life are bad. I don't like negative energy. It's not my way. Once I did an interview on TV. You know Svetlana Khorkina? She won gold medals in Atlanta and Sydney. The interviewer asked me what I thought of her posing in *Playboy*. Well, I had been roommates with Svetlana, but I couldn't understand why this was a question for me. I said it was none of my business."

My initial disappointment gives way to a sense of opportunity, as I realize Elena is really opening up to me. And isn't that what I wanted most of all? Not histories but intimacies. I decide to ask a question I wouldn't have dared to ask before.

"You missed the first time tonight on the Russian swing. Were you angry afterwards?"

"No, it's okay. In the past, yes. But I work on this. Every day I go over me—over my bad mood. I'm a difficult person. But life makes me softer."

And she smiles. "I probably did this twenty times in a row without a miss. I forgot how to miss. But did you notice how I fight the second time? I landed on my knees. In the past maybe I slide off. But I fight and finish. I can feel we are a team. This is new for me."

As I listen to her I try to paint her portrait in my mind, but the girl before me with the fuchsia hair and skin tight shirt seems such a contrast to the reflective soul inside. How do I reconcile them? A minute before one of the guys had come over and asked if she wanted to go to a club. I know she likes to dance; she went dancing with us Sunday night. And tonight is Saturday. But she said no and turned back to me and kept talking.

As if reading my mind, she says she's written a sort of poem, about her thoughts and life. It's in Russian, but if I can find someone to translate it she'd be glad to give me a copy. Later that night she hands me a disk labeled with the words "Elena—My Love" in English. I don't know how to thank her. Or, rather, I do.

Olga invites me up to her room. Alya has offered to talk to me some more about "O", since we hadn't had much time the other day. I have an early flight, but how can I say no? So the three of us sit in Olga's room and talk.

At one point Olga kneels down on the floor and takes Alya's bare foot in her hand. "Look at the line on this foot!" she exclaims. "It is perfect!"

Well, if you never thought a fitness champ could blush, leave it to Olga.

A few minutes later Olga excuses herself to take a bath. She returns wearing blue pajamas, her skin bright pink, and sprawls on the bed.

What am I to make of these people? It's three o'clock in the morning and I'm sitting in the company of two women whose appearance belies their character. Olga at this moment looks like she's eight years old, winsome and helpless. But we know better. And Alya, for all her physical strength, seems to have an even stronger intellect and heart.

I had feared that as I grew to know the people in the Cirque the mystique would fade away and I would cease to be astonished. But watching the show after having come to know the cast only intensifies its allure, and plunging deeper into their private lives only increases my sense of wonder.

"O"

When the Cirque du Soleil started life as a group of Montreal street performers it didn't even have a roof over its head to hang a trapeze from. Then it bought a tent, then it bought more tents, and its shows traveled the world. Then this private Canadian company, headed by Guy Laliberté, with its close-knit creative team and international troupe of performers, these modern, cosmopolitan gypsies did a strange thing—they settled down. They made a deal with the Treasure Island Hotel in Las Vegas and created a new show, *Mystère*, to play in its own permanent theater, a few steps from the slot machines.

Some said the Cirque was selling out, but these critics misunderstood the whole idea of circus, which, unlike the fine arts, was neither aristocratic, elitist or self-referential, but had always been commercial and as responsive to its audience as any form of theater. For Barnum, selling tickets was the whole idea, and if a street juggler can find a sidewalk sheltered by an awning, why should he stand in the rain?

Others worried that Las Vegas and the Cirque were incompatible, but Circus Circus had been one of the Strip's earliest and most successful theme hotels. Sure, the Cirque du Soleil was closer to Lincoln Center than to Coney Island, but it never forgot the roots of the circus as a mass, trans-cultural medium of expression and, for all its success, it never took itself too seriously. Besides, Las Vegas was now catering to a more cultured clientele, with art museums and gourmet restaurants popping up next to strip joints and all-night buffets, a clientele who could afford seventy dollars or more for a ticket and would appreciate the convenience of having the Cirque a chip's throw away.

Mystère was so successful that in 1998 the Cirque created *La Nouba* to play in a permanent theater shaped like a tent in Downtown Disney. And earlier that year they returned to Las Vegas, when "O" opened at the Bellagio.

"O" was Franco Dragone's most ambitious and technically challenging show. An Italian by birth who had grown up in Belgium and studied acting and political science, Dragone came to the Cirque after directing the graduation show for the Canadian National Circus School. His team included set designer Michel Crête, costume designer Dominique Lemieux, choreographer Debra Brown and composer Benoit Jutras, replacing René Dupéré, who had composed the previous shows. The now-familiar Cirque sensibility owes much to their intimate collaboration over the years.

They would create the show at the Cirque's Montreal studio, working with a large team of technicians and those performers fortunate enough to have been chosen for the project. Or perhaps unfortunate enough, because this show would entail new challenges and hardships. The artists would have to become dive certified and learn to make entrances from the water tank beneath the stage and wait for cues while sucking on air hoses. They would have to navigate a slippery stage, perform in wet costumes, dive into the pool instead of a net or mat. One of the human guinea pigs for this new adventure was Alevtyna Titarenko.

Alya was born in Nikolayev, Ukraine to athletic parents. Her mother was a swimmer and her father a biathalete. They lived in their own flat with her grandmother, and life was good. One morning in October when she was thirteen, her grandmother woke her, shouting that there was war in Moscow. It was the end of the Soviet Union. Alya went back to sleep. For a long time her world didn't change.

That world was the gym, the same gym where a future Miss Olympia trained. Alya was practicing acrobatics, but her coach thought she had the right body type for fitness—broad shoulders, narrow waist, not too tall or heavy. Fitness differed from the more traditional bodybuilding and was gaining popularity. Female bodybuilding narrowed the gap between the genders, and steroid use was rampant. But fitness was more well-rounded and performance oriented, and Alya felt she didn't have to compromise her femininity. After posing in a bikini and high heels, female fitness competitors had to perform a choreographed ninety second routine incorporating acrobatics, gymnastics and dance in balanced proportion.

In 1996 she won the Gold Medal in Pairs Acrobatics at the World Championships in Germany, and was asked to represent the Ukraine a week later at the European Fitness Championships. Despite the late notice, she managed to place second.

She met Nico Karsdorf while competing in Germany. They were married in Kiev two years later in a trilingual ceremony consisting of Russian, German and English. "The celebration lasted three days," Alya recalls less than vividly. "The first day was the ceremony, the second day...I don't remember, and the third day was the pool."

She had never heard of the Cirque du Soleil until scouts came to Kiev. She was offered a contract for the creation of "O" in 1997. Nico came in 1999 and was offered a contract for *Saltimbanco*.

Alya's preparation took six months in Montreal and six months in Las Vegas. A mold was taken of her body for her costumes and she had to practice scuba diving as much as acrobatics. Although her mother had been a swimmer, Alya was afraid of deep water.

She didn't have a lot of contact with Dragone. Due to the complexity of the show, he spent more time with the technicians than with the cast. But she remembers how impressed she was one day when he assembled some of them on a stage, and said, "Go there! Go there!" Giving apparently meaningless directions, but then suddenly, out of nowhere, creating a striking tableau.

That was the way he worked. Organically and intellectually. If the Cirque shows seem inspirational it's because they're the products of inspiration. Dragone relies on certain intellectual underpinnings—for *Saltimbanco*: spiritual evolution, an antidote to modern despair, the chakras; for "O": infinity; the four elements of water, earth, fire and air; the history of theater from street buskers to grand opera. But he doesn't write a script. Rather he molds these concepts with the help of the various designers and cast into an expansive tapestry of music, dance and acts.

Of course, that doesn't make life easy for athletes used to a strict regimen. How do you know what's expected of you when the creators aren't even sure? Whole acts would be developed and then tossed out. Artists would be asked to perform a maneuver one way, only to be told to perform it another. Or technical problems would interfere at the last moment, costumes would have to be redesigned, and so on.

But Alya met the challenge, as she met all the challenges in her life. Hard work, sacrifice, dedication. She pushed the Russian swing, she did acrobatics on a barge that floats on the water in the second act, she played a cadaver in Aerial Hoops, lifted into the air and then plunged into the water by nylon fabric held under her arms. There wasn't time to dry off completely between appearances. The water was warmer than a normal pool but the theater was air-conditioned. Fortunately the setting was less intimate than the tent shows and the audience could not see her shivering.

The theater only held eighteen-hundred spectators, while the Grand Chapiteau accommodated twenty-five hundred. But it was twelve stories tall, with a 1,500,000 gallon pool 140 feet wide and twenty-five feet deep. A series of computerized panels and gratings rendered the entire stage solid in a matter of second. So that one minute a swimmer might rise from the depths and the next minute a clown might sit where she had emerged. One moment there would be a rain storm. Another moment rings of fire would sprout from gas jets. Alya's grandmother had always told her that circuses used fake fire. But this fire was real enough, and if a performer weren't careful she could fall through the air, slip on the earth, get burned by the fire and nearly drown in the water, all in a matter of seconds!

Underwater the cast used air hoses to breathe and exited through tunnels, aided by stage hands in scuba gear. Unlike *Saltimbanco*, there wasn't a single artistic tent where everyone congregated, but rows of dressing rooms, a green room with a TV, and two workout studios. The lifestyle too was far different from a touring show. In *Saltimbanco* Alya would have to arrive at the Grand Chapiteau by 1:00 PM on a matinee day and wouldn't leave until after eleven. But in Vegas she could arrive at the Bellagio at 6:00 PM and be home by midnight. She could also work out at Gold's Gym instead of the artistic tent. One of her complaints about touring is that there's no privacy. If you want to develop a new act you have to do it in the artistic tent, where everyone can watch, as I had watched her practice on the tissue that one afternoon in Brussels.

But on the whole she prefers touring, and not only because she's been reunited with her husband. "People pay to travel," she points out. "And we get to see the world for free. We also socialize more. In "O" everybody had their own lives. And it's hard to save money. In Vegas I had a house and a car, which were nice, but expensive. What are our expenses now? Our rooms are free, we can eat at the site, and sometimes the Cirque hires a bus to take us, and sometimes it's close enough to walk.

Alya had never seen *Saltimbanco* before appearing in "O". And she didn't want to watch the video. There was a certain arrogance among the "O" cast. After all, theirs was the newest, most ambitious show. How many years old was *Saltimbanco*? It was a tired show, low-tech, unsophisticated. But when it came to Portland she flew up to see Nico. And she watched the show. And fell in love.

She hoped her husband would stay in the U.S., but *Saltimbanco* was slated to tour Japan the following year. So she decided to join him, and if they wouldn't give her a position she would make one for herself. But first she took a detour home to Ukraine, and then to Rio de Janeiro for the World Fitness Championships. She won bronze, quite extraordinary considering her complicated, transcontinental life.

She then flew to Japan without a contract and trained with Nico in private before or after the show. She already knew how to push the Russian swing, and it was a lot easier with dry hands. But she was afraid of heights and threw up the first few times she tried bungee.

"I don't like deep water and I'm put in 'O'!" she remarked. "I don't like heights and now I'm doing Bungee! I'm living proof of what people can do!"

While training she made all the mistakes one can make. But she watched a lot of videos, and with Nico's help, and some coaching from Sandra, she mastered the bungee cord. As for Chinese poles, she was a natural. No woman was stronger.

When the artistic director came to Japan she was ready for him. How could he say no?

So now Alya is in Vienna, or Brussels, or maybe Madrid. But the Grand Chapiteau looks the same in every city, and the paintings on the walls of their hotel room look the same, and she sits reading her books while Nico watches movies on TV until around 3:00 AM, when it's time to go to sleep.

RINGMASTER

Shakespeare said all the world's a stage, but it's equally true that in the Cirque the stage is all the world. Crossing the psychedelic floorboards of *Saltimbanco*—or flying above them—are performers from four continents, from China and Argentina and France and Poland and Canada, even from Siberia. Even from Harlem.

Yes, Harlem, that breeding ground for circus talent. James Clowney grew up on Lennox and 124th Street, and then, prophetically, on Broadway. His attitude toward clowns was as something undesirable because the other kids teased him about his name. He wanted to be a football player, or a building inspector like his father, who worked for the Health Department. He remembers his dad taking him on jobs, pointing out cracked cornices or rusty fire escapes, and he traces his love of architecture to those outings. He enjoys the opportunity *Saltimbanco* gives him to tour Europe and he often walks through the historic districts at night, photographing the lights and shadows.

"I like meeting people from other cultures," he says. "I tell my friends, there's another world out there."

An interesting statement from someone raised in the world's most cosmopolitan city. Yet in many ways New York is as provincial as Siberia and, for someone living on Lennox and 124th, Lincoln Center, Wall Street, or Ringling Brothers at Madison Square Garden, might as well be across the Atlantic.

A couple years ago I stayed at a hotel in Harlem, on Central Park North. One afternoon I rented a bicycle and circumnavigated the park. When I started I was the only white person on the street and the dress code was a notch or two below business casual. When I reached Central Park South and paused outside the Plaza Hotel the dress code had stiffened significantly. People were carrying tiny shopping bags and walking even tinier dogs. And there were, of course, the famous carriage rides. But the horses had all gotten bottle necked down on the south side because there weren't any carriages on Central Park North.

I had traveled less than five miles. And yet I wondered how many New Yorkers ever made this journey.

Talking to James reminded me of a feeling I always had about New York. That it's a place of tribes, separated by heritage and race, by subway stops and doormen. James had become friends with Wang, the wire walker, even though she only spoke Chinese. Yet he had never had Chinese friends in New York, although New York was full of Chinese who spoke excellent English.

And I recalled the feeling that struck me my first night with the Cirque in Amsterdam. That this group was not merely cosmopolitan, but inclusive. The Russians didn't sit at one table and the French at another. You dressed the way you wanted, acted the way you wanted, spoke the language you wanted, and everyone somehow understood.

When James was seven his mother took him to audition for a new circus school. It was the brainchild of the Big Apple Circus, one of the breed of new smaller circuses that, like the Cirque du Soleil, didn't use animals. They started an educational foundation and the circus school became part of the New York Public School system.

The audition consisted of tumbling, handstands, cartwheels, basic stuff. But James had no formal training in acrobatics and doubted he would be accepted. After all, there were two thousand applicants for a couple hundred places. But shortly his mother received a letter of acceptance and James' life changed forever.

He loved the school. How could he not? What other school taught children how to be class clowns? His name became a source of curiosity rather than scorn. He learned acrobatics and juggling and balancing, but no aerial acts, probably a good thing considering his size. The school put on shows, real shows. They sold tickets and popcorn, and James gave interviews to newspapers in which he was incessantly asked about his name.

Some of the circus school alumni went on to circus careers, and the Big Apple used the school as a source of talent for its own shows. But James still didn't think of himself as a circus performer. He wanted to play football. Unfortunately, the high school he attended after circus school had dropped its football program the year before. Then he went to New York City College, but they didn't have a football team either. So he played for a semi-pro team called the Red Dogs.

Then one day the Big Apple Circus invited him to join, and James became a professional acrobat. He enjoyed working in the show, and the touring was not strenuous because the Big Apple Circus rarely traveled beyond New York and New England. In time, however, personality disputes tarnished the experience and, after seven years onstage, he walked away.

He got married, he moved to rural Pennsylvania, he worked nights in the packing department of a diaper factory and days cleaning home fuel tanks. He was tired but not unhappy. He was making good money, and his mentor, an environmentalist who hired him to clean the fuel tanks, was grooming him to take over the business. His only connection to his circus past was a part-time job teaching gymnastics to children—a job he took to fill the three-hour gap between cleaning fuel tanks during the day and packing diapers at night. James explains his passion for work as a reaction to insomnia he suffered after leaving the Big Apple—both the circus and the city—and finding himself in a small town with nothing to do. Besides, he liked the work, all of it.

One can't say that James Clowney believes in signs, because he seems to have ignored the overwhelming possibility that his fate was inexorably linked with the circus. First there was the hint in his name. Then the circus school. Then the Big Apple called. However, James was like a Greek king ignoring the oracle. But Destiny's convoluted tentacles claimed him again and again. How on earth did they find him in Pennsylvania?

One afternoon when he came home, still in his work clothes and reeking of kerosene, his wife excitedly told him the Cirque du Soleil had phoned. The oracle again. But the caller, as mysterious as the Pythia, left no number. Still, James could have tracked them down. He could have found out from an internet search that the Cirque headquarters were in Montreal, gotten the main number, and asked for the casting director. But he tried to shrug off destiny one more time, and drove to the diaper factory.

A week later the Cirque called again, and this time there was no escape. They were resurrecting *Saltimbanco* in Europe and they wanted him on the team.

James' gifts are ideally suited to the Cirque du Soleil. He might have been a good tight end, but his cheerfulness and curiosity, his extroversion and solicitous smile would have been lost on the gridiron.

The Ringmaster is one of several characters who, along with Dreamer, the Baron, the masques and cavaliers, are neither acts nor members of the troupe. James contends he doesn't do a lot, but his presence is a strong and frequent one, providing continuity in the show. At one moment he struts across the stage with his gold cane and green cape like a master of ceremonies. At another he reverently watches Wang atop the wire or Olga on the trapeze. During Eddy's improvisation he inexplicable runs from one wing to the other, screaming.

And he makes contact with the audience. Unlike the masques and cavaliers, who are expressionless and stay in the background, Ringmaster is as unique and emotional as his bright yellow costume suggests. His lips and eyes are made up in an Oriental style, accentuating his stares and smiles. And because he lingers on the stage longer than most of the cast and has greater freedom in where he roams, he has more opportunity than anyone except Eddy to connect with the audience.

"Every show I try to make contact with at least one person," he says. "It's funny, but sometimes they're scared, they'll look away. They don't know how to take it. But I'll stare them in the eye and I'll come back to them during the show. I know who you are, I remember you."

But perhaps the most important function he performs is the least entertaining, that of spotting. During the Russian Swing and the fixed trapeze he stands ready to catch an errant flyer. I remember someone telling me that when Olga first came to the Cirque and the mat and the spotters were placed beneath her in practice, she suggested intentionally falling to see what would happen. Probably she was just joking. With Olga it's not always easy to tell. But the idea was refuted vociferously.

And it's not just the faller who may be injured. A good spotter takes great risks and often suffers most from a successful collision. James perfected the art during his years in the Big Apple Circus. Since he's bigger than most acrobats, the role naturally went to him, and he studied it the same way he studied a football playbook. Houlden Caufield dreamed of being a catcher in the rye, of standing at the edge of a cliff and catching children about to run off. But Houlden's charges are running, not falling from heights up to thirty feet.

If it weren't so perilous, James could make an act out of spotting, showing the full range of his talents, perhaps catching crash test dummies flung from catapults.

"The circus is more dangerous than football," he asserts. "In football people are coming at you on a flat surface, they aren't falling out of the sky. In this show people are flying every moment, in all directions. Head first, or twisting, or tumbling. Or two people fall and you have to decide which one to catch. You have to learn to go against your instincts. When something's falling, your natural reaction is to turn your head away, but you can never lower your head if you're spotting. You have to keep your eyes on them. The first thing you do is look for their head. Where's the head? That's what you have to protect above everything else. And the problem is, when people fall they reach out. So I'm trying to catch you and you're putting your hand in my way. I've gotten poked by a lot fingers and elbows working in the circus. I can't count all the bruises and cuts and black eyes. I like to box, but the punishment I take spotting is worse. But my attitude is, I'm gonna catch you even if I get hurt."

If only we could all be so lucky to have James Clowney catch us when we fall.

MADRID

When a trapeze star for the Cirque du Soleil flew by me at the Paradiso Club I knew it was an act of serendipity, and I did what I could to keep her within reach. But I couldn't have known then how incredibly fortunate my timing was and how narrow the window of opportunity for what was to follow. For *Saltimbanco* had just returned to Europe after a three-year hiatus and Amsterdam was the first city on tour. And it was Olga's first city with the Cirque as well, after having trained for six months in Montreal. And by year's end she would be gone.

I had followed them in their journey so far, from Amsterdam to Barcelona to Vienna to Brussels. Madrid would be the first city I would miss, saving my money for their next stop, the Royal Albert Hall in London.

"You should have come to Madrid!" Arthur would tell me by phone a week after they had arrived. "It's gorgeous here. Much nicer weather than London."

But I had already seen the Cirque in Spain and, since I didn't yet have a book contract, I was paying my own expenses.

"Olga misses you," Arthur says. "Every time someone knocks on the door she thinks it is you!"

Only later do I learn she isn't performing. She re-injured her knee and is scheduled to go to Montreal for surgery. But she isn't in pain. "I can run," she says in a surprisingly buoyant voice. "Only when I jump— then my God! What you need for London?" she then asks. "Who you want talk? Where you stay?"

In the meantime she works on her choreography and keeps in shape by running. She's unsure what to expect from the surgery. "I know one girl who have knee surgery and after six months she can still hardly walk!"

I take advantage of my medical connections to reassure her she'll probably be walking within a week and running in two to three months. As for the trapeze—well, what are her plans anyway? The last I heard she was retiring after London. Now, of course, she won't be going to London. She thinks she'll stay in Montreal and use the Cirque's facilities for rehab, which may take four to six months. And after that?

She hasn't renewed her contract but informs me they've offered to let her stay on and perform galas and other special events. She won't have to tour. It sounds to me like a good opportunity, and she seems interested. Since coming to Madrid I haven't heard her mention the school she wants to start, and she's no longer complaining about the Cirque.

"Mark, Cirque take all your life!"

She no longer complains of loneliness now that she has Arthur. But I also realize the toll of doing all eight to ten shows. In Madrid the twins are only performing half the shows, while awaiting a replacement soloist. No trapezist does every show.

Of course, now that Olga doesn't have to be on site, she goes willingly. She watches the twins. She even talks about Dasha.

"Dasha going to Montreal to study trapeze," she tells me.

I maintain a judicious silence.

One night she tells me in a mock serious voice, "Mark, I pregnant!"

"With twins no doubt?"

"Doctor he say maybe with three! But Arthur don't want three. So if I have three will you take one? What you prefer, boy or girl?"

I thought she might be depressed, no longer performing, facing knee surgery, her future uncertain. But her voice is radiant.

"Mark, if I has twins will you be godfather?"

"I would be honored."

"But you know what it means? If something happens to Arthur and me, you has to take care of kids!"

And she laughs and laughs.

She asks me to help her write a letter to the casting director—the man from the Cirque who had first contacted her in Australia—explaining why she ran away. She knows she hadn't communicated as well as she could have in the past and this gives her a chance to put her thoughts in order and formally address Cirque management. She talks for an hour and I condense her sentiments into the following:

Dear Fabrice,

I wanted to write you because you have known me longer than anyone in Montreal. I don't want to give a long explanation of what happened in Vienna. Let me just say I had problems that were not solved. I have devoted my life to the trapeze. I love her more than anything in the world. I don't give up easily, but I can't perform less than one hundred percent. It is too dangerous. In Vienna I could not sleep for a week and needed time off, not just from the trapeze but from everything. I hope you can understand.

I also want you to know I'm glad to be in Brussels and happy to see the twins. I love the Cirque du Soleil and appreciate the chance it gives me to perform.

"Mark, you ever dream of writing?" she asks.

"All the time."

"Really?"

"But it never comes to anything. The ideas are always bad, or incomprehensible."

"Well guess what? Last night I dream about trapeze! Mark, I never dream about trapeze. But last night I have dream. People put me up on bar. I take off hands and start flying like bungee and then I catch trapeze... And this feeling... I just wake up. I feel very close, very deep, like my child."

I don't know whether she means she feels like a child or the trapeze is like her child, but I find it more remarkable that she has this dream so seldom. "You mean you never dream of flying or falling?" I wonder. "It's a common dream."

"No. I never have such dream."

Christmas has passed, and New Year's. The tent has folded up and moved north to Bilbao, where it will await the Cirque on its return from London. But Olga and Arthur are still in Madrid. Her surgery had been scheduled weeks ago but the Cirque had been unable to get her a visa on time.

"This is why I hate to put my life in other people's hands," she complains. "If I know this was going to happen I would have surgery in Spain! All this time and I doing nothing."

I don't understand the delay. "But the Cirque's a Canadian company," I point out. "I would think Canada would grant you a visa immediately."

"But one question on the form was not answered correctly," she replies. "You know the questions, 'What countries have you traveled in the last five years?'" And she laughs.

But she hasn't exactly been idle. One afternoon she had happened to see a family of performers in one of the public squares. Street entertainers, not unlike the sort of people who had started the Cirque du Soleil on the streets of Quebec. Except this was a family.

"They has seven kids!" Olga says. "Can you believe? They from England and they come to Spain because they want their kids in circus school. They want them learn trapeze."

"You're kidding!"

And I think it's another one of her elaborate jokes. But the next time we speak she talks about them again, and Arthur confirms their existence.

"They live in a caravan," she says. "It parked outside our hotel. Can you believe? Nine people in a caravan!"

She's been teaching the children trapeze in the Retiro Park. "Not a real trapeze, you understand? But we put a swing over a tree every day and I give them lessons."

"In the middle of the park?"

"Yes, why not? Mark, you should have seen... We go to store to buy swing, the father and me. And he puts all his coins out to pay! It take his last coin to buy trapeze! And today I let the girl—she twelve—take shower in my room. Because you know they don't have shower in caravan. And after she hides under my chair and doesn't want leave. You know what she say? She say if she didn't have parents she want live with me!"

I realize this is more than a diversion for Olga, but a true labor of love. The children's gratitude is part of it. But I think the real reason she's expending such an effort on an impecunious family of nine is captured in something she tells me one night.

"Circus is family," she says. "Do you understand? Every circus begins with a family." And I realize how, perhaps in the twilight of her own career, encountering this family of true believers has made her nostalgic for her youthful journey to the circus. For it's the children she talks about at length, the children she identifies with.

"The oldest girl, she only has one arm! Can you believe? But she in act. They all in act. They do real show in street, thirty minutes! Acrobatics, everything. Mark, you should write about this family!"

I try to imagine Olga giving trapeze lessons in the park. Do these people realize how fortunate they are? But to listen to Olga you would think she were the beneficiary of their generosity.

"I been teaching the two youngest kids, a boy and girl. They have some talent. But Mark, they so hungry to learn. I teach them every day. Two, three hours. Even in the rain. They never complain. You know when I teach in Australia I never have students like these!"

Incredibly, there's even a *Saltimbanco* connection. It turns out the father had once worked for the show, not as a performer but in some other capacity.

"And that's when the girl with one arm lost arm!" Olga exclaims. "They were in Vienna. And you know the boy Max, in Adagio? Well, then there was another family. And she was friends with boy. And one day they playing by railroad and she climbs fence, but this fence have electricity and she touch and fall!"

"How terrible!"

"But she beautiful girl! Never complain. She can do everything with one arm. They want go to America and get her arm. Not real arm, you understand? Father tell me someone help them go to America and she get arm and they work in hospitals, traveling from one hospital to next doing show."

"That's a great idea."

"For Christmas Cirque give everyone in show CD of *Varekai*. And this boy who friends with girl, he grown now and in *Varekai*. I give my CD to family and girl look at pictures and say, 'That's Anthony!'"

I wonder if this family, or even Olga herself, realizes the literal meaning of "saltimbanc"—from old Italian: an itinerant street performer.

One afternoon I get a call at work. Our assistant is out, so I answer the phone myself.

"Dr. Schreiber's office. Mark speaking."

And I hear laughter, pure laughter.

"You so funny!"

And she laughs some more.

"Are you busy?" she finally asks.

"I'm never too busy for you."

"Good. Because I want you do me favor. You know this family I tell you about?"

"You mean the same family you talk about every time I call you?"

"Yep. Well they ask me to write letter. You understand? I go soon and they have letter from me. But I not so good writing. And you so good..."

"What do you want to say?"

"I don't know."

"Well what's it for?"

"I not sure."

"I mean, do they want a letter of reference for their kids to get into circus school, or to show prospective employers, or the U.S. Consulate?"

"Yes. But they have no address. They live in caravan. So can you e-mail me today and I give them?"

Olga finally has her visa and I talk to her one last time before she and Arthur leave for Montreal and I go to London, where she has been kind enough to make arrangements for me.

I would have been happy to pay for a room, but Olga insisted on asking the performers with spare rooms if I could stay there. "Alya not sure," she says. "And Sandra and Sam, it's not possible. But twins' father say you can stay with them. They not in hotel. Families stay in apartments. I think you be very happy there."

How could I not be? I had been concerned about my reception in

London without Olga to break down doors for me. But now I can't wait. Teenage twin trapezists. Does life get any more exotic than that?

Before we go I ask if she's seen the *Fire Within*. It's a Cirque documentary about the making of *Varekai* and they've just started showing it here on the Bravo channel. In fact Olga has seen part of the documentary on video. "I was training in Montreal when they was doing this," she tells me. "One day I was on trapeze and they want film me, but I tell them go away!"

Who else in Olga's position would devote weeks of her time to training a family of street performers, even letting them use her bathroom and choreographing their act? Who else, newly arrived at Cirque headquarters for her own training, would refuse to be included in a prestigious documentary that will be seen by millions?

The Mother Theresa and Greta Garbo of the aerial world.

I can no longer say I'm surprised.

THE BOLSHOI CIRCUS

After graduating from the Moscow Circus School, Olga's travels began in earnest. The journey from Siberia to Moscow might have been, as Olga puts it, like going from the earth to the moon. But she still had never flown on a plane. In the years following her graduation, however, her voice and image would become indelibly stamped in the memories of customs' officials across the globe. She would travel with her trapeze packed in a large wooden crate. During her first trip to Australia she would check in with an expired passport. And she couldn't understand why it wasn't possible to take a desktop computer as a carry-on item.

Olga's professional career would take her to Belgium, England, Germany, Italy, the Persian Gulf, the island of Mauritius, Australia, Canada, and back to Europe, with holidays in Florida and Siberia. Her mother was a geography teacher, and Olga would send letters describing the cultures of the countries she toured. How could Mrs. Sidorova have imagined that one day Olga would visit many of the distant places she taught her daughter about in class?

But the truth was Olga didn't really care where she was. She didn't prefer Italy to Germany or England to Spain. Rainy days were the same as sunny ones, historic capitals no more interesting than provincial resorts. All that mattered was the feeling of flight and the caliber of her performance. And neither the applause she received nor the money she earned nor the glamour of seeing the world relieved her inner turmoil.

She had not wanted to graduate. She was content training with her coach. She felt they were a team and aspired only to create something magical together. When people came to watch them, students and coaches from the circus or visitors, she felt the impertinence of their gaze, as though they might rob her of her freedom, bring her back to earth. And her coach, too, surprisingly, never pushed her to perform and compete. He knew what it was to pursue a passion for its own rewards.

But she couldn't stay in school forever, so she perfected an act for final exams. She received first prize in all the school and was profiled on state television. A doyen of the circus proclaimed that everyone would know her one day, that Olga had no rival on trapeze, that she represented the future.

Most graduates work their way up, often beginning their professional careers in provincial circuses. But Olga received numerous offers from all over the world and the Bolshoi Circus promised to start her at the highest pay scale. She accepted, but turned down an invitation to the prestigious circus arts festival in Monte Carlo.

"I don't need compliments," she would explain. "I don't care about being best or winning medals. For me it's not about being good, but just to be there!"

The trapeze coach for the Cirque du Soleil, who had also worked at the Moscow Circus School, would one day tell Olga, "You're a different person when you're up!"

"The trapeze is like the cosmos," Olga would agree. "I go somewhere and come back. And when I on ground again I like ghost."

For her first few months with the Bolshoi Circus she was happy. She traveled within Russia and her coach came with her. But then the troupe was sent to Belgium and she felt cut adrift. The awards and praise meant nothing to her. She felt inadequate and ashamed. She began to fall. She phoned her coach every day. "I no good for trapeze!"

And then one night in Brussels she fell and kept falling. Her assistant didn't pull on the safety in time and she hit the stage. Not full force. But enough to tear the ligaments in her knee. Somehow she managed to go back up and finish the act, although the pain was unbearable and she couldn't put any pressure on her right foot. Afterwards she crawled from the stage like a lizard.

She wasn't taken to a hospital but simply given injections to relieve the pain and swelling. Incredibly, she continued to perform. She cut half her tricks and received more cortisone. Only after the run was over did she return to Moscow for surgery.

Her professional career had only just begun and now it seemed over. But her coach wouldn't let her give up. "We will start again training!" he said. And she returned to circus school.

She also enrolled in Moscow University and took courses in stage production. By the time her knee had healed she was prepared both mentally and physically to return abroad.

A Latvian gynecologist now living in Mauritius wanted to bring a circus to the island and she asked Olga to be the first person ever to perform trapeze in this Indian Ocean paradise. For four months she performed three shows a day in a tent used for weddings. It was more primitive than the circus school in Tyumen but she felt liberated and confident because the show had energy and the natives, who had never seen trapeze, were enthusiastic. "The Indian people touch me like I'm something gold," she would reminisce.

LONDON

I come to London without expectations. True, I'm supposed to be staying with trapeze twins, but there's a father as well, a Ukrainian father. A stern taskmaster perhaps, a Karamazov, with doppelgangers in tow. Breakfast might be a scene out of Dostoevsky, with porridge and curses flying and I, the intruder, the object of every superstition. I don't know the living arrangements, but what if I share a room with the father and the walls are thin and I can't sleep due to jet-lag and have to muffle my coughs for fear of waking the trapezists? Maybe intimacy, in this case, is the worst part of valor, and all of us would be better served had I reserved a room at the Victoria Park Plaza.

But these concerns take a back seat to my astonishment that this man is allowing me to stay with them, and that the daughters have consented, for while it was probably not their decision, I'm sure if they objected the father would have declined. I doubt that I would host a stranger were I in his position, his daughters still new to the Cirque, performing in a strange city under the intense scrutiny of the British media. What lies did Olga tell him about me?

In truth I'm touched almost to tears by this act of kindness and faith, and only hope I don't get in the way. Olga had warned me not to try for too much on this trip. But it's a little late in the day for that advice. I won't be able to watch the show backstage because of limited space. There will be no artistic tent in the Royal Albert Hall, just dressing rooms, a small green room and a commissary. I might not be allowed backstage at all because the Royal Albert has its own security staff. As for tickets, Olga tells me last minute seats aren't available and she tries to order me an advance ticket through the Amsterdam office, but still hasn't received a confirmation number by the time I leave for London.

Not that it really matters. Sure, I'd like to see the show in the Royal Albert Hall, and watch the twins perform. But that isn't essential. What's more important is to renew acquaintances and perhaps make new ones. To say goodbye to some, who are leaving the show after London: Marie-Claude, Sandra and Sam, Sue Daly. And who knows if I will return?

But what excites me most is the unexpected opportunity to live with a circus family. When I first decided to write this book the Vintilovs were among those artists I wished most to meet. And I was fortunate to get to know Igor Issakov and his daughter. But I hadn't observed a family at home, on a daily basis. And now Olga and Vitaliy Bazaliy were giving me this great chance. I recalled what Olga told me when relating her adventures with the street performers in Madrid: all circuses begin with family.

Of course it's also exciting to be in London. Not only is London much larger than the other cities on the schedule, and the Royal Albert Hall nearly twice the size of the Grand Chapiteau, but the West End, along with Broadway, is the heart of the theater world. The Cirque hasn't stopped here in three years, when *Alegría* played the Royal Albert, and despite the competition from hit musicals and plays, the evening performances of *Saltimbanco* will nearly all sell out and, as I would personally discover, even the standing room gallery would be full.

But first I have to get off the train that takes me from Gatwick Airport to Victoria Station. It's called the Gatwick Express but the doors take a long time to open. I look for a button to push, a handle, a lever. For once I'm in a country where English is the native language and I can't open the damn train door! Then a man behind me pushes down the window, reaches out and pulls the handle on the outside of the carriage.

"It's archaic, I know," he says apologetically.

I don't have a key or a phone number, just an address to hand the taxi driver. Mr. Bazaliy had the phone disconnected because it cost too much, but Olga sent him an e-mail telling him when I was arriving.

They live in a serene corner of Westminster, just a block from the cricket grounds of the famous school of the same name, in a six floor building of furnished luxury flats. I ring the bell and true to Olga's word he answers. He can't buzz me in, so I wait for him to come down.

He's a slight man with gaunt, youthful features, who might have once been a gymnast or acrobat himself. His smile is affable and demure and he welcomes me in halting English as though we were old friends.

Their flat is the sixth floor penthouse, and you need a key to reach it by elevator. But for some reason his key doesn't work, so we get off at the fifth floor and take the stairs. There his key does work to let us into the corridor and to open the door, directly across from the elevator.

I've never seen anything like this place in England—except in Hugh Grant movies. Frighteningly large for central London, bright, modern, with hardwood floors, soundproof windows, central heating, three bedrooms, three bathrooms, a dishwasher in the spacious kitchen, satellite TV, gleaming chrome and glass tables.

But my favorite feature is the wrap-around balcony, and Vitaliy takes me out to admire the view. From the living room we can see the spire of Westminster Abbey and the Eye, the Millennium Ferris wheel that won't revolve once during my entire stay. From the bedroom we can see the yellow brick tower of Westminster Cathedral rising gracefully beyond the cricket field. I don't see any pedestrians and only one or two cars passing through the straight, narrow streets. It's ten o'clock on a Friday morning in January and I feel as though I'm in the English countryside.

I imagine I'll be spending a lot of time on the balcony, but the weather will turn colder, it will rain from one day to another, the wind will howl, and the balcony door will remain locked for the remainder of my stay.

Vitaliy proudly shows me the satellite TV. He likes to watch the Indian music video channel. He shows me the two controls, one for the television, one for the satellite, and which buttons to press for each. Then he carries my bag down the hall, past the two closed doors where the twins have their rooms, and sets it in the master bedroom.

I protest vaguely. "*Nyet, nyet...*"

But he assures me in broken English that he likes to sleep on the blue fabric sofa in the living room, serenaded by Indian dancing girls.

He opens another door in the hallway and points to a switch on the wall by the water heater. It seems the central heating is a kind of myth.

The bedrooms in fact have radiators and this switch is an hour timer, but it has a habit of not resetting after midnight, so despite the staggering sum this penthouse must cost to rent, I'll have to dress as warmly for bed as though I were staying in a Pimlico bed and breakfast.

We end up in the kitchen, where I learn his great hobby is cooking. He points to a jar of sour cabbage. "Try! Try!"

Then he tells me he's making *plov*. Have I ever eaten *plov*? It's a Ukrainian dish made with marinated beef, rice, tomato sauce, onion and garlic. The pot he's making will last all week. He stirs the meat in, lets it simmer while we talk, and then leaves it on the stove to marinate. In the meantime he offers to make me tea, sweetened with real Ukrainian honey. He doesn't drink alcohol except for red wine, a glass of which he'll have for breakfast.

Vitaliy is what my father calls a "process person." Motives, goals, agendas aren't important to him. None of this—"Who are you? What are you doing here? These are the house rules..."

Instead he points to the sour cabbage and says, "Try!" as though the reason I enthusiastically crossed the Atlantic and the reason he intrepidly agreed to host me was so that I might explore the pungent subtleties of Ukrainian cuisine.

It isn't even noon and I feel we're old friends.

I've kept my voice down because I assume the twins are still sleeping. Their doors are closed. But Vitaliy makes a lot of noise in the kitchen. I ask what time they have to be at the show.

"They're already at show."

It turns out they have to go to school for a couple hours six days a week. Not a normal school, of course, but an improvised school taught on-site by a tutor. So instead of being able to sleep until noon on a matinee day and have most of the afternoon free on days when they only have one show, a car comes for them at ten o'clock, and they spend twelve hours at the Cirque.

This explains why they are so tired when they come home just before midnight. They're both wearing their Cirque jackets and flash identical smiles. I was looking forward to talking to them, but they excuse themselves and instead I follow Vitaliy into the kitchen.

"They have homework," he says with a shrug.

"Homework!" Isn't performing two shows on trapeze enough?

However one of the twins soon appears in the kitchen—Ruslana, and says she can talk for a few minutes while waiting for her sister to get out of the shower. She's wearing loose clothing which hides her muscular physique. My eyes are drawn to her feet, because they hang from each other's bare feet, both in the fixed routine and while swinging.

"Who hangs from whom?" I ask, not having yet seen them perform, but recalling the Canadian twins I had watched seven years ago in Amsterdam.

"Usually Tais hangs from me, but sometimes we change."

She stands by the wall while her father prepares more *plov* at the stove. I thought I would just be able to say a few words to her, but she talks to me for twenty minutes, and Vitaliy shows unusual respect in a parent by not interrupting.

Her English is excellent, and she explains that when the Cirque brought them to Canada their school lessons consisted solely of English for the first few months.

She had been a gymnast prior to joining the Cirque and had participated in competitions in the Ukraine, but not before large audiences. I ask her how all these people watching her now, especially in the cavernous Royal Albert Hall, affects her.

She shrugs. "It's not a problem. I'm not nervous," she replies, as though she has been performing as long as Olga. "It was harder in Montreal when we gave a demonstration for the top people."

"For Laliberté?"

"No, he wasn't there."

"Did it go well?"

"Yes, it was fine."

"Did you have any problems adjusting from gymnastics to trapeze? To the height, for instance?"

"No."

Her unwavering smile belies a critical cast of mind. She calls her home town of 500,000 a village, which draws her father's protests. She's evasive when I ask if she had Olympic potential as a gymnast. She likes *Saltimbanco*, but was less impressed with *Dralion*, which the Cirque flew her and her sister to Dallas to see while they were in training so they could gain an appreciation for a live show. And here in London she walked out on a musical because the dancers bent their legs when they kicked. She found Disneyland Paris boring. She wasn't overwhelmed meeting the King of Spain in Madrid, and when I ask about British celebrities she tells me, as if it were a matter of complete indifference to her, that Madonna and Sting were supposed to attend but canceled.

"And what do you think about Olga?" I finally ask.

Her smile widens into a grin and finally she has something positive to say. "I like Olga. She's crazy!"

Being called crazy by a fellow trapezist is no small accomplishment. "So trapezists are not all the same?"

"I think there is no one like Olga!" she declares.

The twins may be the quietest teenagers this side of Tibet. No loud music, no yelling, no running down the hall. I thought teenagers were hard to wake up on a Saturday morning, but I don't even hear their alarm. They don't eat breakfast and I find them already standing in the foyer, wearing their Cirque jackets, slipping on their shoes.

"Bye!" one of them says.

I eat *plov* with Vitaliy while Indian dancers gyrate on Channel 286. We have a panoramic view from the balcony but the sky is unremarkably gray and the narrow streets below eerily quiet. Andrei, the son of the Russian family with whom the twins lived during their training in Montreal, is supposed to arrive today from Paris, where he is now studying. But after a while Vitaliy says we should leave. He too has a contract with the Cirque and even receives a small stipend as guardian. His responsibilities include being present on the site during the show.

I go to the Victoria Park Plaza to drop off the new profiles I've written with the concierge and to see if anyone's around. I spot Jesko sitting in the cafe with someone from Marketing. If I had any doubts as to the welcome I would receive in London sans Olga, he quells them with startling vociferousness for a mime.

"Fucking amazing!" he shouts, leaping from his chair. "I was just thinking about you! This is so weird! I was just this very moment thinking about you!"

It turns out there was a problem with his e-mail and he never received the profile, or my note that I was coming to London. I tell him I left his profile with the concierge.

"I'll read it tonight!" he promises—or threatens.

I ask him how he likes the Royal Albert.

"I'm still getting used to it," he admits. "How long have we been here? One week? The space is so big it's hard to project, and there are technical adjustments. I can't use all the aisles, for instance. It's a dream to play there, of course. But it's not as well suited for the show."

The conversation eventually turns to Thailand, where he plans to travel after London for a yoga retreat. And he talks with relish about the strict diet he'll follow to replenish his body. No meat, no sugar, no alcohol, no caffeine, vegetable enemas.

"Your body reaches such a state of harmony, you never want to eat fast food again," he proclaims with an earnestness that nearly convinces me to give up chocolate. But then he pauses and the closest thing I'll see to a grin escapes from his lips. "However the other day I was really craving a steak!"

I attend the show that evening. It's sold out, but Vitaliy has given me an all-areas pass. I can't watch backstage because of limited space, but the Royal Albert has a standing room gallery one flight above the cheap seats. However first I have to get inside, and none of the ticket takers wants to let me through. I'm told to go to Gate 6, then to Gate 4, and I finally wind up at the backstage entrance. While there a woman with her face made up for Chinese Poles steps out. It's Sandra. She recognizes me before I recognize her and gives me a big hug. She asks me how I'm doing and when I got in and how long I'm staying. It's thirty minutes before curtain and she's chatting with me! Maybe I should work harder on my juggling and run away to a circus. I've never been so well greeted in publishing.

The Royal Albert Hall was built in 1871 at the request of Queen Victoria's husband, Prince Albert. A round structure of red brick and terra cotta it accommodates up to eight thousand, depending on the configuration. The curved corridors are lined with photos of past events, from Royal galas to rock concerts. Even tennis tournaments are held here.

One commercial advantage of the Royal Albert is the space available for advertisements. There are no advertisements plastered in the Grand Chapiteau, but here the gates are filled with the sponsor's posters, featuring the twins in a mirrored pose from their fixed routine. And a movie screen sized banner hangs above the grand staircase. It's very impressive, but neither they nor their father seems affected by their larger-than-life debut in the London theater world. The girls would say the picture is not so good and the father merely smile, as though embarrassed.

The top tier originally served as a picture gallery and consists merely of a tiled floor and iron railing. But due to renovations, only the right side is open. The standing crowd is young, casually dressed, and enthusiastic. There are even a few children. I squeeze against a pillar and peer down.

When the show begins I feel as though I'm watching from a balloon. Despite its energy and ambition, *Saltimbanco* was created for an intimate space, and even though the Grand Chapiteau seats 2,500, the last row is still within plain view of the stage. The Royal Albert not only seats twice that number, but the galleries are much higher and the ceiling dwarfs the rigging.

Nevertheless, I watch with great interest, as the Royal Albert presents a unique opportunity to look down on the aerial acts. I've always gazed up as Wang ascends to the double wire, but tonight for the first time I can see the small platform that serves as her base. There's a compartment to stash her umbrella, and when she makes her exit, by sliding down a third wire stretched from the platform to the edge of the stage, I observe that she first places a short guide over the wire and stands on this rather than on the wire itself.

The twins had performed the matinee, so aren't on the schedule tonight. Instead I watch a Canadian trapezist, the same woman whom Olga had replaced. It's disconcerting to hear Olga's music but see a much taller woman emerge onstage. Her act, however, is completely different. As she finishes her fixed routine and begins to swing I reflect on the strange fact that after all these months I am still here with the Cirque, that Olga is the one who is gone.

Afterwards I go backstage. The Royal Albert may be glamorous, but the backstage areas are dingy and cramped, with a conspicuous absence of the red velvet so prominent above. One might be forgiven for thinking he's in the bowels of a hospital or school rather than an entertainment palace. There are too many corridors and doors. I don't even know in which direction the stage lies. How different from the large communal space of the artistic tent. The Royal Albert may have a grand dome, but the backstage area is a basement, the ceiling of which is probably too low for Masha to practice her juggling.

The rack of masks sits in the corridor, outside the modest green room. I peek inside and see Vitaliy sitting by one of the two computers. He smiles and shows me to the commissary. The performers are still changing, so I take a seat at one of the round tables and wait.

Marian is one of the first to come in and greets me warmly, asking if I want anything to eat. He brings me an orange juice and we talk for a few minutes, as the tables begin to fill up. I then chat with Igor Issakov and Elena Grosheva and say hello to the Vintilovs. Oxana gives me a hug and I ask about Dasha, who has just gone to Montreal to train for trapeze. But Max is still here and she introduces me. I've never actually talked to him and he shakes my hand with a wide grin.

Vitaliy then asks if I want a backstage tour, and he shows me the famous organ with its ten thousand pipes and leads me to the stage. I'm reluctant to walk out, but he encourages me, so I step onto center stage and gaze up at the curved tiers, my eyes coming to rest on the pillar in the standing gallery where I had stood an hour before.

Vitaliy then shows me the alcoves where the equipment is stashed. He tells me to touch the aluminum Chinese poles. They're warm and extremely tacky. He asks me to climb on the Russian swing for a photo. Then he points out Masha's juggling platform. I can imagine her wrath if I so much as leaned against it and wisely keep my distance.

Back in the green room he introduces me to Andrei, the son of the twins' hosts in Montreal. He was formerly the Canadian junior chess champion but has given up the game to study engineering in Paris. I find him surprisingly personable for a prodigy and I talk more to him than to the twins as we walk past a white stretch limo to the bus stop.

I wonder if Paul McCartney and Bob Dylan and the Who took the bus after performing here. Masha walks with us, laughing with the twins. Earlier in the year she had taken Dasha under her wing, and now that Dasha is gone she has befriended the Bazaliys.

We ride atop a double decker to Victoria Station and then walk a mile to the penthouse. I don't think the twins are even aware of the contradictions inherent in their life in London. Walking past posters with their image on them without once being recognized, taking public transportation to a Westminster penthouse. On the contrary, rather than being spoiled by fame and luxury they seem to relish simple pleasures. I had offered to hire a taxi, but when I see them scurry to the front of the bus's top deck I realize the limitations of convenience.

The girls go to Taisiya's room and I peek inside. I am struck by how spartan it is. A stuffed animal, a single photo on the dresser, nothing on the walls. How different from the other performers and crew, who personalize their rooms with mementos and photographs. Except for Olga, I realize, who keeps her past in drawers.

They're all sitting on the bed, looking at photos from Spain. I stand by the dresser, reluctant to intrude. But after a moment Taisiya asks if I want to see the pictures. I'm struck by one of Olga standing between the twins onstage. They're not in makeup and Olga actually appears tall between them. The twins flash their characteristic smile and Olga beams radiantly. I ask if I can borrow it to make a copy.

Masha is flipping an empty soda bottle in her left hand. Earlier, on the bus, I had noticed her flipping a coin.

"I want you to know you've inspired me to juggle," I tell her during a pause in the conversation.

She couldn't care less, but Taisiya asks how many balls I can juggle. "Three?"

"Four," I tell her.

"Four!"

She seems impressed, but Masha doesn't even look at me. I had thought after our long talk in Vienna we might become friends, but she has since retreated to a polite reserve.

"I want to juggle five," I then say, trying to temper my ambition with modesty. "How long does it take to learn?"

"I'm still learning five," Masha confesses without any trace of irony.

The twins are staying with Masha at the hotel this weekend and I walk back with them, hoping to see James Clowney, who earlier had offered to go out for a drink. But he's not among the Cirque people in the lobby or cafe.

Jesko tells me he liked the chapter but wanders off when Sandra approaches. "You were with women, I didn't want to bother you," he would later say.

I talk to Sandra and Alya, but Sandra excuses herself because Sam is sick. Alya and I sit on one of the couches in the lobby and talk for almost an hour.

She and Nico are planning to go to Oxford tomorrow after the second show with Sandra and Sam, but Sam is the only one who knows how to drive on the left side of the road and Alya doubts he will recover in time. More importantly, Sandra and Sam are leaving the show after London, and Alya will miss them dearly.

I myself had sensed a more serious, anxious mood among the cast than in the other cities and Alya confirms my suspicions. "It's the end of the contract year, people are tired," she says. "And friends are leaving. It's sad. And I don't know what it's going to be like in Bilbao with so many new people. It's hardest for the troupe, we work so closely together, we get used to each other. And the weather's bad. People are sick. And we can't practice and warm up as usual because we don't have the tent."

Then she asks about Olga. Everyone has asked me about Olga. It's a measure of how far I've come that I know her better than they do, and I realize that despite the friends Olga's made here, I might form the only lasting link between her past in *Saltimbanco* and her undecided future.

And I think about my own links to the show. Alya, like Jesko, had been on the perimeter of my radar when I first began following the Cirque. I hadn't spoken to her at all in Amsterdam or Barcelona. But, as with Jesko, we were now becoming friends. And I found our conversation tonight particularly poignant. For while I had talked to her alone and at length in Brussels, that was for the book. Tonight she was talking to me as a friend. I never imagined I would form such bonds with the cast, and yet just as I was beginning to achieve genuine intimacy, I was approaching the end of my own road. I couldn't follow the show forever.

London might be my last city. I reflect that one of the reasons circus life is so insular is that the grueling schedule and continual travel make it extremely difficult to maintain ties with those not traveling the same road. True, there was the telephone, and e-mail, but Olga hadn't contacted any of her friends since parting in Madrid and I doubt anyone from the show had written her. There's a psychological tent as protective and opaque as the Grand Chapiteau. And Alya and Nico may be best friends with Sandra and Sam. And they might have trained and worked together for years. But in a couple weeks Sandra and Sam will bow out from *Saltimbanco*, and how will their friendship endure? They might send postcards and e-mails and even visit each other if their paths veer near enough. But for how long?

Friendship is no less a discipline than fitness or juggling. As Olga says about gymnastics in her video, "You has to practice every day, every day, every day!"

I find it ironic that after following the Cirque for almost a year, the first sustained words I hear about fear relate not to trapeze or bungee or the high wire but to chess!

"For Bobby Fisher, the hardest move was always the first," Andrei tells me late the following night as we drink tea in the Bazaliy's living room. The girls are again staying at the hotel with Masha. Vitaliy sits on the sofa watching Indian music videos.

"Fisher was terrified to sit down at the board. Imagine, he had only lost a handful of times in his entire professional career. So the pressure he faced every time he played was enormous."

And he tells me how the greatest players, the masters and grandmasters, are haunted by ghosts—by phantom bishops and rooks crossing in their minds. But these are ghosts not of the past but of the future, and the best players, even though they look three or more moves ahead, can be terrified almost to paralysis by an overlooked pawn or a knight unaccounted for.

"Many grandmasters go mad or quit playing," he tells me. "Haunted by these ghosts."

Olga would later tell me she never feels afraid on the trapeze and dislikes performers who make the audience uncomfortable by focusing on the danger of their act. The twins appear to share her attitude and play down the risks of their new career. I realize I've never seen a chess grandmaster smile as exuberantly as they do. Perhaps Ruslana was wise, when she lived in Montreal, to refuse Andrei's offer to teach her chess.

Vitaliy also has an unexpected perspective on risk and fear, which I discover over breakfast Monday morning. It's their day off, but the twins are spending it with Masha.

"Do you like Masha's act?" I ask him, since she and his daughters have become good friends.

I haven't yet perceived any trace of concern in Vitaliy's conversation or demeanor. He trusts his daughters and their trainers. He doesn't analyze their performance as so many parents do. He watches, or doesn't watch, their act with apparent equanimity. Only now in response to my question about Masha do I observe tension in his features.

"Oh, I think she's very good," he answers. "But it makes me nervous to watch her."

I can't believe what I'm hearing. The father of two young trapezists can't bear to watch a woman throw a few balls in the air from a platform only four steps high?

"My daughters wear a safety," he continues after I beg him to explain. "But in juggling—the balls are so close! It's so easy to make a mistake!"

I want to point out that when a juggler makes a mistake it's the balls that fall, but when a trapezist makes a mistake, it's the trapezist who falls.

Later that day I take him to the Tate Gallery, which is just a few blocks from the penthouse. I had escorted Olga's sister to the museums in Vienna, why shouldn't I do the same for the twins' father? Maybe I could write a book about accompanying the relatives of circus performers to the world's great art museums. Vitaliy certainly shares Tatiana's thirst for culture and has already visited the National Gallery and the British Museum. We linger at the Tate until closing, Vitaliy most impressed by the iconic paintings and the gallery devoted to Biblical etchings by the poet William Blake.

On Tuesday there's no matinee, so Vitaliy doesn't have to be at the

Royal Albert until six. So we go to the Tower of London and spend four hours walking in a suitable downpour between the ancient buildings. I'm beginning to feel useful playing the role of tour guide. Vitaliy hadn't even heard of the Tate Museum or the Tower of London. I'll take him across the Tower Bridge as well. But first he asks if he can go back and look at the jewels again. I seek the Royal Cafeteria.

Olga delivers on her promise of tickets and I find myself that night craning my neck to glimpse the standing gallery where I had watched the show on Friday. I'm sitting far below, in the eighth row, center aisle, and when I lower my gaze I notice a young man with teen idol looks sitting directly behind me. In fact he is a teen idol, and I even recognize his blond girlfriend from newspaper photos I had seen the day before.

At intermission a woman scurries along my row with an outstretched *Saltimbanco* program. "Gareth! Gareth, could you please sign?"

A minute later Gareth and his girlfriend are hedged in by autograph seekers. I'm tempted to ask for *her* autograph. It must be unsettling to be a pretty girl all dressed up, surrounded by aggressive males all staring at your boyfriend. Yes, the men outnumber the women here. Not a teen in sight, crushed out by the scrum of middle-aged managers in dark suits assaulting him from the box seats, sacrificing their staid dignity for the chance to win the approbation of their daughters.

When they finally clear away I'm tempted to flash my all-areas pass and offer to take him backstage to meet the artists. "I'm with the band."

But now comes the moment I've waited for. The twins. I haven't seen Duo Trapeze since the first time I attended *Saltimbanco*, seven years ago.

The music is different from Olga's, more upbeat and energetic. The twins are carried onstage and climb to the trapeze on parallel ropes. I don't recall the fixed routine at all, but Ruslana will later tell me they changed the choreography. She will also be surprised when I describe the fixed routine as very fast. She thinks the fixed is slow. In any case, it's entrancing, as they mirror each other on the bar and then take up opposite positions, with one standing and the other hanging. Their timing is impeccable. One can see why the Cirque wanted twins.

Then they begin to swing. And this part I do remember, as one drops to the bar on her hands, then holds the other by her waist and, most dramatically, slides down and locks her bare feet to her sister's.

The audience gasps and applauds. Say what you want about juggling balls and chessboards, few sights are more thrilling than that of a human being hanging precariously from a height—upside down.

I hadn't planned to see the show again, but on the walk home Ruslana—or Taisiya?—asks if I want a ticket for tomorrow afternoon. Second row. They won't be performing, but still, how can I refuse?

After the matinee I go backstage and compliment the solo trapezist on her performance. She's not as demonstrative as Olga in her reaction to praise, but equally dismissive.

"Oh, I don't know," she says with a smile, standing by the coffee machine. "There were problems."

Somehow she knows who I am and asks about the book. "I'd like to read it," she says, still smiling.

I offer to include her, but she declines. "But I'd like to read it," she repeats.

I sit down at a table with Sue Daly, whom I hadn't had a chance to talk to yet, and Sandra, who has caught her husband's cold. I had always wanted to know how they manage to perform when ill. Olga was no help at all, telling me she never got sick. Now here's my chance.

"It's not fun," she replies with a wearied look. "But you gotta do it."

"You did Bungee too?" I ask incredulously.

"Not Bungee," she says with a weak laugh. "I would have barfed for sure!"

I hadn't asked for autographs since that first night when Olga signed Vika's program. But on my last day I decide to ask the twins to sign for my brother, who collects autographs. Vitaliy offers to take the program to the show and get everyone to sign. I object, but he insists, and when he returns that night he hands me a touching keepsake of my year with the Cirque. Everyone has signed.

"It was great seeing you again. Good luck on the book," from James Clowney. "Good luck for your book!" from Marie-Claude. "Fly high!" from Sandra. "Good luck with your book!" from Alya. "Dearest Mark, I wish you well with your book," from Sue Daly. Oxana drew a stick figure

Adagio and wrote, "With love and all the best for good memory from the Vintilov family." Jesko wrote all around the perimeter of his page. "...I look forward to getting a hard copy of your book when you are published and enjoyed your interest in our work and our conversations..." And on Olga's page: "Hi Mark, I'll write on Olga's page—but I am not her. I am solo trapeze though. I heard you are writing a book about it. I would love to read it some time. Good luck. Anna."

The following morning I'm on my way to Hamburg to visit a writer friend. Vitaliy insists on accompanying me to the station, where I'll catch the express train to Heathrow. I don't know when I'll be back, or if I'll be back. Not to London, but to *Saltimbanco*, which will return to Spain for a run in Bilbao, then Geneva, Cologne, Oostende in Belgium, Zurich. But so many of the people I've met on this journey have left the show themselves, including of course Olga, and Vitaliy may trade places with his wife before year's end. But whatever happens, I hope it's not the last time we meet.

He gives me a strong hug. "Thank you for everything!" he says.

AUSTRALIA

After finishing the Moscow Circus School, Olga was offered a contract with the Royal Australian Circus. She turned the offer down, as she rejected most offers, without giving it serious consideration. She didn't even look at a map. Australia was so far away. Why would she want to go there?

But after England she was ready for a change of climate. Cultural more than physical. She was tired of the Russian mentality, the circus tent claustrophobia, the self-aggrandizement and unrelenting competition. Of course, with the paradoxical ambivalence that characterized most of Olga's actions, she would seek out Russians in Brisbane and Melbourne. But that was later.

Although she was now a cosmopolitan woman of twenty-four, she knew almost nothing about Australia. The world's smallest continent had not been among the exotic lands studied in her mother's geography class. Much as we might think of Siberia as a frozen wasteland, so Olga thought of Australia as a desert wasteland crawling with crocodiles and surrounded by sharks. It might seem odd that a young girl who had journeyed from Ishim to Moscow with no thought for her personal safety should be frightened by a place called the "Gold Coast." Maybe it wasn't an oversight that she forgot her documents and only realized when checking in at Heathrow that her visa was in her new passport, and she had brought the old one. She rushed back to the circus. Like a gypsy battling consumerism, she was always leaving things behind. Trapezes, expensive rigging belts, costumes, clothes, passports.

Despite this inauspicious start, she would eventually come to view

Australia as home, even more than Russia. She would become involved with a native and finally learn English. And in Melbourne she would lead something resembling a settled life, with an apartment and a car and fixed place of employment.

But that was later.

First she came to Brisbane, on the Gold Coast, to perform solo trapeze in a variety show entitled *Inneurve* at the Conrad Jupiter, a 603 room casino resort. She was no longer a waif hitchhiking with a mangy dog but a star performer esteemed throughout the circus world, financially independent, accustomed to taxis and fine hotels. And yet when she came to Australia she came alone, without even a dog for companionship. She had left her boyfriend in Moscow, she had left her circus, all her friends and acquaintances. Even when she ran away to Tyumen she had not felt so vulnerable.

When the driver picked her up at the airport she cried in the car. Where I go? she wondered. Where people bring me?

Actually, to a sparkling resort hotel less than a mile from the beach. But Olga only saw dry land, the island of the stage, and with the single-minded devotion that marks so many in her profession, she literally threw herself into the trapeze.

After her first month Down Under someone mentioned going to the beach.

"Where?" Olga asked.

"Here."

"You have beach here? Why I never see?"

Olga's favorite leisure activity would become surfing, which she would learn from her boyfriend. Indeed, Olga was so adept at the sport that he grew jealous of her proficiency and turned in his own board for a set of golf clubs. Over the course of our friendship I never ceased to be fascinated by the allure of the trapeze for her. She didn't sky dive or hang glide or bungee jump. She had learned high wire in circus school but never spoke of it. She wasn't even interested in other forms of the trapeze, such as flying to a catcher. I realized she wasn't an exhibitionist. She didn't need to perform for attention or praise. And she wasn't drawn by the danger and thrill. She had always talked about wanting to fly. But I found her answer incomplete. The time between letting go of the bar and grabbing back on is only a breath or two. Surely there are other, less momentary, ways to fly?

"Yes," she finally said to me one night. "But not where you control. Bungee is wonderful, but you are tied to bungee cord. If you sky dive you have parachute. In trapeze, trapeze don't move. You have to make it move. And when you let go it is only the control over your body that keeps you from falling."

And when I asked her what activity most resembled those precious seconds in the air, which she had dreamed of since first seeing the circus as a girl of twelve, she answered, "Surfing."

It was in Australia that she first saw *Saltimbanco*. She had heard of Cirque du Soleil but had never seen it or even considered applying for a role in one of the shows. But when she saw *Saltimbanco* she knew she could perform in this show. Still, she didn't take action. She was under contract to the hotel. Even when the Cirque later offered her a place in *Saltimbanco* she declined due to pressure from her boyfriend, who didn't want her to leave Australia.

Had she gone she might have saved herself from the most desperate days of her life. After learning of her boyfriend's infidelity she fell into a state of shock. She drove without watching the road and crashed. Fortunately she was driving slow and no one was hurt. Of course, she was already hurt. She drove to Sydney and checked in to a hotel intent on killing herself.

How does a trapezist kill herself? She took a razor blade to her wrist but couldn't bring herself to apply pressure. She considered hanging herself, but in the end she fell asleep.

She returned to Brisbane and rented a U-haul trailer. She threw in her clothes, her costumes, her photographs and other mementos from her singular life, and most importantly her trapeze. She drove alone to Melbourne, where a coaching position had been offered to her at the National Institute of Circus Arts.

But she not only trained others, she trained herself as well. She sought out Russian gymnastics coaches in Melbourne because she wanted to combine gymnastics with trapeze. Suddenly the Russian mentality had its uses. Olga not only taught trapeze to students seeking degrees in the circus arts, but gymnastics to children, and she had no patience for the parents, who would ask her after six months when their girls would be ready for the Olympics. "In Russia this will never happen!" Olga would proudly tell me. "In Russia parents give their children to coaches. They will never ask, 'Is my child good?' 'Is my child for Olympics?'"

Nevertheless, she enjoyed coaching and developed good relationships with the administration. And in the evening after everyone had left, the studio was hers. With only a fellow coach or assistant in attendance to hold her safety, she worked far into the night perfecting her art. And when the casting director of Cirque du Soleil called again, she was ready.

MONTREAL

I call Arthur in Montreal the day of Olga's knee surgery.

"The surgery went fine, but she's in a lot of pain," Arthur says. "She was yelling at the nurses, yelling at me, screaming and crying. They keep giving her morphine."

I pause. "Do you think I should still come?"

"Oh yes, of course. "

Olga's home the next day when I call.

"Oh Mark, I in so much pain. I never been in such pain. I wonder what it like for someone who in accident or war who lose an arm or leg. I try tell myself I love my pain, but that doesn't work. Nothing works, not even morphine. But today I much better. Arrrtuuuuur!"

Two days later I arrive on a standby ticket. Montreal is cold and snow-covered, but the skies are blue. Olga's two-bedroom apartment, which the Cirque provides, is in the suburb of Fleury, in the northeast part of the city. Fortunately I had visited Montreal years ago because I won't see much of it now. The Cirque headquarters, the inside of taxis, narrow streets with plastic canopies over the driveways to keep out the snow, the neighborhood grocery and liquor store, a computer shop God knows where.

I arrive in the early afternoon. Olga is just waking up. She offers to make me breakfast. I tell her I didn't come here to watch her standing over a stove. But in fact she's doing remarkably well. Standing easily. Walking without a limp.

"What are those for?" I ask, pointing to the crutches propped in the corner.

"They for Arthur."

Olga pulls on a bright red one-piece ski suit over leotards and a printed shirt.

"People wear ski suits before the knee injury, not after," I tell her.

Arthur calls for a cab and we go to Cirque headquarters, a sprawling steel and glass complex built on landfill in the St. Michel district. The architecture is bright but severe, with hard surfaces, straight edges, towering ceilings, softened somewhat by photo galleries and life-sized costumed mannequins hanging overhead. A large trophy case graces the lobby across from the cafeteria. Beyond it lies the cozier weight and physiotherapy room.

This is where Olga is supposed to go, of course, but first she takes me on a tour. This is her first day back since surgery and everyone comes over to say hello. I stand aside but she introduces me to everyone.

"Mark, where are you? Come here! I want you meet...."

And this scene repeats continually throughout the day. One tall, well-dressed man with long hair speaks to her for a several minutes. Afterwards I ask her what he does and she says he's high in the organization. I ask about his position in relation to the artistic director, which is the top management job in a particular show.

"He higher than artistic director," Olga replies casually, and proceeds to give a warm hug to a secretary.

If I hadn't appreciated Olga's stature before, this afternoon would leave me in no doubt of her importance in the world of circus and Cirque du Soleil. Everyone is friendly, but deferential. One young woman who turns out to be an aerialist in another show nearly accosts her as we exit an elevator.

"Are you Olga Sidorova? I'm so happy to meet you! I saw you here last year. I'd love to talk to you sometime...."

Olga seems unconcerned by all the walking and only uses her crutches as a kind of decoration. She takes me to the building where they make the costumes. We can't go inside but have to peer through the window at racks of dresses and women hunched over sewing machines. Olga points to the mannequin heads. Every performer has a cast made of his or her head. I can't imagine Olga sitting still long enough for hers, but she assures me it's in there somewhere.

There's a building where the sets are designed, there are administrative offices on the upper floors and even a small shop in the basement that sells discounted Cirque merchandise on Fridays. But the most impressive spaces are the cavernous studios, which resemble gymnasiums, but larger and with higher ceilings. We peer into one that is dark and empty and Olga explains that this studio is used for creating new shows—at the moment for the show that will be resident at hotel New York, New York in Las Vegas. The other studio is filled with activity. This is where performers train, and the space is large enough to accommodate several aerial acts at once. The ceiling is gridded with complicated rigging. There are trapezes and ropes and rope swings and the fabric called "tissue" hanging above mats and nets and piles of Styrofoam cubes. There's room as well for acrobats and dancers, for Chinese poles and Russian swing, even a contortionist or two can squeeze in.

And indeed, I quickly realize that as impressive as this state-of-the-art facility is—probably the best training center for circus arts ever built— what is more impressive still are the people hanging and soaring and tumbling within it. The artistic tent at *Saltimbanco* is a snapshot of a particular show at a particular moment. But Cirque headquarters represents the fluidity of the Cirque du Soleil as an entertainment empire and encompasses all the shows, and the past, and the future.

It's ironic that I have come here at the end of my road, because for the artists this is their beginning. This is where they audition and train, their first home before going off to Las Vegas or Orlando or Europe or Japan. When I first met Olga and told her which shows I had seen, she replied that she knew performers in all of them. And now I can see how. At a single table in the cafeteria might sit someone from *Quidam* and *La Nouba* and *Mystère* and the new show, not yet named. This is where everyone starts, but it's also a way station for those who are injured or switching shows. And it's the world's most vertiginous retirement home, for people like Vladimir, who used to perform High Bar in *Alegría* and now works as a rigger, or the trapeze artist who now works for a different troupe but still comes here to train.

"Remember Mark," Vladimir will tell me with a confident smile, during my second trip to Montreal, when I say this might be my last, "the circus is a ring. No matter how far you go, you will always return."

I gaze up at a woman in the corner wrapping herself in the tissue and letting it unravel. Beside her another woman is practicing a horizontal twist on a rope swing with the assistance of her coach below. The only male aerialist in the studio at that moment is practicing straps, soaring in a high circle in the middle of the studio. And in the far corner I see Dasha, hanging from a trapeze. Lower down and just a few feet away a Mongolian contortionist balances on one hand.

Olga talks to an older Russian man named Viktor for a few minutes and then calls me over. Olga knew him from the Moscow Circus and he's one of the pre-eminent trapeze coaches in the world.

I labor to absorb it all. When you've lived your whole life without expectation of ever meeting a contortionist and then you shake hands with three in the space of five minutes it's a bit overwhelming. How do you shake hands with a contortionist anyway? And then you meet a couple more trapezists, Shana from San Francisco, someone from New Zealand, a dark-skinned aerialist from Sweden. And then in the lobby Olga introduces you to a former teammate of Elena Grosheva's, who is slated to join her friend in *Saltimbanco* next month. And you meet on your own a lovely blond woman raised in Japan who will soon be performing in that very same country as the female half of a hand-to-hand act in *Quidam* called "Vice-Versa." And at last, to give rest to the rash of new faces and names, you spot one quite familiar, the amiable Cambodian Jean-Paul Boun, doing chin-ups in the physio room.

Yes, the physio room. It's going on four o'clock and Olga is finally ready for her 1:30 appointment. She sets her backpack on the floor and lies down on the table, immediately striking up a conversation with the woman beside her.

The physiotherapist unwraps the gauge for inspection. "It's very important to use your crutches," she reminds Olga.

"Yes, I always use crutches."

I had come here to help Olga with her recovery, but she has other ideas.

After getting her knee re-wrapped and learning some exercises she leads me to the library, filled with books and magazines on the circus arts, and videos of the shows.

"Maybe you find this interesting," she says, showing me bound reviews.

And then she points to a PC with internet access. "Can you check on my computer?"

It's a long story. Olga had spilled wine on her laptop in Europe and needed a new computer. But she didn't want a laptop. I suggested an iMac, since she wanted to make videos. James Clowney was supposed to bring her one from New York. But that fell through. Then she tried to order one in Canada on Apple's 800 number, but her credit card limit was too low. So she asked me.

I ordered it yesterday on my own card and told her it would probably arrive Friday. But she was rightly suspicious and asked me to check. So I use the computer in the Cirque du Soleil library to track its progress through Canada. But like an illusionist's rabbit, it had disappeared. So I call the 800 number and spend the next forty-five minutes in high-tech purgatory as a host of computers search in vain for the computer I ordered for Olga.

On our way back through the lobby Olga stops at another computer and asks me to help her write some e-mails. One is to the artistic director. They had had their differences in Vienna, but now Olga is grateful to him for authorizing her surgery and wants to write a letter of thanks. Olga dictates like a seasoned executive and I shape her thoughts like a ghostwriter and type them like a harried secretary. It's a dangerous partnership. This isn't the sort of collaboration I envisioned when I decided to write the book. But Olga deserves whatever services I can provide. Besides, she has promised to host a dinner party for me Saturday, inviting only women.

One of the women Olga has invited is a young Russian contortionist training for the new show in Las Vegas. I met her briefly in the physio room and she immediately reminded me of Vika, although in truth they were quite dissimilar. Vika was blond and tan, this girl pale with dark hair. Olga took her hand and spoke with her for several minutes in Russian while I stood by.

Back in the apartment, while peeling onions for dinner, Olga turns to me and says, "I like this girl very much. She not like most girls her age. She real and true. She remind me Vika."

I'm sitting at the table drinking tea. Arthur has gone jogging. I want to wipe my eyes, but it's not the onions. I feel a devastating sense of longing and regret. And irony. A year ago, how could I have imagined that I would one day be staying with Olga, and that Vika would be gone?

"I didn't think you remembered her," I say, struck also by the coincidence of our observation.

"Of course I remember her."

"But you meet so many people..." I protest. "Do you remember your conversation that first night, at the Paradiso?"

"I usually don't like meet Russians," Olga confides. "But I can tell at once she doesn't have Russian mentality. I see a little bit myself in her."

Now the onions really are getting to me.

The next day I go alone to the studio with Olga. Arthur, who perhaps has glimpsed Olga's mood, claims an urgent need to run errands.

"Don't let her walk too much," he tells me as Olga zips up her jump suit. "Make sure she uses her crutches."

Why is he telling me and not her? Olga won't even let me help her up the stairs and she hobbles across the icy walkway as if it were gravel. When the taxi pulls up to Cirque headquarters I innocently ask if she wants me to pay. Yesterday she had used a voucher.

But Olga takes offense. She assumes I understand that she has to pay for the vouchers and thinks I am being inconsiderate. After all, she's bringing me to the Cirque, introducing me to people. I thought I was here to help her with her knee. But no matter, I realize I should have simply paid the fare.

But Olga has no patience for apologies. "I hate stupid men!" she declares.

Of all the times to get a taxi driver who understands English. I pay with a shrug, as if to say, "She's Russian, she's a trapeze artist, she's on pain killers," and help her out of the cab.

"Please don't call me stupid," I mutter as we walk to the entrance.

It's the first time I've ever said anything to her in anger. I've lasted a long time I think. Perhaps longer than anyone who's ever been closer to her. But she deserves my forbearance, I remind myself, as I open the door for her.

She changes out of her jump suit and leads me into one of the adjoining buildings, carrying her backpack, which contains my manuscript.

"I think you not my real friend, you just want write book," she proclaims, looking ahead, maintaining her pace.

This is the first time she has ever accused me of ulterior motives. I expected such challenges earlier in our relationship, and they would have been understandable and deserved a response. But not now.

The anger I felt a moment earlier threatens to explode. It was obvious that Olga had done a lot for me. More than I had done for her. But I was trying to give back now, and had come to Montreal at my own expense to help with her recovery. Of course I wanted to see Cirque headquarters, but didn't she know I would have come anyway?

As we continue to walk along the empty corridor four options present themselves to my anguished mind:

1. Impale her on one of her crutches.
2. Storm off.
3. Compare her unfavorably with Ivan the Terrible.
4. Walk on.

I walk on. I don't even know where we're going. We take an elevator in silence and enter a conference room. Olga peeks into an office and greets a woman who works for Cirque du Monde, a non-profit organization partly funded by the Cirque du Soleil, which conducts circus workshops and other activities around the globe.

Olga shows her my manuscript. "This my friend Mark Schreiber," she says with a smile. "He wonderful person. He write book about people in circus. Maybe it's interesting to you."

If I didn't know Olga, I'd say it was the morphine.

But she will turn on me again in the physio room. That damned computer. Customer service blithely tells me Apple canceled the order. A big box with pictures of apples on it won't be arriving in the studio this afternoon. Never mind that I put it on my credit card, that I spent hours on this misadventure. What matters to Olga are results, not intentions. She may complain about the Russian mentality, but this is a familiar trait of Russian coaches. You don't get points for trying.

"I told you they won't take foreign credit card!" she yells as the physiotherapist massages her leg.

A similar problem had occurred when Olga tried to order the computer with her Australian card. But her limit was also too low.

"I specifically asked when I placed the order," I reply. "They said there was no problem with a U.S. card."

She pouts. "So how I get my computer?"

"Don't worry. You'll get it tonight. I'll buy one here."

"But they more expensive here!"

Despite my lack of culpability, I still feel responsible. It was important not only to buy her a computer, but to get it while I was here so I could help her set it up. So I return to the library, not to look through the stacks of interesting circus literature, but to thumb through a Montreal *Yellow Pages*.

I receive a welcome respite back in the physio room. Olga is nowhere to be found, and the room is deserted except for Jean-Paul Boun, who is quietly doing chin-ups. I'm surprised that he can do chin-ups after back surgery, but he tells me with a laugh that chin-ups are easy. However sometimes he can't tie his shoes.

When I first started following the Cirque I wondered how these artists could perform so many shows without injury. I've since learned that they often perform with minor injuries, and that major injuries are not uncommon. And yet I've never heard a single complaint. Igor Issakov laughed when he showed me the photo of his neck in a cast. Olga was crying for morphine not even a week ago, yet I spotted her earlier dangling by her hands from a horizontal bar. And Jean-Paul appears in remarkably good spirits, wishing only that he could be back in the show. They've come to remind me of football players, who consider injury and surgery occupational hazards and never doubt the rewards worthy of the risks.

After I set up the computer in the living room, Olga compensates me with a ballet lesson. Four days after knee surgery and she's doing ballet!

I had asked her once if she would give me a session as a personal trainer. But Olga, like Vitaliy Bazaliy, is a process person. A process person from hell. She won't say yes or no. She'll look at you as though you've asked her to shine your shoes. But then one night you find yourself lying face down on a mat, slowly raising your back as she counts to thirty.

I've never done ballet exercises, but I'm eager for the chance. Following the Cirque has made me rededicate myself to fitness and sport. I've taken up juggling. I've improved at squash. I've started doing chin-ups.

One doesn't have to know much about ballet to appreciate Olga's proficiency. The daughter of her Moscow coach was a member of the Bolshoi Ballet, and Olga appears fluid and strong enough to have been a professional dancer had her aspirations been to leap and not to fly.

Straining to follow her quick commands, I feel I'm receiving an authentic experience of the Russian ballet.

"*Dis vay! Dis vay!*"

The night ends with that other staple of Russian culture—Monopoly. Olga and Arthur play to test their relationship and tonight they compete for my alliance. I make a bad trade with Olga and bow out early. Soon after, Arthur concedes, and they proceed to argue for several minutes, because he always concedes and she wants to play to the bitter end.

"I want see you bankrupt!" she says.

All of Saturday is given to this mysterious dinner party. Olga says she has invited only women, but I don't know who, or how many. But she's cooking for twenty. Several enormous salads and two whole chickens. And a special honey cake, a family recipe that she hasn't made in years.

"I make it for you!" she says.

Later in the afternoon Arthur informs me the oven has gone out. The chickens are still cold. The burners work, so it can't be the fuse. Nevertheless we check the circuit breakers and pull the oven out from the wall and examine the wires. Finally, he knocks on the other apartments, hoping we can borrow a neighbor's oven for two hours. But no one is home.

I dread Olga's reaction. This is certainly one time I could not fault her for yelling. But when I break the news she merely shrugs and says we can eat the salads. I find her equanimity hard to believe and am not so willing to give up myself. I suggest offering to pay the pizzeria next door to cook it, but the pizzeria is inexplicably closed. I find a Chinese restaurant two blocks away and evoke peels of laughter from the hostess when I make my request. They only have woks, she explains. If it were up to me I would just order a few servings of orange chicken, but Olga rejects the idea.

When I ask if I can pay for groceries she says I can buy the wine. There's a liquor store around the corner. Olga wants red wine, but I feel I should get a bottle of white as well. And vodka—there are bound to be Russians present. I feel under intense pressure. Many an otherwise excellent party has been ruined by a scarcity of alcohol.

I return with several bags, having spent over eighty dollars U.S., but alas the most popular drink will be the grape juice I bought at the supermarket. Olga will drink wine from an already opened bottle, and my own won't even be touched. None of the guests will drink at all.

In fact there are only two guests. A trapezist from New Zealand who came all the way to Canada to train privately with Viktor, and a female aerialist from *Quidam*, also recovering from a knee injury. It's just as well, because Olga only has three chairs. We spend several hours at the table eating the salads and drinking water and grape juice. The biggest hit is Olga's cake, which doesn't survive the night.

The next afternoon I attempt to leave. But I'm flying standby and my flight is full. So is the next one. They offer to re-route me through New York, but the incoming plane is delayed and I will miss my connection. I feel a sense of deja-vu, but there's no Botel to return to. It's with no small degree of trepidation that I phone Olga to tell her I'm still here.

"Yes, of course you can come back," she says. "Do you need Canadian money?

Three weeks later I return. Olga wants me to stay for a month but I can only manage four days. Arthur has returned to work in Amsterdam, so it will just be the two of us, a proposition I might have wished for months ago but which now fills me with terror. Don't fight back, I keep telling myself in anticipation of whatever epithets she might hurl at me this trip. Don't lose sight of the sweetness of her soul.

I go straight from the airport to Cirque headquarters and we have lunch in the cafeteria, which is filled with artists rehearsing for the new show at New York, New York. Olga appears to be doing very well and is quite happy to see me.

"I have so much work for you!" she says.

There seems to be nothing I can do for her knee, but she has questions about the computer, and e-mails to answer and she wants to revise her web site. As we're leaving, she tells me in an offhand way that the Cirque has asked her to do Solo Trapeze in "O".

"O? Oh? When?

"This summer."

I wait for more, but she is silent. I want to shake her and say, "Take it! What an opportunity! You can always coach in Australia afterward."

But I too remain silent, and merely gaze at her with admiration. Cirque scouts scour the globe for talent, and twice a year athletes and artists come to Montreal from all over the world to audition. World champion gymnasts and acrobats, the world's best aerialists. And here is Olga, no longer young for a trapezist. She ran away from the Cirque. She's recovering from major knee surgery. She's made it known she doesn't want to return to *Saltimbanco*. And yet they ask her for "O". How good must she be?

She doesn't want to take a taxi and the bus comes in a few minutes. She runs ahead of me on the snow-covered pavement. Runs! Why can't she be like Greta Garbo in *Grand Hotel*, the prima donna with her car always waiting out front? Can you imagine Greta Garbo nudging her companion in the back of the bus. "Darling, you need get transfer!"

At home she shows me my office for the next few days—the computer in the living room, looming over a low square table a mere foot from the wall. She has placed a blanket on the hardwood floor for comfort.

"How am I supposed to sit here?" I ask, trying to squeeze in.

"I always put my feet on each side," she says.

I tell her that's not an option and sit on my knees. She makes tea and kneels beside me. Right beside me. I might think how lucky I am to have achieved such a degree of intimacy with her, but then this isn't the intimacy of a lover but the intimacy of a secretary on a working holiday.

First a year of e-mails. Yes, there's an e-mail over a year old. A fan wants to know why she doesn't wear shoes on the trapeze.

Olga replies—through her humble medium—that it's mostly a matter of preference. She hates shoes and never wore them while training. And she pauses to show me a photo taken of her with a pile of black slippers. She explains that in *Saltimbanco* you couldn't walk onstage barefoot, so the costume department provided black slippers for those who weren't wearing shoes. Well, Olga hates shoes. She would put the slippers on to walk onstage, put them back on after her routine, stuff them under her dressing table and forget about them. A couple weeks later she stormed around the artistic tent, asking for slippers. She finally lifted the flap under her table and about twenty pairs tumbled out! One of the cast insisted on documenting the occasion.

There are e-mails from talent and booking agencies, including one from India. She wants to reply just out of curiosity.

"Mark, you want go India with me?"

And she laughs again and tells me about a booker in Turkey who proposed she tour the countryside in a caravan.

"Can you imagine? In a caravan?"

Well you do take the public bus, I want to say.

She wants to write a reference for her dear friend the artistic director. He hasn't asked for one, but she wants to do it anyway. Also for the woman who appealed the insurance's initial denial of her surgery.

What about the bus driver? I'm tempted to ask.

There's an e-mail from the director of the National Institute of Circus Arts in Melbourne, where Olga coached before joining *Saltimbanco*. She tells Olga they'd be glad to have her back. They'd also like to have her former coach from the Moscow Circus School. Who wouldn't? Olga has me reply that her plans are still undecided and her coach is unfortunately working in Japan until January. But she tells me it would be a dream to work with Gennady again. Maybe there's a place for him in "O", I want to say.

There's an e-mail from Marie-Claude Lecroix, the boleadoros dancer who left the Cirque to join her boyfriend in Oxfordshire. I answer that with pleasure.

"Now, I want write something for my meeting with Cirque du Monde," she says as night falls. "You want first eat?"

"Yes, let's go out. I'll treat you," I eagerly offer, rubbing the sleep from my legs.

"No, stay here. I cook."

Olga plans to meet with the director of the Cirque du Monde to suggest closer ties with the National Institute of Circus Arts. It's her own idea and she's pursuing it, as she does many of the projects in her life, with pure and noble intentions:

> ...I believe circus can change your life because it changed mine. I understand perfectly the idea of Circus for Life, because this was my own experience. I didn't come from a circus family. When I first saw a circus I thought—this is for me. I wasn't thinking of a career. I didn't even know a career was possible. I was thinking, this is a way to challenge myself, to become something more, to fly.

It's midnight by the time we get around to redesigning her web site. We're supposed to meet with a Russian programmer tomorrow and she wants to have everything decided. I tell her you can't design a web page in one evening, but she wants it off her hands.

She brings out her photo albums and we look through them with a critical eye, trying to find a picture suitable to replace the rather vague full-body image on her home page. I'm reminded of the first time she invited me up to her room in Barcelona and we looked at these same photos on her bed.

The next day we go to the home of this Russian programmer. Poor guy. I thought we would be there for just an hour or two, but it takes six hours to decide everything. The resolutions of the night before have eroded into suggestions. We sit on opposite sides of him in front of the computer, tossing ideas back and forth. Olga is excruciatingly deferential.

"What you think? Which photo you want?"

"It's your web site," I remind her.

I'm numb and starving by the time we leave, but it's worth it to see

Olga happy. And I've achieved my objective, she hasn't run away from me. In fact I've done such a good job I may not be able to get rid of her.

We go to the Chinese restaurant around the corner, the one that only has woks. Olga complains she's not properly dressed—this from a woman who thought a bathrobe sufficient for the Danube Hilton. But I'm too hungry to go back home and we take our seats. Ten months ago I couldn't have dreamed of spending two days in the exclusive company of this rare and wondrous creature. Yet I've endured it like a punishment. Only now over our long dinner do I relax enough to remember how fortunate I am.

What does one do when alone with a trapezist on a Friday night? Play Monopoly, of course. I myself would have preferred Chutes and Ladders, but Olga has a limited library of games. We watch *Quidam* simultaneously on the computer's DVD and she provides a running commentary. She wins again, and perhaps her capitalistic prowess encourages her to ask a strange favor.

"I want have contract with you," she says in all seriousness at two o'clock in the morning, as we sit next to each other on the floor. "I want you be my secretary."

I laugh. "You don't need a contract for that. Besides, I won't take money from you."

"I don't give you money. I helped you with book, so now you help me write letters."

"Ah!"

Olga has never asked for anything in exchange for helping with my book. And she has trusted me completely, more than I would have trusted a writer were I in her position. Arthur would later tell me over the phone, "Don't sign anything with Olga!" But I'll give her whatever she wants.

"I suppose I will have to write the contract as well?"

"Of course."

I quickly type something up. She seems surprised by my acquiescence. I don't think she realizes it, but I've never said no to her.

"It's a test, isn't it?" I then suspect.

"Yes," she admits. "But I also want call you when I need advice or want talk."

"You do that now. I'm always glad to hear from you."

"Yes, but someday when you have girlfriends all over the world and they answer phone and tell me you busy, I can say, 'I have contract!'"

The oven is working again, and Olga puts a chicken in for this dubious dinner party. She also sends me out to the grocery to buy rice vinegar and cucumbers for sushi.

"I learned make sushi in Australia," she explains. "I loved sushi but it so expensive. So one day I go to a Japanese grocery and ask them what I need buy to make sushi. It's easy really, and I make all different kinds. With chicken. With pork. But my favorite is salmon."

I had told her before I came that although I appreciated her offer to throw another dinner party for me, I didn't want her cooking all day. Now she admits that as a result she didn't invite many people, and she didn't give them her address.

She leads me across the street to an ATM, where she withdraws enough money to pay me for the computer. It hasn't been necessary to remind her. Then we take a bus to a money exchange, and she gives me the amount in dollars. She doesn't thank me. But then generous people are often rude beneficiaries.

I ask if she wants to go to the French Quarter—I still haven't seen anything of Montreal these two trips. But she says we need to go home in case anyone comes.

"Who is going to come?" I ask.

She disconnects the internet to free the phone line, but no one calls. I talk to her in the kitchen as she rolls the sushi in a bamboo mat. She takes out the chicken and brings everything over to the table. Suddenly we're eating.

"I guess no one's coming," I observe.

"You told me you didn't want party."

"Yes. And I'm just as happy to be alone with you."

A few minutes later there's a knock on the door and Vladimir walks in with a bottle of wine. He remembers me but I don't recognize him at first. He works at the Cirque and lives upstairs. He's Russian, originally from Kazakhstan. Olga points to a chair and prepares a plate for him.

Then she shows him my manuscript and he reads the table of contents with interest.

"The Bolshoi Circus!" he exclaims.

Olga tells me he was with the Moscow Circus and performed high bar there. *Alegría* hired the whole troupe. High bar is an aerial act with two trapeze hanging at opposite ends of a cage of aluminum tubing. Three men take turns leaping from the top of the cage into the outstretched arms of one of two catchers. Vladimir was a flyer.

I'm surprised to learn he never performed any other form of trapeze. I ask him if he's a thrill-seeker but, like Olga, he seems more interested in the technical achievement than the adrenaline rush.

I ask him if he likes heights.

"Not at first. But now. And as rigger I work higher than I ever did as an artist. But I'm always a little afraid. The people who aren't afraid, they're the ones who get hurt. The first time I did high bar, I was just supposed to climb to the trapeze and let go. But I couldn't let go! The bar is hard metal, you know. Well, when I finally let go I looked up, and I could see the image of my hands on the metal!"

Olga proudly shows him a textbook on rigging she borrowed from the Cirque library, and Vladimir gets a length of rope for her to practice on.

"She might make a noose and hang someone," I say warily.

"I have one upstairs," Vladimir boasts. "Do you know the joke—a Russian man is standing on a chair about to hang himself. But after he puts the rope around his neck he sees a bottle of vodka on the table and says to himself, 'I'm about to die, why shouldn't I have one last drink?' And he gets down and pours a drink. And then another. And by the time he's finished drinking he can't climb the chair to hang himself!"

Back at our own table I ask him about *Alegría*. He has fond memories of the show and loved touring. I ask him why he works as a rigger at the studio and not at the show.

He replies that he has a wife and two children, and that the Cirque school only teaches the children of artists. "You don't see many people on the crew who have families," he points out. "It's too expensive."

"Do you find that people treat you differently now that you're a rigger than when you were an artist?"

"No, not here. But when I performed with the Moscow Circus the crew couldn't eat with the artists."

The buzzer rings. I hear Olga talking to someone and a minute later Gyula, the Russian contortionist, appears. The girl who reminds us of Vika.

"Hello Mark!" she exclaims with a perfect smile.

Another performer joins us as well. A male aerialist from *Alegría*, recovering from shoulder surgery. I can't believe Olga's subterfuge, the lengths to which she went simply to create this moment. I'm the happiest secretary in Montreal.

Russian pop music is playing on the stereo and Gyula starts singing the words and dancing. She seems to feel very much at home. And after all these long stressful days, so do I.

When we're all sitting at the table, five people on three chairs, Olga gives Gyula the letter from me. The letter!

The last time I was here, on the day of that dinner party, Arthur had walked in from one of his sorties with a dozen tulips. Olga told him to give one to me and Arthur suggested I give it to the contortionist. Later that afternoon, during one of my own sorties to the corner supermarket, I noticed a rack of French Valentine's Day cards and got one for my mother. I also contemplated getting one for Gyula, but then reconsidered and selected a blank card and wrote my own simple offer of friendship.

But she didn't come. So I asked Olga if she would give it to her Monday when she went to the studio. Olga said of course. But later that night, as we sat alone in the kitchen, she turned to me with an exasperated shrug and said, "Mark, why you always want girls ten years old? You need find woman gone through life. Know what life is. To tell you truth, if I Vika's age I hurt you so much! Why you think this girl be interested in you?"

Rather than attempt a defense I went to my room and turned out the light. A few minutes later Olga knocked on the door and peeked in.

"How you doing?"

"I'm trying to sleep."

"Have sweet dreams."

The next day, before I went to the airport, she asked me for the card. I told her I had thrown it away.

"Why you do that?"

So I rescued the card, but decided not to attempt any further contact with Gyula or even ask Olga about her reaction. But how could she react at all? Olga had kept the letter all this time.

And now Olga gives it to her in front of witnesses. And to compound my embarrassment, Gyula asks if I will read it to her! Her English is good but she claims she cannot read well. So I read, and Olga translates the words she cannot understand. She rewards me with another perfect smile. And when she leaves she'll blow me a kiss.

But first we eat. And make toasts with wine and grape juice. When it's my turn I steal Olga's line and say, "May all your dreams come true!"

Then I ask Gyula about performing at the Moulin Rouge and coming to work for the Cirque. After a few minutes she says, "Please, I trained all day, can we talk about something else?"

Vladimir turns to me with a grin. "Mark, there is a joke about circus people. A group of friends from the circus are having a party. And everyone is talking about the circus. So one man finally says, 'Enough! How can anyone relax when everything's about the circus twenty-four hours a day?' And he puts an empty glass in the middle of the table. 'The next person who speaks about the circus has to put a coin in the glass.' And everyone agrees it is a good idea, and they began talking again. By the end of the party the table is covered with glasses filled with coins!"

SHANA

I'm on the roof with two trapezists. Olga, of course, who walks from edge to edge with the insouciance of a pedestrian crossing a country road, and Shana Carroll, the original soloist in *Saltimbanco*.

Shana is showing us the view of the courtyard from atop her new home, an odd arrangement of connected apartment buildings in the St. Henri district of Montreal. Decades ago the apartments were converted into a convent. When the nuns left, the church had a difficult time finding a buyer for this assortment of worn structures, ill-suited for any imaginable type of inhabitants—unless they happened to be aerialists, acrobats, contortionists and clowns.

It's like walking through an Escher drawing. Down stairways, turn, up stairways, through corridors. The same rooms keep reappearing and yet here's a bedroom I haven't seen before, and here's an open closet brimming with toys. Here's Shana's husband, Seb, working on the wiring in a kitchen stripped bare. An acrobat who met Shana in *Saltimbanco*, he developed the diabolo routine which now serves as *Saltimbanco's* backup act. Here's the courtyard at last. We've reached bottom. Or perhaps not. Down some concrete steps. Here's a long muralled room where the nuns ate. Here's a submarine-like chamber where they slept on bunks like sailors. Here's the basement chapel, now equipped with DJ equipment for parties but too low to rig a trapeze.

We knock on closed doors. And what surprises on the other side! Here is a student of the national circus school, renting a room. Here is an infant acrobat crawling around. On Shana's cue she raises an arm and leg. Here's Patrick, Seb's new partner in diabolo, which is an hourglass-shaped object spun like a yo-yo on a long string and caught on that same string after being tossed in the air. He's building a shower. Shana explains there's a race to install the first shower. It's a mystery how the nuns bathed. Here's Isabelle, a petite woman with pale skin and large dark eyes. I shake her hand and move on, only to learn as we ascend yet another stairway that she was a teenage contortionist in *Saltimbanco*, then an aerialist who performed the tissue act in *Quidam*.

These former Cirque du Soleil artists have chosen to live together, and to work together again in a show of their own design. It's a risk, Shana admits, investing together, living in such close quarters. But born in 1970, Shana arrived at the tail end of the commune craze in her home town of Berkeley. And who better to revive those hippie traditions than the sort of people the hippies emulated in the first place? Circus folk. One of the residents is even named "Gypsy."

Their new show is entitled, *Les 7 Doigts de la Main*, a French expression which means seven fingers of the hand. The two other fingers reside elsewhere. Samuel, who performed hand balancing in *Alegría*, and Faon, who literally grew up in Cirque du Soleil, her mother having been one of the street performers who formed the core of the original company.

Many Cirque veterans have tried to start their own company without success. But Shana and her friends have already staged their show, to critical acclaim, and are now in the process of booking an international tour.

When Olga first told me about the show, before she had seen it, I envisioned something threadbare, unconnected. A group of talented artists doing their own acts in a former convent—the show and residence having fused in my imagination, so that I saw them performing to a small group of devotees and then going to sleep in the rooms above. But later Olga actually attended a performance and phoned me to say how beautiful it was. Knowing how critical Olga can be, I immediately became intrigued. The show had finished its run by the time I returned to Montreal, but I was determined to gain a more accurate picture from Shana herself during our afternoon together.

So after the tour of the house she leads us back to her room and shows us a trailer for the show on her computer. I ask to watch it twice more, I'm so enchanted. I realize I'm being shown yet another branch in the evolution of the circus. Just as Cirque du Soleil breathed sophistication into the circus arts, marrying them with music, dance, choreography and narrative, so the *Seven Fingers* joins circus to modern theater. The result is something completely different from the productions of their former employer. Cirque du Soleil is sprawling and exotic; *Seven Fingers* is intimate and familiar. Cirque du Soleil is a journey to another world; *Seven Fingers* a homecoming.

Guests enter through a refrigerator. The stage is a modern urban loft. There are no masks, no elaborate sets. The artists wear white night clothes, address the audience directly, take as their props ordinary objects such as an apple, a television. The music is an eclectic mix of rock, pop, and tango, the finale a rendition of "There's No Business Like Show Business."

Shana wanted to perform since the age of four, when her mother took her to see *Guys and Dolls*. Although musical theater was her first love, in high school she dove into the deeper, darker world of drama. When she met Gypsy she was living on her own on Post Street in downtown San Francisco, going for auditions as well as teaching and directing at the Drama Studio.

But, she says, "The problem with goals is they have shelf lives, and by the time you reach them they have already expired. In Rilke's *Letters to a Young Poet*, there's a line about not seeking the answers but living the questions. So from a family of brainy writers I tried to turn off my brain and ignore logic and literally get into the swing of things."

Gypsy Snider was the daughter of the founders of the Pickle Family Circus, a small resident circus in San Francisco. It was through her friendship with Gypsy that Shana began to study trapeze. After performing with Pickle's, she studied for two years at École Nationale de Cirque in Montreal, then followed her trapeze coach to a school outside Paris, before returning to Canada and joining Cirque du Soleil.

Originally *Saltimbanco* did not include Solo Trapeze. Shana created the act herself with the help of the choreographer and artistic director and it was taken on as a backup to the Steben twins, the original duo trapeze artists. Only years later was Solo Trapeze given equal status.

Most trapezists come from circus schools or circus families and learn performance skills later, if ever. Shana was unusual in that she came to trapeze from a theater background, the ideal resume for her innovative new employer.

After *Saltimbanco* staged what was thought to be its last show at the Royal Albert Hall in London in 1997, Shana went back to Montreal and joined Cirque Eloize.

A year later *Saltimbanco* was resurrected for an Australian—Asian tour, and Shana packed her bags once again. It was while preparing for this tour that she met Sebastien Soldevila, her future husband. Seb wanted to perform the entrance dance to her act with her, but Shana wasn't enthusiastic. But he was persistent and she finally challenged him, "If you do the dance you have to fall in love with me!"

He did and she became pregnant and announced her retirement. She stopped performing trapeze but took additional cues during the show.

Three months later she lost the baby. The artistic director wanted her to stay and offered to let her take as much time off as she needed. But Shana realized she was entering a new period of her life and declined. They were in Japan now and she was still performing. She scheduled her departure to precede the intended arrival date of her replacement. She had just lost her baby and she found herself facing, so painfully soon after, the loss of the act she had given birth to.

There have only been three solo trapezists in *Saltimbanco*. Shana, Olga, and Anna Ward, who returned to the show after Olga was injured in Madrid and whom I saw perform in London.

It was Anna who came to replace Shana in Japan. But she arrived early, before the break between cities. Of course, Shana didn't have to stay those last weeks, but she wanted to cherish her remaining time. Besides, Seb was still in the show, and the two of them had been working late into the night on his diabolo act, Shana doing the choreography.

So Shana continued to walk through the flaps of the Grand Chapiteau. But now someone else wearing an identical costume stepped out to the music that had become such a part of her life for the last eight years, and ascended to the solitary trapeze.

Ever the workaholic, Shana went on to perform at a festival in Venice, then taught at the Circus Center in San Francisco, as well as leading workshops and choreographing a show for the New Pickle Circus. Finally she returned to Montreal to start *Seven Fingers*.

The circus is a ring, and relationships between artists and employers are rarely completely severed, as they are in the outside world. Shana had quit the Cirque but continued to train at the Cirque studio. And after Olga ran away in Vienna, they asked Shana to fill in. When Olga came back to the show in Brussels and the two met for the first time, I assumed Shana would feel wary and perhaps resentful, but the two became friends. And when Olga came to Montreal for her surgery, she volunteered to help Shana train. And Shana, older by a few years, became a beacon for Olga, proof that life for the solo trapezist existed after thirty.

And what does the Cirque think of *Seven Fingers*? When computer programmers leave a Silicon Valley giant to start their own company, they aren't allowed back to headquarters to use their former employer's equipment. But circus relationships are more complicated. After beginning their search for funding, Faon suggested going to Daniel Gauthier. Gauthier co-founded the Cirque with Laliberté and served as president until Laliberté bought him out. Gauthier was a kind of father figure to Faon and expressed interest in helping the new troupe. When word got back to Laliberté, he asked why they hadn't come to him as well. So a week after I left Montreal, the seven former Cirque artists went to a meeting at the studio. Laliberté wasn't there, but many of the top people in the Cirque du Soleil were, and Shana found herself in yet another new role, fielding questions about expense items and revenue projections.

Her relationship with the Cirque over the years had been at times difficult, at times disillusioning. But as she spoke to the familiar faces at this meeting, including members of the creative staff who asked about the artistic content and seemed interested in more than just bottom lines, Shana realized how different they were from the other corporations they had approached for funding. "They really understood what we wanted to do and were completely supportive," she later told me. "It really hit me at the meeting that these were the good guys."

Nothing has surprised me more about the artists in Cirque du Soleil than how much they have to say of interest to people beyond their profession, and how articulately they express themselves. None more so than Shana, who refuses to ever respond to a question with yes or no but settles into charming, impassioned monologues. We are lucky for the chance to listen:

I believe in circus the way someone can believe in God. Sure, there is a magical and admirable quality to circus artists, but it is the circus that makes them that way. Circus is so rigorous that you make yourself second to it, you break yourself down so violently, in every sense, that the inflated egos and illusions of invincibility that other performers have to wrestle with is just not a factor.

Circus builds character the way any rigorous training would, and yet in its performance (okay I'm from California, but I do mean this), circus is about love. Okay, okay, that sounds so hippie and hokey, but after performing through my childhood in various forms of theater, I had never encountered as generous a performing art, where performers perform with so much love for their audience and for their craft. There's a quote about circus performers risking their lives to be beautiful, for the pleasure of their neighbor. This is inherent in the circus arts. You learn in circus this strange nobility, risking your life to be beautiful. Nothing in the world is more important than your audience, and delivering for them every day, lovingly.

And I do think there is something empowering about pushing your limits on a daily basis, that risk-taking in life is all interlocked and you overcome one fear in one corner of your world and it transfers over. That you live as a stronger and braver person when you push your limits with that sort of regularity. And yet unlike random thrill seekers, there is a cause, this sense that you are doing it to make people happy, and that gives your life a momentum and purpose that many lack.

It is the circus itself that creates extraordinary individuals. Sure there are people like Olga who in their drive and courage were already a lot farther down that road, but I've seen people who were not, who were ordinary self-involved teenagers, transformed by the circus arts.

The other thing I believe in is the circus life. Living as part of a com-

munity, and yet not in some designed, affected way as in many modern com-
munes, but as a natural by-product of the lifestyle. I remember hearing once
that depression is a modern thing, a city thing, that tribal people do not get
depressed and take Zoloft. Every individual, of course, needs to feel they mat-
ter, that they serve a unique purpose, that they have a function in a greater
whole. When you live in a community, that happens naturally. Everyone has
a purpose. Even people like Olga who try to keep to themselves, understand
that within the show they contribute to something larger.

My love of trapeze is related to the fact it is distinctly feminine. I was always
a strong girl but I was always a feminine girl, as Olga is too. I spent my life
wrestling with trying to be both and to be viewed as both. I remember so well
the first time I saw a trapeze artist, how she was so womanly and graceful
and yet doing something that so graphically required enormous strength and
courage. I was beside myself!

The first time I did my own solo trapeze act, the costumer put me in a
bird costume. The next year, when I was trying to articulate what I loved
in trapeze and what was important to have the audience feel, I came back
to this symbol of woman as strong and independent, yet sensual and longing,
searching. That when you can't go left and you can't go right, you go up. That
every woman needs to fly. I even believe that the pendulum rhythm of the
swing is that of a woman's sexuality.

The smoke machine snorts out a few puffs of ambiance. I am waiting in
the "hole," the tunnel beneath the bandstand. The floor light points outward
through the hole, backlighting this underworld entrance ramp. It fades in its
blue light, and that's my cue.

First a sort of rolling intro on the guitar, before the melody comes in. I
walk down the ramp. This was my favorite moment. The nervousness that
I thought, only seconds earlier, would implode inside of me, is suddenly fun-
neled and focused and transformed into pure energy. For a second I am
blinded by the smoke, but once I come through I spot that red light in the
sound booth. Right foot, left foot, right foot, on the music, three more steps
and suddenly I am swept up by this man, this man that represents everyman,
and yet in the Pacific tour also happened to be my one and only man, the
man that I love.

Seb and I have four dance moves or so during my hypnotic walk towards the red light in the sound booth. He tosses me over his head, turn me and stops me horizontal, inches above the ground. He catches me as I launch myself forward and we float there in counterbalance.

Each movement ends with me pushing him out of my way, sometimes aggressively, sometimes tenderly, until the final move that leads me directly from his shoulders to the hand loop, the express-line to the trapeze.

I wanted my number to be about becoming a woman, and I personally could not paint a portrait of that journey without the presence of a man, defining that womanhood both with and against him, his interference both helping and hindering my progress.

Men are what make womanhood such a challenge. At the time I put the number together I was at a period—before Seb—when I knew I had to keep leaving the men I love to live something greater. I knew that I had to fly, and that I had to fly alone. And after following those passions to their ecstatic outer limits, I could come back to the man I love. Because he let me go in the first place, I came back to him.

The entrance for me was the determination, the strength and decisiveness that led to finding myself alone in the air. The fixé was the searching, the questioning, the complexity of a woman's deeper emotions. And the swing was freedom, triumph. Ecstasy.

But I was only really complete when I slid back into his arms at the end, like I'd never left.

Now my routines are going in a slightly different direction. As opposed to attempting to portray the ultimate woman looking for the ultimate something, I'm trying to deconstruct all that, break down from a pure feminine image to something wild and free. But in the end I'm still floating around those same themes, and the trapeze for me is still the place to demonstrate that limitless spectrum of womanhood.

My dad wrote a column called, "Just Grateful for the Dead Spot," based on what I explained to him about trapeze technique. Every maneuver is done using the dead spot, the point of weightlessness in the swing, the apex when the trapeze changes direction. If your timing is impeccable you can use this weightlessness to execute moves otherwise impossible. But a millisecond off *and you need to compensate, get yourself somehow back onto the bar.*

Lately I've felt a bit in the dead spot, waiting for the swing to take off in the other direction, waiting for momentum to hit me and to once again hold on for dear life through its adrenalin-charged swoops. But for the moment I'm tumbling weightlessly, effortlessly through my days. Yet the lack of direction is giving me a kind of vertigo I never knew on the trapeze. There is direction, but it is not the jet-fueled direction of tour life, traveling light and burden free and thus highly aerodynamic. Cities marking your calendar instead of seasons, visas pasted into your passport as proof of a life in perpetual motion, straddling continents and oceans...

Saltimbanco. *When I told you about my departure from the show, I didn't mean to imply Anna was callously plowing over me. My only point was that she had such a rightful need to forget what came before and make the act her own. My most graceful and respectful stance, when she arrived, was to make myself very sparse. All to say, that it was a difficult way to end, after all those years, trying to make yourself invisible, trying to help others forget your work at the one moment you need to celebrate and remember it. A month later it would have been okay, but the timing made it difficult to swallow. All to say, because this is the real point—I was stunned the way Olga chose to receive me when she returned to the show in Brussels. To ask me endless questions about the source of the act, to acknowledge this shared experience as something sacred. It allowed me to love the number again, because I was free to talk about it and relive its moments with her. With her something came full circle.*

I felt I had the tremendous honor to have someone like Olga stand where I stood, and for that matter the tremendous honor to suddenly have her in my life, and to share with her something that for me was very intimate. I've spent only a fraction of the time with her that you have, but she has entered my heart with the same speed and thoroughness.

Even if that was all that was left after my years at Saltimbanco, *it was so much more than enough.*

Saltimbanco... *Salty, but oh so sweet* Saltimbanco. *The strongest memories I have are of singing "Kumbalawe," under the umbrella, smelling the ingredients of that night's meal on everyone's breath. But I have very few memories* of my number. When your focus is so inward, when you are so concentrated, when your internal monologue narrates your every move, you do not observe, you do not contemplate. You spot the same marks every night, the exit signs, the seam on the canvas of the tent, the stage left follow spot, the red light in the sound booth—though you don't even know, after 1,500 shows, what that red light in the sound booth is even for! You look for people with glasses—the light reflects off them—trying to make some kind of eye contact, whether you are upside-down or right side-up or horizontal or vertical. The multi-colored interlocking circles of the stage, upon which you have mapped out the last five years of your life, whiz through your gaze.

The memories are like excerpts of very surreal dreams. Sometimes you can't even describe the details. But the general sense haunts your days.

There was one show that will always stand out in my mind, from my first year on tour with Saltimbanco. My former husband had disappeared. I was up all night crying, believing he had gone back to his ex-wife. I had not slept. Tears ran inadvertently down my face all the way to show call. I couldn't possibly imagine how I could do my number. I could barely put on my makeup. I knew that the dance and the fixé could be a release—anyway its very themes were these tumultuous female emotions, and it had certainly been an emotional outlet for me at other times. But the swing... How could I possibly swing? The concentration it demanded, not to mention the joy I should be projecting to my audience, felt so far from my actual state of mind and heart.

But I started. The fixé, of course, was turbo-charged with emotion and defiance. I am woman, hear me fucking roar! But when the swing came, I took a deep breath, and all of a sudden I recalled a conversation I'd had with some friends about trapeze years before. She said it must be a metaphor for so many things. And he said, so accurately, so perceptively, "Yeah, it's a metaphor for everything, except when you're on it, and then it's just a trapeze."

Well, that day, for the first time in my career, I sat on the trapeze in front of 2,500 people, and instead of thinking, "Okay, just breathe," or, "Look into their eyes, look ecstatic," or, "Remember to let go of the ropes before twisting," or, "Do I still have rosin on my hands? How will my grip hold up?" or, "Did I lock my carabineer?" or, "Where am I on the music? Slow down! No, speed up!" or, "Save energy for the evening show," or, or, or...

Instead of all these things, I thought: THIS IS MY ESCAPE. Life is com-

plicated. This is trapeze. The trapeze will not change direction mid-swing. It will not change its moods, its laws. With the metronomic regularity of my own beating heart, it swings back and forth, back and forth...

LAS VEGAS

In frigid Montreal I shared a rooftop view with two trapezists. Now in blistering Las Vegas I share a Mustang with two contortionists. Can life get any better?

Let others have their high stakes tables, Ferraris, suites at the Bellagio. I have the two artists who will perform the opening act at the Cirque's new show, *Zumanity*, bending over the table in my garden room at the Tropicana, perusing *Las Vegas Apartments*.

Gyulnara is here—yes, Gyula. I've seen her since the surprise dinner party, during a subsequent trip to Montreal in May. Olga and I took her out to dinner the night after our journey through Shana's house. And then Sunday afternoon, before I left for the airport, we went to Mont Royale and ate cafeteria food on a park bench overlooking the pond. The snow had finally melted and it was nice to see something of the city after having spent so much of my time in Quebec sitting cramped behind Olga's computer.

The two women spoke to each other in Russian and I was content just to watch the scene reflected in Gyula's sunglasses. At one point Olga looked up and informed me that I can write a chapter about the contortionist.

"Why not?" Gyula said. "You are free. I am free."

There are degrees of freedom, however, and I remained an indentured volunteer to Ms. Sidorova. I think few things in her life have given her more pleasure than to have her own secretary, and what I assumed would be an occasional request to help her write an e-mail became a daily habit. After I returned home my workload only increased because she's going back to Australia. She still isn't sure what she will do, whether she will stay, if she will perform again, or coach. Much depends on her knee. As for Arthur, he will propose to her on what passes for a mountain in Holland, and she, after a garrulous detour, will accept, and he will patiently let her find her way. In the meantime there are many e-mails to send Down Under, to circus schools and agents and realtors and friends. One day she even asked if I could find out about apartments in Las Vegas for Gyula. She kindly points out that I'm not required to comply, since I don't have a contract with Gyula. But I couldn't think of a better way to fill in the afternoon.

Of course, I had hoped to see *Zumanity* once it opened in August. But now I realized I might be of assistance to Gyula before, and it would give me a chance to see her again. So I told her I would be happy to come out to Las Vegas for a long weekend, if she wished, and help her get settled.

Before departing for Australia, Olga told Gyula, "I give Mark to you. But only for one month. And to no one else!"

One thinks of Las Vegas as a twenty-four hour town, but most swimming pools close at ten. I learn this unusual detail because the top priority for Gyula in an apartment, second only to cost, is a spa she can use after the show. Zorigtkhuyag Bolormaa, her Mongolian partner, wants a quiet studio. It was Bolormaa I had seen practicing in Montreal, but we had only talked briefly then.

She and Gyula had shared an apartment there and trained together every day. Soon they will be performing together, in a water tank not much larger than a Jacuzzi, two shows a night, five nights a week. So it's understandable they don't want to share an apartment.

Alya had told me about the differences between touring and working in a resident show. One could live a more normal life in Las Vegas, strange as that may sound. But it was harder to save money, and if you had never lived in the U.S. and didn't speak English fluently, the challenges could be overwhelming.

The Cirque helps them get visas, social security numbers and bank accounts. They put them up in a hotel for the first month, give them a thick binder with information on everything from health insurance to area attractions, and show them two apartment complexes. However, Gyula and Bolormaa hoped for something cheaper, so I stop at a convenience store to pick up an apartment guide and, after checking in to my hotel, we're on our way.

First, let's get one thing straight. Contortionists cannot bend their arms back at the elbow and their legs forward at the knee. "Those people are called double-jointed," Bolormaa informs me as we drive to apartment number five, or six. Contortionists are extremely flexible but they train interminably at it from a young age. Bolormaa's mother was an acrobat, but Bolormaa didn't want to be in the circus herself until she was eleven, when she discovered contortion. Before coming to Cirque du Soleil she had worked all over the world, including a tour with the Hanneford Family Circus in the U.S. As a teenager she had been awarded a silver medal in the junior festival in Monte Carlo.

Gyula Karaeva came late to contortion. Unlike Bolormaa, who has broad shoulders and muscular limbs, Gyula is slight and her strength deceptive. At the age of six she was chosen by an acrobatic's scout for special training. Because she lived in Moscow she didn't have to leave home, as many athletes do. But by her early teens she was traveling to Europe for international competitions. She participated in pairs acrobatics with another girl and at age thirteen won a silver medal. A year later they won gold.

Not many people can claim to be the best in the world at what they do, but Gyula talks about her acrobatics career without pride. She recalls more clearly the silver medal because their coach believed they should have won gold the first time around.

She always worked hard, a trait she inherited from her mother, who had to support the family after the death of Gyula's father. Her route to the Cirque began when a former member of *Saltimbanco* developed a contortion act in water for her and became her producer. There was no act in the world like it, and Gyula performed at festivals, including the Mondia du Cirque de Demain in Paris. The Moulin Rouge gave her an award, and she performed there for a single, magical night.

The Cirque wanted her act for *Zumanity*, but they envisioned it as a duo contortion. They asked one of the performers in *Alegría* for a recommendation. This man had been urging Bolormaa for years to send her tape to the Cirque, and now here was her chance.

And several months later here they are, driving down the Strip in Las Vegas. I point out the hotels, but Bolormaa recognizes the sign outside the Mirage for *Siegfried and Roy*. She saw it when she was nine.

"My mother was in Ringling Brothers," she tells us. "And I toured for a while with her."

"You lived on the train?"

"Yes."

From the infinite plains of Mongolia to the cramped quarters of a circus train. A hundred questions come to mind, but more pressing matters draw my attention. For contrary to the belief that Las Vegas is a twenty-four hour town, most leasing offices close at five.

We spend all Thursday afternoon inspecting apartments. Friday as well. For Saturday I had suggested a picnic in Red Rock Canyon, but as Olga had earlier pointed out when I asked her what Gyula liked to do for fun, "How she can have fun in new country with so many things to do? You need help organize her life."

So Saturday we visit a couple more complexes, straying farther out on the southwest side of town. But by mid-afternoon these two very thrifty and thorough twenty year olds are no closer to a decision than on the first day, and Gyula throws her head back against the seat and moans, "Ma-ma!"

I venture to ask what was so bad about the first apartment, the one the Cirque showed them, where many of their friends are staying. Their main objection was price. But we have now visited fifteen apartments, and haven't found anything suitable for much less.

So we return to the Cirque recommended site and this time I accompany them on the tour. The Jacuzzi is open twenty-four hours and there are washers and dryers in the apartments, plush carpets, soundproofed walls. I have served perhaps inefficiently as a guide, but well as a guru, having revealed to them what was all along before their eyes.

During the cool nights we toured the Strip hotels. They had noticed the sign for David Copperfield, who's appearing at the MGM. They have seen him on TV and are big fans, so I secretly bought tickets for Saturday night. Gyula runs around the car when I show her.

I park at the Tropicana and we walk across the street to the MGM. From here we can see the stylized skyline of the New York, New York on the far corner, where *Zumanity* will soon be playing. The girls are talking with excited anticipation about Copperfield. I interrupt to tell them that what they are feeling now is what thousands of others will feel when they walk to the New York to see their show. I tell them I know there will be days when they feel exhausted, overwhelmed, under-appreciated. And I remind then how special their gift is. That for many who see their show, it will be the highlight of their trip to Las Vegas, and few will ever forget their contortion in water. Just as we will never forget David Copperfield making a car appear onstage.

"Mark, now I can see why you are a writer," Bolormaa says with a smile. "You think deep about things."

I expect them to be tired after the show. They are still training on their own two hours a day even though they are not in rehearsal, and the day-time temperature has been triple digits. But they are full of energy and we walk to the Luxor and back. On the walkway between the Excalibur and New York, New York, they point out the digital sign announcing *Zumanity*. And as we walk across the overpass, Gyula stops and spreads out her arms to the throng below and proclaims, "Welcome to my city!"

Of course I wouldn't be here if it weren't for Olga. Gyula isn't shy, and she's one of the warmest, most amiable people I know. But I would never have gained a place in her life had it not been for Olga's machinations.

After the surprise dinner party in Montreal, which Gyula had attended, I had given Olga a big hug. "Thank you so much!"

"Did you like party?" she asked with a smirk.

"I've never had a better one."

"I think nobody come," she said.

"How did Gyula know my name?" I asked. "We only met that one time at the studio and didn't really talk."

"I tell her about you. I say you good person to have in your life."

"Did you tell her she's too old for me by ten years?"

"Mark, sex with contortionist nothing special."

"For the woman probably."

"For the man too."

"How do you know? Besides, who said anything about sex? Can't I cultivate her as a friend? Like you?"

But I'll never have a friend like Olga. How could I?

And what about *her* friends? Olga lives resolutely in the present. She's superstitious of the future and leaves the past behind. She left Siberia, and Moscow, and now she's left the show. When I told her Bazaliy had invited me to Geneva she asked what was in Geneva. She didn't even know the show was stopping there.

"Aren't you sad you have no connections left with *Saltimbanco*?" I asked her.

"I have connection," she answered at once.

"Who?"

"You."

JOY AND DEDICATION

imagine...

You've entered a room with one Russian woman, lost her, found another. Could it be a hall of mirrors, deceiving you with distorted reflections? Or maybe it's a dance club in Amsterdam, or a hotel in Barcelona, or a tent that wanders the world like an impecunious refugee or an aristocratic traveler. Wherever you are, the Earth keeps spinning, and you keep losing your balance, falling. A world filled with tragedy and sorrow. Every joy you reach for eventually spins away from you, as the stars spin away from one another, and the universe gets darker, colder.

And yet you've found an invisible thread, a lifeline, your safety, that keeps you from hitting bottom, that winds you back from lonely hotels and rooms with inscrutable walls to that circular stage beneath the Grand Chapiteau. And you could be in Holland or Spain or Austria. You could be listening to any language. The masked character you watch could be a man or woman, black or white or brown, a fellow countryman or a runaway from Siberia. Do you really need to know?

For all the strange uncertainty, the roles unspoken, the messages only hinted at, you take comfort in the knowledge that in some time zone, at 7:30 in the evening, Dreamer is ringing the bell that begins *Saltimbanco*. And you may never see it again. You may never see her again. But still you'll always be there, connected by a strand of memory. To that wondrous place where the world, for once, makes sense.

Now that I've been there, I can look back. And I see friends where once I saw masks. That first night with Vika, the man in the box office trailer who gave us our passes, wearing a goatee and wire-rimmed glasses. I can now say that's Remi, from France. And the man walking through the aisles after the show, talking into a headset. That's Robert from Wales, chief of security. We had a beer at the Renaissance later that night. And the woman backstage riding the stationary bicycle. Oxana, of course. I didn't think she ever smiled. How wrong I was. And the boy and girl jumping from the horizontal bars to the mats, Max and Dasha. And the diminutive tornado who whirled out to us still in makeup and invited us for dinner—well, maybe, for all our intimacy, I know her least of all.

Two images from those first two nights backstage in Amsterdam stand out in my memory as emblematic of the joy and dedication these men and women and even children bring to their profession.

From the first night: I'm waiting in the commissary tent as the performers leave in groups. Masha, the juggler, is alone, however, and lingers. She takes an orange from a bowl of fruit, to eat later, and as she walks out she repeatedly tosses it into the air and catches it in her right hand. Perfectly straight tosses to the same height, landing effortlessly in her palm. I am the only witness to this strange performance. I suspect she doesn't even know she's doing it herself. Any more than she's aware of her breathing.

And from the second night: Standing by the stage after the show, waiting to be ushered back. Suddenly two figures emerge, dressed as cavaliers. I recognize one as Dasha. She seems to be taking a lesson from the other, for she follows her—or him—around the stage, walking slowly in a circle with measured steps. Then she works on maneuvering the light that shines on the end of a long arcing metal tube attached to a harness worn around her waist. She's twelve years old. She could be playing, or eating, or sleeping. After all, it's past ten and she's had a long day. Surely there are other times she could practice. But she follows her teacher around the stage, silently, patiently, as if there couldn't be anywhere else in the world she would rather be.